"Business, and especially tourism, can be a force for good and drive positive change. *Social Entrepreneurship in Hospitality: Principles and Strategies for Societal Changes* celebrates the power of entrepreneurs and the critical role they play to drive innovation within the industry. The case studies provide real-world examples to inspire students, academics and professionals to think outside the box and help the industry to change and evolve as a result of the COVID-19 crisis."

— **Dr. Anne-Kathrin Zschiegner,** Technical Assistance Advisor, The Long Run

"This book takes a brilliant look into the importance of social entrepreneurship. A company should have purpose beyond enriching shareholders. It is excellent that students have an opportunity to learn about the benefits of progressive businesses' social and environmental impact."

— **Sonu Shivdasani,** CEO and Joint Creative Director, Soneva, Bangkok, Thailand

"While glittery hospitality establishments are teeming to epitomize the practices of corporate social responsibility, such as an embryonic concept of social entrepreneurship, the work by one of the most talented, prominent leaders in hospitality sustainability Professor Legrand, and his colleagues serves as a practical guidepost for hospitality managers hankering for best practices and a timely overture to scholarly discourses in social entrepreneurship."

— **Joseph S. Chen,** Professor, Indiana University (Bloomington), USA

Social Entrepreneurship in Hospitality

This innovative book is the first to explore social entrepreneurship in the field of hospitality, introducing students to the principles of social entrepreneurship motivation, finance, sustainability, issues and challenges, and how these can be successfully implemented in a range of hospitality settings.

The hospitality industry offers a particularly fruitful framework for social entrepreneurs, partly due to the low barriers of entry and opportunities to enhance social and environmental wealth. A variety of international case studies are integrated throughout to showcase the challenges and successes of social entrepreneurship in the hospitality industry in a wide range of settings. Discussion questions, further reading suggestions and exercises at the end of each chapter help the student to explore these concepts further. Insights into the industry's role during and potentially beyond the COVID-19 crisis are offered in the concluding chapter.

This is a timely addition to the literature, written by a team of highly regarded professionals and academics, and will be essential reading for all current and future entrepreneurs in the field of Hospitality Management.

Willy Legrand is professor of Hospitality Management at the IUBH University of Applied Sciences, Bad Honnef – Bonn, Germany.

Miguel Angel Gardetti is Director of the Center for Studies on Sustainable Luxury, Buenos Aires, Argentina.

Robert Schønrock Nielsen is Ph.D. in Business Administration at the Ministry for Education, Culture, Church – Government of Greenland.

Colin Johnson is professor and Chair, Department of Hospitality and Tourism Management, and Co-Director of the Center for Ethical and Sustainable Business, Lam Family College of Business, San Francisco State University, California, USA.

Mehmet Ergul is professor of Hospitality and Tourism Management, Lam Family College of Business, San Francisco State University, California, USA.

Social Entrepreneurship in Hospitality

Principles and Strategies for Change

Willy Legrand, Miguel Angel Gardetti, Robert Schønrock Nielsen, Colin Johnson and Mehmet Ergul

LONDON AND NEW YORK

First published 2021
by Routledge
2 Park Square, Milton Park, Abingdon, Oxon OX14 4RN

and by Routledge
52 Vanderbilt Avenue, New York, NY 10017

Routledge is an imprint of the Taylor & Francis Group, an informa business

© 2021 Willy Legrand, Miguel Angel Gardetti, Robert Schønrock Nielsen, Colin Johnson and Mehmet Ergul

The right of Willy Legrand, Miguel Angel Gardetti, Robert Schønrock Nielsen, Colin Johnson and Mehmet Ergul to be identified as authors of this work has been asserted by them in accordance with sections 77 and 78 of the Copyright, Designs and Patents Act 1988.

All rights reserved. No part of this book may be reprinted or reproduced or utilised in any form or by any electronic, mechanical, or other means, now known or hereafter invented, including photocopying and recording, or in any information storage or retrieval system, without permission in writing from the publishers.

Trademark notice: Product or corporate names may be trademarks or registered trademarks, and are used only for identification and explanation without intent to infringe.

British Library Cataloguing-in-Publication Data
A catalogue record for this book is available from the British Library

Library of Congress Cataloging-in-Publication Data
A catalog record has been requested for this book

ISBN: 978-1-138-73408-1 (hbk)
ISBN: 978-1-138-73411-1 (pbk)
ISBN: 978-1-315-18736-5 (ebk)

Typeset in Arno
by codeMantra

Contents

	List of figures	ix
	List of tables	xi
	List of case studies	xiii
	Preface	xv
	Organization of the book	xvii
	Acknowledgments	xxi
1	The evolution of sustainable development in the hospitality industry	1
2	From entrepreneurship to social entrepreneurship	33
3	Social entrepreneurship: definitions and concepts	46
4	Social entrepreneurs: characteristics and motivations	73
5	Social impact assessment, social return on investment and networks & certifications	94
6	Hospitality social entrepreneurship: the nexus of hospitality, sustainable development and entrepreneurship	128
7	Hospitality and tourism as natural agents of social change	163
8	Hospitality environmental entrepreneurship	189
9	Funding and financing hospitality social ventures	211
10	A world of change in hospitality: a concluding statement	237
	Index	239

Figures

3.1	Hiç entrepreneur Ms. Duygu Ozerson at the olive farm	57
3.2	Areal view of Chumbe Island	59
3.3	Chumbe eco-bungalows: living in the open with a near-zero environmental impact	61
3.4	Chumbe's head ranger, Omari Nyange, on boat patrol	63
3.5	Chumbe's environmental education (EE) program takes local school children snorkeling in the protected reef. Most of the children don't know how to swim and need life jackets and training before exploring the coral reef	63
3.6	Chumbe Reef Sanctuary – a protected coral garden of high biodiversity value	65
3.7	The closed forest reserve on Chumbe Island is home to a large population of coconut crabs (*Birgus latro*), the largest terrestrial crab in the world	66
3.8	Zanzibari students learning about marine ecology on Chumbe Island	68
4.1	Areas of opportunities for social entrepreneurs	82
4.2	Inkaterra Hacienda Concepcion: sheltered by the forest's canopy	84
4.3	Inkaterra Reserva Amazonica: 35 wooden cabanas inspired in the Ese'Eja culture. 540 bird species have been inventoried in hotel grounds, deep in the rainforest	84
4.4	José Koechlin, social entrepreneur and founder of Inkaterra	85
4.5	Artisanal fishing	89
5.1	Differentiating TBL and QBL (adapted from Rachel, 2012; Bremser, 2014; Knowles, 2014, Sood et al., 2014; Zahringer, 2014)	99
5.2	Hospitality social entrepreneurship within tourism social entrepreneurship	110
5.3	Baiazinha aerial view	114
5.4	Cowboys	116
5.5	Pantaneiro festival	117

x FIGURES

5.6	Cordilheira outdoor space	119
5.7	A jaguar	120
6.1	Hydrology analysis of the Peninsula Sanctuary – a luxury sustainable tourism resort in Nicaragua	150
6.2	An ecopsychologist conducting a 'Forest Connection' workshop with the client, consultants and indigenous stakeholders (Mayans) for the Master Plan for Chaa Creek Reserve, Belize	151
6.3	A metaphysical workshop participant conducting a 'sound' sensorial site immersion	152
6.4	Sustainable biodiversity and tourism master plan for Lapa Rios Reserve. (Photo Credit: HM Design)	153
6.5	An illustrated conceptual site plan for Plataran Menjangan Lodge and Spa	155
7.1	Field working with the communities	175
7.2	Monitoring natural and cultural places with local communities	176
7.3	Cultural activity with the younger generation	178
7.4	Organising field working with local authorities	182
8.1	A view of Peuma Hue	199
8.2	Peuma Hue in Winter	199
8.3	Peuma Hue's Master Suite	203
9.1	A room at Borana Lodge	226
9.2	Borana Lodge	227
9.3	A Black Rhino on Borana Conservancy	228
9.4	Horse riding on Borana Conservancy	230
9.5	Breakdown of how conservancy fees are spent (2011–2019)	232
9.6	Total funding from 2011 to 2020	233

Tables

1.1	Explaining the nine planetary boundaries	6
3.1	Abu-Saifan's unique and common characteristics of profit-oriented entrepreneurs and social entrepreneurs	54
3.2	Research areas addressed by articles on social entrepreneurship (in percent)	55
4.1	Summary of 'pull' and 'push' factors	76
4.2	Summary of factors of motivation of social entrepreneurs	77
4.3	Summary unique and common characteristics of traditional and social entrepreneurs	80
5.1	Prominent stakeholder of social entrepreneurship	98
5.2	Methods for the identification of social entrepreneurs	98
5.3	The six steps in SROI	101
5.4	B Impact Assessment	103
5.5	Step one of the global social venture competition and social impact assessment	106
5.6	Advantages and disadvantages of social impact assessment methods	107
5.7	Authenticitys' B Corp performance	113
7.1	Comparison of leading hotel companies, 1975–2018, by number of rooms	165
7.2	Goals and progress of Hilton	171
9.1	Eight challenges in social enterprise financing	212
9.2	Source of financing and funding options for social entrepreneurs	214
9.3	EU funding for social entrepreneurship	216
9.4	Differences and similarities between business incubators and business accelerators	220
9.5	Selection of social incubator and accelerator organizations	221

Case studies

1.1	Role and responsibility of the hospitality industry towards global challenges	20
2.1	Social entrepreneurship classic: Muhammad Yunus and Grameen bank	42
3.1	The Hiç Olive Company, Urla, Turkey	56
3.2	Chumbe Island Coral Park Ltd. (CHICOP): Lessons learned from setting up the first private Marine Protected Area	58
4.1	Inkaterra pushing the boundaries of eco-friendly luxury hotels: from Amazon sustainable landscape corridors to a marine reserve in Peru	83
5.1	Authenticitys – the first travel company in Europe to become a certified B Corp	112
5.2	Reviving and celebrating local culture: a case study of the Caiman Ecological Refuge	113
6.1	Case study: Soneva – when environmental and social involvement meets luxury	143
6.2	Physical master plans: a roadmap to developing sustainable destinations	147
7.1	Thinking outside of the box for community and business sustainability: a case study of Nomad Lodges	174
7.2	"Le Marche in Valigia" (Le Marche in a Suitcase)	182
8.1	Estancia Peuma Hue: An environmental and conservation project on luxury sustainable ecotourism in Argentina	198
8.2	Mashpi lodge: A socio-environmental project on biodiversity, education and local community in the Ecuadorian Amazon	203
9.1	Establishing a financially sustainable conservancy: Borana Ranch case study	226

Preface

There is a strong momentum for change in the hospitality industry, supported by external events and internal forces. The adoption of the UN's 2030 Agenda for Sustainable Development along with the Sustainable Development Goals (SDGs) and the Paris Agreement provide a global framework to tackle the major challenges faced by civilization: ending extreme poverty, fighting inequality and injustice and mitigating climate change impacts. Tourism in general, and the hospitality sector in particular, has the potential to contribute, directly or indirectly, to all of the 17 SDGs (UNWTO, 2014).

At the same time, the 2020 COVID-19 pandemic has put a halt to the unprecedented growth of international tourism. The industry has shown resilience in past crises and the expectation is that a similar pattern will take place; while the timeframe for a 'bounce back' of travel is difficult to predict at this stage, demand for travel will grow again in the future, but alas possibly of a different type.

Whether in pre- or post-pandemic world however, large hospitality organizations are often involved in the tweaking of current processes to 'try to adapt' to new demands; the most innovative solutions are led by the many social entrepreneurs in the hospitality industry. Social entrepreneurship can be defined as "identifying or recognizing a social problem and using entrepreneurial principles to organize, create, and manage a social venture to achieve a desired social change" (Balambika, Subrahmanyam, Tamilmani, 2013). Social entrepreneurs measure performance, taking into account the positive return to society.

Social entrepreneurship and the hospitality industry go hand-in-hand for multiple reasons as both concepts have shown to be drivers for social change, not least because the hospitality industry has few barriers to entry.

This book, *Social Entrepreneurship in Hospitality: Principles and Strategies for Societal Changes*, is a timely addition to existing literature and is designed as an essential read for current or future entrepreneurs, as well as students and academics in the field of hospitality management and business entrepreneurship. Additionally, social enterprises have shown to play a critical role in society facing large-scale challenges in the past, including during and post the 2008 global financial crisis, and will do so in post the corona crisis of 2020. Through the latter, the world of business has shown resourcefulness and citizenship. Indeed, the hospitality industry has proven to be one of the most innovative sectors in times of crisis, adapting to keep operating: from providing emergency housing, coronavirus quarantines and daytime offices to hotel-to-hospital conversions. Lately, the industry has also assumed a role in keeping spirits high across the communities it operates in. Businesses with strong social values and social enterprises are key to creating innovations that shape communities and society at large during and after a crisis.

Willy Legrand Department of Tourism, Hospitality & Event Management, IUBH University of Applied Sciences, Bad Honnef – Bonn, Germany.

Miguel Angel Gardetti The Center for Studies on Sustainable Luxury, Buenos Aires, Argentina.

Robert Schønrock Nielsen Government of Greenland. The Ministry of Education, Culture, Church and Foreign Affairs

Colin Johnson San Francisco State University, Lam Family College of Business

Mehmet Ergul San Francisco State University, Lam Family College of Business

References

UNWTO. (2014). *How Tourism can Contribute to the Sustainable Development Goals (SDGs)*. http://www.e-unwto.org/doi/pdf/10.18111/9789284417254.

UNWTO. (2015). *United Nations declares 2017 as the International Year of Sustainable Tourism for Development*. http://media.unwto.org/press-release/2015-12-07/united-nations-declares-2017-international-year-sustainable-tourism-develop.

Organization of the book

The evolution of sustainable development in the hospitality industry

Chapter 1 provides an overview of the general concepts of sustainability and sustainable development. A review of the evolution of sustainable development thinking is presented. A discussion on the role of businesses in achieving sustainability as well as a description of the role and responsibility of the hospitality industry is provided. The chapter concludes with a case reviewing the role and responsibility of the hospitality industry in global challenges, using examples of current best practices. A set of exercises is provided at the end of the chapter, which are based on individual or group research and discussions.

From entrepreneurship to social entrepreneurship

Chapter 2 introduces key theories linked to the entrepreneurship phenomenon and reviews traditional approaches for generating entrepreneurial opportunities. The chapter also examines the links between entrepreneurship, market instability, corporate social responsibility and social entrepreneurship. A discussion on the limitations and gaps associated with traditional entrepreneurship as well as market inefficiencies is provided. The chapter introduces various definitions and descriptions of social entrepreneurship. It concludes with a classic case of social entrepreneurship: Muhammad Yunus and the Grameen Bank. A set of additional exercises is provided at the end of the chapter, which are based on individual or group research and discussions.

Social entrepreneurship: definition and concept

Chapter 3 explores the origins and development of the field of social entrepreneurship. It examines the definitions and boundaries of social entrepreneurship, including social entrepreneurs, social entrepreneurship, sustainable entrepreneurship and ecopreneurs. It also discusses perspectives on studying social entrepreneurship and provides an overview of the research areas addressed by social entrepreneurship articles. The chapter concludes with two case studies reviewing the challenges and successes of social entrepreneurs in setting up their endeavors. A set of additional exercises is provided at the end, which are based on individual or group research and discussions.

Social entrepreneurs: characteristics and motivations

Chapter 4 explores the key attributes or characteristics of social entrepreneurs and the reasons or motivations behind why some individuals decide to invest in social entrepreneurship ventures. 'Push' and 'pull' motives as well as the concepts of 'necessity' and 'opportunity' entrepreneurship are reviewed. A well-established typology of social entrepreneurs is presented. The chapter concludes with a discussion on the role of social entrepreneurs in being 'change agents' towards building a better world, supported with the case of Inkaterra. A set of additional exercises is provided at the end of the chapter, which are based on individual or group research and discussions.

Social impact assessment, social return on investment and networks & certifications

This chapter discusses the concept of social impacts, assessment methods and social return on investment. An overview of the existing global and regional networks of social entrepreneurs as well as existing certification systems is provided. The chapter also reviews tools to identify tourism and hospitality social entrepreneurs. The chapter concludes with two case studies discussing the management of social impacts from different perspectives. A set of additional exercises is provided at the end of the chapter, which are based on individual or group research and discussions.

Hospitality social entrepreneurship: the nexus of hospitality, sustainable development and entrepreneurship

Chapter 6 explores the linkages between sustainability innovation and entrepreneurship. Following a brief review of entrepreneurship and social entrepreneurship concepts, the chapter explores the attributes of social entrepreneurs. It also investigates the ways in which hospitality has become a major activity in society and an increasingly important sector in terms of economic and social development. In particular, it discusses tourism, luxury, sustainability, and the role of social entrepreneurs in guaranteeing a cohesion between these concepts. The chapter concludes with example of the nexus of hospitality, sustainable development and entrepreneurship from the perspective of luxury tourism and destination development. A set of additional exercises is provided at the end of the chapter, which are based on individual or group research and discussions.

ORGANIZATION OF THE BOOK xix

Hospitality and tourism as natural agents of social change

Chapter 7 examines trends and changes in the hospitality and tourism markets in relation to social entrepreneurship. It opens with a discussion on the role of hospitality and tourism in developing tourism destinations. It also discusses the role and responsibilities of larger corporate players in achieving change, even if this sector is not usually considered within the social entrepreneur realm. The chapter concludes with an evaluation of the enhanced role of hospitality in tackling global societal and environmental problems, illustrated with two cases of change agents. A set of additional exercises is provided at the end of the chapter, which are based on individual or group research and discussions.

Hospitality environmental entrepreneurship

Chapter 8 chapter starts with a discussion of the ethical issues facing the hospitality industry and expands on the concept of sustainable tourism. It explores the impacts of tourism on climate change and biodiversity collapse, with a focus on identifying opportunities in environmental entrepreneurship, and discusses best practices in that field.

The chapter closes with two case studies that tackle those challenges via their mitigation strategies. A set of additional exercises is provided at the end of the chapter, which are based on individual or group research and discussions.

Funding and financing hospitality social ventures

Chapter 9 identifies methods to fund and finance social enterprises. In doing so, it reviews the most traditional and emerging sources of funding and financing, and discusses the challenges linked to social-enterprise financing. It also discusses social business incubators and accelerators, supported with prominent examples. The chapter concludes with a detailed case study on establishing a financially sustainable conservancy. A set of additional exercises is provided at the end of the chapter, which are based on individual or group research and discussions.

A world of change in hospitality: a concluding statement

Chapter 10 concludes the book with a few considerations on social entrepreneurship in hospitality but also on the role of business in building resiliency in light of the 2020 COVID-19 pandemic.

Acknowledgments

First of all, we thank our families and friends for their support, who relentlessly encouraged our endeavor and shared our effort in assisting this book project. More specifically, a special thank you goes to Jakob Rametsteiner, who supported the preliminary research for this book with his time and passion for the hospitality industry. We express our gratitude to Claudia Langer, who co-authored Chapter 5 of this book and provided invaluable insights into the topic of social impact assessment and social return on investment. We extend a special thank you to Anne-Kathrin Zschiegner, Technical Assistance Advisor at The Long Run, for the generous support in contributing some of the case studies and facilitating contact with the many entrepreneurs who are making a difference in this industry.

We are grateful to our affiliations; the IUBH University of Applied Sciences, Bad Honnef – Bonn, Germany; the Center for Studies on Sustainable Luxury, Buenos Aires, Argentina; the Ministry of Education, Culture and Church, Government of Greenland; and San Francisco State University, Lam Family College of Business, who have supported our research efforts concerning sustainable hospitality management. We are intellectually in debt to those colleagues leading us to a new scholarly horizon.

We are grateful to all social entrepreneurs in hospitality who constantly strive to improve business in a sustainable manner and have provided this book with so much valuable material.

Finally, we pass on our sincere thanks to the all students around the globe who have, over the years, provided valuable support in terms of research, ideas and discussion on the theme of social entrepreneurship in the hospitality industry.

Chapter 1

The evolution of sustainable development in the hospitality industry

In the last thirty years, the concept of sustainable development has received great attention from the academic, political and corporate sectors. However, the ambiguity of the sustainability definition has resulted in a wide range of interpretations and new definitions.

This chapter explains how sustainability integrates both the short and long term. And although sustainable development could be actually defined as a paradigm that includes actions, attitudes, thoughts and projects based on values – which have a social, economic and environmental impact – a long evolution was necessary to approach this concept that started in academia back in the early 1970s. This evolution in thinking and approaches is reviewed also within this chapter incorporating concepts such as the planetary boundaries, sustainable development goals and the impact and responsibilities of businesses. The chapter discusses the hospitality industry's approaches towards environmental, social and economic challenges.

The chapter concludes with a case reviewing the role and responsibility of the hospitality industry towards global challenges using examples of current best practices. A set of exercises is provided at the end of the chapter, which are based on individual or group research and discussions.

2 OVERVIEW OF SUSTAINABLE DEVELOPMENT IN HOSPITALITY

Sustainable development: concept & characteristics

"An important motivation behind the sustainable development discussion is that of a just bequest to future generations" (Costanza & Daly, 1992, p. 39). Written three decades ago, these words from Costanza and Daly still resonate today when the global community is faced with probably its greatest once-in-a-generation trial – that of mitigating climate change and biodiversity collapse. Historically speaking, the concern for the environment has been approached from various perspectives, with the purpose of reaching an agreement on how to make improvements. This may be due to the fact that, from a conservative point of view, the economic interests of various sectors are in competition with the objectives of sustainable development. This is connected to the remarks of Gardetti (2005), who argues that due to the "needs and aspirations" of these groups, organisations and individuals, there is quite a variety of definitions of sustainable development that can be categorised by their constituents. Sustainable development is a responsibility and a challenge to be tackled at multiple levels – those of the individual, family, community, institutions and businesses.

Defining the concept

The Report of the World Commission of Environment and Development (WCED), *Our Common Future*, also recognised as Brundtland Report,[1] was released in 1987.

This report presented – but did not define[2] – the concept of sustainable development as that which satisfies the needs of present generations without compromising the abilities of future ones to satisfy their own needs.

Since then, several authors have explored and (re)defined sustainable development. For instance, John R. Ehrenfeld, Professor Emeritus at the MIT, in a paper called "Cultural Structure and the Challenge of Sustainability," stated,

> Sustainability is a possible way of living, of being in which individuals, firms, governments, and other institutions are responsible for taking care of the future as if it belonged to them today, for equitably sharing the ecological resources on which the survival of human and other species depends, and for assuring that all who live today and in the future will be able to satisfy their needs and human aspirations.
> (Ehrenfeld, 1999, p. 230)

It can be noticed that this definition has a more detailed, hands-on approach compared to the one provided by the WCED.

Some authors (e.g., During, 1992; Marcuse, 1964; Redclift, 1996; Robertson, 1990) contest the emphasis around the concept of 'growth,' pointing out that growth (as a qualitative increase in production) is not the same as 'development' (as a qualitative improvement in the lives of people). It is also argued that, in many cases, growth has not led to development, but instead to a significant decrease in the quality of life. In contrast, Daly (1996) argues that if sustainable development is to be meaningful, we need to conceive the economy as part of the ecosystem and, as a consequence, to abandon the ideal of economic growth (Gardetti, 2005). Finally, sustainable development is not only related to intergenerational equity (equality between generations), but also with intergenerational equity (equality between members of certain generations) (Schaltegger, Burritt, & Petersen, 2003).

As Elliot points out, "The idea of sustainable development is not new but has a substantial history" (Elliot, 1999, p. 32). The concept of sustainable development is defined on a contextual basis. In fact, it is estimated that there are more than seventy definitions of 'sustainable development.' At the same time, this sets out guidelines for the appropriate behaviour with regard to, for example, the environment, water, energy, and animal and human rights.

The evolution of the concept of sustainable development

In his book titled *In Earth's Company*, Carl Frankel (1998) explores the evolution of the concept of sustainable development and concludes that sustainability is characterised by the harmony of three elements: the economy, environment and social equity.

Throughout history, discussions have been based on a process of definition. Instead, it can be suggested that we should understand how to have a healthy relationship with our environment. Academics' discussions about this subject can have a constructive approach as long as they try to comprehend what sustainable development is all about and, even further, how to apply it. Indeed, a priority is to agree on an approach based on sustainable development, and have it reflected in awareness-raising actions and concrete actions. Furthermore, to change our paradigm we should bear in mind that the attitude taken until now towards social, environmental and economic developments has not entirely worked out to build a better life experience or higher levels of happiness (Helliwell, Layard, Sachs, & De Neve, 2020).

Most of the literature on sustainability and sustainable development agrees on limiting reductionism (scientific thinking for understanding and managing the environmental crisis). As an alternative to this limitation, a significant number of authors have based their arguments on ethical considerations. Nevertheless, in recent years another group of authors has begun to recognise the complementarity between reductionism and holistic thinking.

Nonetheless, and although the research goes back two decades, Paul Gilding argues in his paper "Sustainability – Doing It" (Gilding, 2000, p. 42) that by just revising social and environmental aspects, a great deal of sustainability complexity is lost. He also affirms that global trends should be considered within the decision process – for instance, the evolution of the environmental movement, rampant capitalism, role changes in governments, the evolution of civil society's role in developing regulations and policies, globalisation, technological development and the communications revolution (Gardetti, 2005). In the paper "Tomorrow's Markets – Global Trends and Their Implications for Business," the World Resources Institute (WRI), in alliance with the United Nations Environment Programme (UNEP) and World Business Council for Sustainable Development (2002), argues that these trends have consequences in business. According to Allen, Bonazzi, and Gee (2001), sustainable development is a controversial expression, on whose significance few people can generally agree. It is a "conservative" notion crossing over social, environmental and economic considerations. These authors go on to explain that everyone can take the term and "reinvent" it by looking at their needs.

Finally, it should be stressed that an inherent characteristic of sustainable development is flexibility, as it needs to adapt to circumstances, events, societies and behaviours throughout its implementation. It can be argued that describing and understanding, rather than defining, sustainable development is more effective. Notwithstanding that, the Brundtland Report can be considered the baseline for discussions about sustainable development, whereby it constitutes a major political change (Gardetti, 2005).

Brief historical perspective

The discussion about the consequences of human activities on the environment dates back to Greek and Roman philosophers who "already reflected on the diverse and sometimes complex relationships between humans, and in particular human activities, and ecosystems in which those activities take place" (Legrand, Sloan, & Chen, 2017, p. 20).

However, an in-depth discussion on 'sustainable development,' a term used in the management of forests in Europe during the 18th century, is considered to have begun in the 1970s, when the Club of Rome[3] used the term "Global Problem" to refer to the dynamic connections and interactions between several aspects of the then environmental crisis and its consequences worldwide (Reid, 1995; Rockstrom et al., 2009).

The social, political and economic dimensions and the associated cultural, spiritual, psychological and intellectual implications of such crisis could have originated in the rise of capitalist economics from the scientific and industrial revolutions in 19th-century England (Carley & Christie, 1992; Merchant, 1980; Spretnak & Capra, 1985). Springett and Redclift also argue that the new scientific paradigm at the centre of the Enlightenment that transformed the relationship between humans and nature, besides the capitalist model of production and consumption, created such a degree of change and scale of degradation that had not been possible until then (Merchant, 1980). To this we can add the process of North-South domination through colonisation, in search of resources, markets and lands – and later extended through the globalisation of trade, technological experience, money markets and communications (The Ecologist, 1993).

Warhust (2001), quoting Bansal and Howard, explains that sustainable development can be described as a process to reach equal, connected, prudential and safe development. Connectivity embraces ecological, social and economic interdependence. 'Equality' suggests justice, within and beyond generations and species. 'Prudence' means duty of care and caution in a technological, scientific and political way. 'Safety' implies the care of everyday threats and damages, because, to a certain extent, sustainability is about social and environmental justice.[4]

Since the 17th century, several thinkers including Bacon, Malthus, Marx, Shelley, Stuart Mill, Leopold, Carson and Anne and Paul Ehrlich, among others, have addressed the consequences of economic growth on natural resources and the environment (Dresner, 2002). But it was only in the period between 1977 and 1981 that the then-US President Jimmy Carter, concerned about the 'energy crisis,' ordered an investigation that concluded in a report called "Global 2000 Study," which projected environmental until the year 2000 and concluded the following:

> If present trends continue, the world in 2000 will be more crowded, more polluted, less stable ecologically and more vulnerable to disruption. Serious stresses involving population, resources, and environment are clearly visible ahead. Despite greater material output, the world's people will be poorer in many ways than they are today.
>
> (Barney, 1981, p. 1)

Today, the planet is crowded and the use of natural resources is beyond its capacity. This means that the availability of resources is not sufficient to meet the needs of all of us who live on it. This has negative social and environmental consequences. However, some sections of the population are more affected than others. In many cases, those with fewer resources are more affected by environmental pollution (Agyeman, Bullard, & Evans, 2003; Dobson, 1998; Faber & O'Connor, 1989; Martinez-Alier, 2003). In fact, it is argued that Earth has several 'boundaries,' as presented by Johan Rockstrom and colleagues at the Stockholm Resilience Centre in what is called the 'Planetary Boundaries Framework' (Rockström et al., 2009a). The idea is simple and brilliant – within a finite world, we operate with a series of budgets called 'planetary boundaries.' Nine boundaries have been identified (see Table 1.1), in which four are being trespassed, or are over budget, including climate change, biodiversity loss, and the nitrogen and phosphorous cycles (the four boundaries are highlighted in Table 1.1 – note: the boundary 'biochemical flows' is split into two sub-boundaries, 'nitrogen' and 'phosphorous' cycles).

Table 1.1 Explaining the nine planetary boundaries.

Planet Boundary Name	Threshold Explanation	Planetary Boundary
1. Climate change	Impact of human activities on carbon dioxide emissions affecting the loss of polar ice sheets; regional climate disruptions, loss of glacial freshwater supplies and weakening of carbon sinks.	To ensure that atmospheric concentrations of carbon dioxide do not exceed more than 350 parts per million (ppm).
2. Biosphere loss	Extinction rate or extinctions per million species per year	To maintain 90% of biodiversity
3. Biochemical flows (3.1 nitrogen and 3.2 phosphorus cycles)	The addition of phosphorus (e.g., mined from rocks and used in fertiliser production) and nitrogen to the world's crops and ecosystem such as leakages into oceans (e.g., via industrial intensive agriculture).	To limit the use per year of about eleven million tonnes of phosphorus and thirty-five million tonnes of nitrogen per year
4. Land-system change	The percentage of global land cover (e.g., forests, grasslands, wetlands) converted to cropland which has affect carbon storage, biodiversity and various biogeochemical processes.	To limit the global ice-free land surface conversation rate to cropland to less than 15%.
5. Novel entities (chemical pollution)	The impact on the ecosystem and human health resulting from emission or concentration of various pollutants such as plastics, micro plastics, heavy metals or nuclear waste.	Scientific evidence is available, however the global boundary is still to be determined
6. Ozone depletion	Severe and irreversible ultraviolet radiation (UV-B; responsible for delayed tanning and burning; promotes the development of skin cancer, (WHO, 2020)) radiation effects on human health and ecosystems.	To maintain at a level of less than 5% below pre-industrial level of 290 Dobson Units (DU)
7. Atmospheric aerosol loading	The overall concentration of particulates (microscopic particles) in the atmosphere which affects human health, climate change, freshwater sources and other living organisms.	Scientific evidence is available, however the global boundary is still to be determined

(Continued)

Planet Boundary Name	Threshold Explanation	Planetary Boundary
8. Ocean acidification	Roughly 25% of all human-made carbon emissions are dissolved into the oceans. This alters the ocean chemistry, decreasing the pH (Potential of Hydrogen) of the surface water. Ocean biodiversity is affected as some have difficulty to grow and survive in such environment.	To sustain 80% of the preindustrial aragonite (carbonate mineral) saturation state of mean surface ocean. This is linked to climate change boundary (see above).
9. Freshwater use	The possibility to use up to 4,000 km^3 of freshwater per year	The possibility to use up to 4,000 km^3 of freshwater per year

Source: Based on Rockström et al. (2009a, 2009b) and Stockholm Resilience Centre (n.d.).

As Rockström et al. (2009a, 2009b) write, "Although the planetary boundaries are described in terms of individual quantities and separate processes, the boundaries are tightly coupled. We do not have the luxury of concentrating our efforts on any one of them in isolation from the others." (p. 474). The planetary boundaries framework makes it clear; the need for sustainable development is more critical than ever before. Sustainable development also means that we need to change objectives and priorities over time, as it is an open process (Gardetti, 2005). A real transition to sustainable development requires a new way of thinking (Presas, 2001). As boundaries are trespassed, it is necessary to employ a collective learning mechanism for all types of environments and stakeholders, and to create the necessary space for structured dialogue about what our vision of a sustainable society is all about and how it can be implemented.

This reinforces the idea put forward at the outset: as we begin to understand what sustainable development is all about, we can define it. But in fact, sustainable development is now more about actions, not words. To add a layer of complexity, however, it also requires attention to the concept of economic development.

Traditionally, the organisation of economic systems has altered some concepts, such as 'quality of life' being mistaken for 'purchasing power.' Redclift and Springett (2015) point out that after the Second World War, ways of exercising power over people and nature have been strengthened by globalisation, with the creation of dominant structures and institutions such as the World Bank, the International Monetary Fund and the World Trade Organisation (Brack, 1998; Esty, 1994; Lang & Hines, 1993).

However, sustainable development is a challenge that must be faced by ordinary people and decision-makers around the world, rather than by some institutions in isolated regions (Redclift and Springett, 2015). While individuals, as well as empowered communities, can exert pressure on government decisions, it becomes more evident that sustainable development is everyone's responsibility. Both challenges and opportunities for sustainable development require a commitment at all levels – individual, institutional and community. At the same time, we need to gain openness in communication and vision, so that we can correct past mistakes. Unfortunately, the solutions that were in place a decade ago would not be effective today, or even worse, they could be harmful. Sustainable development should be about finding the best way to live together in the current context and to be able to constantly adapt and maintain a healthy relationship with the world around us.

Sustainability is feasible if there is a clear reduction of the environmental burden. This can occur by reducing human population, decreasing wealth levels (consumption) or through a radical change in the technologies used for wealth creation. One of the challenges remains finding ways to develop a sustainable global economy that can be endured indefinitely by the Earth.

Business organisations can drive sustainability and, more importantly, a new group of leaders and entrepreneurs are including sustainability, efficiency, sufficiency, justice, equity and the community as the highest social values of their ventures. Four decades ago, environmentalists Paul Ehrlich and Barry Commoner made a simple but effective observation of sustainable development: the overall environmental burden created by human activity is the product of three factors – population, wealth (understood as synonymous with consumption) and technology (understood as the ways to create wealth).

To create a resilient society, we need a system of trade and production in which every act is fully related to its restoration capacity. For this, businesses need to integrate economic, biological and human systems, creating a sustainable system of trade. Sustainability implies integrating the economic, ecological and social aspects. It is also about integrating the short and the long term, which requires a multidisciplinary approach. The strategy to respond to the demands of sustainable development must begin with a real commitment from the entire organisation.

To conclude, Dyllick and Hockerts considered the three pillars, environmental, social and economic, in defining the roles and responsibility of businesses whereby:

> A company is economically sustainable when it permanently guarantees sufficient cash flow to ensure liquidity while producing positive returns to its shareholders. A company is considered ecologically sustainable when it uses only those natural resources that it consumes at a lower rate than reproduction. Furthermore, it does not cause emissions that accumulate in the environment in greater quantities than the absorption of the natural system. And it does not engage in activities that degrade ecosystem services. Finally,

a company is socially sustainable when it adds value to the communities where it operates by increasing the human capital of its individual "partners" as well as the social capital of the community. This capital is managed in such a way that stakeholders can interpret their motivations

(Dyllick & Hockerts, 2002, pp. 133–134)

Business and sustainable development

The World Summit on Sustainable Development (WSSD) in 2002 and Rio+20 in 2012 witnessed real institutional change. Among the different topics addressed, climate change, deforestation and biodiversity prevailed over population, trade, poverty and financial crisis. However, these topics were dealt with in alternative scenarios. This means that there is an agenda with pending issues (Redclift, 1996). It was also perceived that non-governmental organisations (NGOs) had committed to legitimising a process that many were originally opposed to. Sustainable development is essentially a political project, with the power to generate social change and the ability to challenge the ideology of neoliberal capitalism. It calls for emancipation, a more equitable distribution of power and resources, changes in human behaviour and the redemption of the roles of public, private and political institutions. The potential for sustainable development to change paradigms and demand structural change would have been radical enough to isolate businesses completely, providing corporations with an even stronger drive to take responsibility for the sustainable development agenda (Springett, 2013).

The Industrial Revolution

The Industrial Revolution, which took place in England between the mid-18th and mid-19th centuries, consisted of changing the ways of production and consumption, as well as impacting the population and the use of resources, trade, political and economic relations. Previously, the form of production was agrarian and artisanal, the form of government was an absolute monarchy and most people lived in rural areas. This revolution, which emerged during a liberal monarchy and started from a liberal economic system, somehow contained a probable political revolution, such as the ones that had been taking place in other countries including the independence bid from the thirteen British colonies in the Americas and the French Revolution. From that moment on, Great Britain would lead the economic, financial and commercial fields (Hosbaum, 1988). For instance, Springett and Redclift state that the "the transformation of England into an industrial society through the power of capitalist industrialisation provided a microcosm of today's global money economy and prevailing paradigm of profit and domination" (2015, pp. 3–4). The authors also discuss a "global crisis management," which led towards the use of fear and threats to legitimise a militaristic and technocratic approach, leaving the world with a "profound absence of vision and leadership."

Role of businesses

Historically, Western industrial societies have operated a system with a main goal of obtaining profits and wherein both goods and people are quantitatively observed. Productivity and output are key performance indicators. Therefore, the values within which production and consumption patterns operate have led, largely, to the degradation of both the environment and the societies the system works in. That is how society and the environment were immersed in a system that offers economic growth in the name of (and in exchange for) individual fulfilment (Jacobs, 1996; Redclift, 1996; Springett & Redclift, 2012). This way of operation led societies to coexist. However, narcissism, pride, selfishness, greed, competition and addictions are also components of such societies, who are required to equally deal with potential destructive forces.

Within a society, industry is also required to change towards a more collaborative paradigm, focusing on the real *needs* rather than creating *wants* to sell products. A societal and industrial transformation built on a perspective that is beneficial to all stakeholders may not be, at first sight, for 'everyone.' The world is a very crowded place after all. But positive change can happen and businesses can drive that change. In fact, change must and will take place, whether we like it or not. Planet boundaries will dictate the process. The illusion that accelerated economic growth, global overconsumption, markets and technology will solve environmental problems has been challenged by a series of events over the past century.

Major disruptions in the economic development model have been felt around the globe several times already. The 2008 financial crisis was driven by the individual greed of many bankers and financial managers and fuelled by the almost uncontrolled low-interest lending and, in this regard, the lack of sustainability made most consumers an accomplice to the model. The financial crisis revealed that this model is completely unsustainable.

BOX CASE 1.1

The modern food system: unsustainable?

The food industry, which is closely related to the hospitality industry, was developed to meet the needs of developed countries, where technological changes and the growth of domestic markets started industrialised agriculture (Goodman & Redclift, 1991). In the 1970s, the prevailing view was that food production could not keep pace with population growth. To some extent, the success of the much-praised "Green Revolution" in staple grains was to discredit this rather simplistic view of boundaries. In the 1970s and 1980s, impressive gains were made in the productivity of staples – especially rice, corn and wheat – helped by improved irrigation systems and chemical fertilisers and pesticides.

Springrett and Redclift (2012, p. 13) explain that

> today about 12 per cent of global cereals are traded between states on the international market: about half the 300 million tons annually between the North and the South. The South is still a net importer of cereals: not Latin America but much of Asia and North Africa experience net deficits in cereals. In 2006, the United States exported 32 million metric tons of cereals, compared with 22 million metric tons from the European Union. Projections for the year 2020 suggest that the United States will trade about 119 million metric tons of cereals by this date (SCOPE 2009). The drivers of cereal imports in the South include population growth, changing diets (which substitute grain-fed animals for vegetable protein) and non-food land uses, particularly the development of biofuels. Additional factors, which are likely to drive the import of cereals to developing countries, include increasing energy and fertilizer prices and climate change effects in the tropics.
>
> In addition, biofuel production has made the prospect of serious food shortages much worse than it might otherwise have been. The United States embarked on a very large-scale ethanol production programme under President George Bush, not primarily to address climate change but to provide an alternative source of energy to hydrocarbons. Biofuel production requires heavy use of nitrogen-based fertilizers and often diverts land away from food production or forest/grazing land. The increase in biofuels production thus reduces carbon sequestration from the atmosphere and serves to jeopardize climate change from a land use perspective, while making only small gains from substitution of hydrocarbons in energy systems. Biofuels are not 'carbon positive' in that nitrous oxide emissions increase with only modest benefits in reducing carbon emissions – the new effect on greenhouse gas emissions is negative.
>
> The most serious effect of the growth in the biofuels market is that land and water uses are transformed in ways that increase food and water insecurity. The conversion of land from forests and grasslands to biofuels production is one of the key factors. However, biofuels also make enormous demands on scarce supplies of fresh water and contribute to air pollution by increasing vehicle emissions of nitrogen. Another important effect is the runoff from nitrates that contributes to water pollution, and has been a major factor in the water sources ending in the Gulf of Mexico. Finally, biofuels are very land-intensive: three and a half times as much energy can be produced from grassland as from biofuels conversion.

There are also a number of major new challenges, resulting from the dependence on cereals in the developing world, including newly industrialised Asian countries. Firstly, China, South Korea and some Gulf States are acquiring land. In addition to the crops that the Global South grows to trade with the Global North, in particular soybeans, these countries are buying land to supply their own domestic markets and the poorest countries in these regions are the least able to take advantage of this potential, putting their own domestic food supplies at risk. There is also a persistent problem of trade barriers raised by the industrialised world against cheap food and imports from the Global South.

Credit expansion in much of the developed world, and the associated levels of personal and corporate debt that have affected most financial institutions since September 2008, led to economic constraints and, in 2014, a period of recession in parts of the world in which it had yet to emerge. The characterisation of climate change as a "market failure" immediately gave economists, businesses and governments a lifeline (Stern, 2007). Rather than requiring costly and comprehensive restructuring of supply systems, or even a reduction in production and consumption volumes, Stern's neoclassical view that sustainability could be achieved through increased consumption of certain types of products, while feeding the economy, has come to characterise the dominant discourse of sustainable consumption while, at the same time, turning sustainability thinking onto its head. In addition, such developments in economics and public policy pose some uncomfortable questions for our understanding of sustainable development and the political discourses that have characterised the field. There is very profound literature (Hobson, 2002; Jackson, 2005; Seyfang, 2005) that suggests that there is still considerable confusion about the most effective way to achieve more sustainable consumption.

And there are struggles ahead. The industry was forged and nurtured in a purely economic environment and its actions were based on the possession, accumulation and exploitation of resources (and other living beings) and human labour. It was (and still is for many) an era based on possession.

However, because societies are evolving, this paradigm is slowly changing. Ultimately, it changes the industry, the people who work in it and the people who interact with it.

Describing the hospitality industry

A description of the industry is best captured as the following:

> When describing a phenomenon such as the hospitality industry, it is difficult to define not only its size and activities but also its role in society. The diversity of its products and services, from luxury hotels, to cruise ships, casinos,

catering firms and even hot dog stands outside sports stadiums, defies the conventional definition of an industry as being a set of firms offering the same or similar products. Naturally, the provision of hotels falls within the general context of hospitality, an aspect of human activity which has important social dimensions as well as meeting the physiological needs of shelter and comfort. From an international perspective the notion of a hotel is understood as a culturally bound phenomenon that represents a certain set of assumptions. Managing a hotel in the twenty-first century is a challenging task. Welcoming and taking care of guests from different backgrounds and offering food and shelter are always constant but the demands made on hoteliers have drastically changed. The modern day hotelier requires an in-depth knowledge in the traditional fields of operations, finance, marketing, customer relationships, branding, media and communication but also in stakeholder relationships and increasingly over the past decade: environmental management, ethics and social responsibility. Many hotels now consist of multiple units including restaurants, bars, clubs, entertainment facilities, spas and recreation facilities operating 24/7/365 and consequently have a relatively high environmental impact and may cause a strained relationship with people both locally and internationally in the global market place. The expansion of the hotel industry is dramatic with dozens of new properties opening weekly. This expansion is a response to increases in prosperity and the desire to travel. The result is direct pressure on non-renewable resources both in the 'design and construction phase' and the 'operation and occupation phase' of hotel properties. This is where innovative and sustainable buildings and management systems are needed to relieve the unrelenting pressure on the natural environment that is reaching the limits of its carrying capacity in many destinations.

(Legrand et al., 2017, pp. 16–17)

Over time and throughout its entire life cycle, the hospitality industry has been a considerable contributor of greenhouse gases (GHG), exacerbating climate change. The industry interacts with the food (food supplies, gastronomy), textile (staff uniforms, white goods, upholstery, carpets), technology (property management systems, servers) and transport industries (buses, airplanes, cruise ships, automobiles). It is a large producer of waste, plastics and user of fresh water. Since the hotel sector relies on guests traveling to and from a destination, an impressive carbon footprint is allocated to transport. The same applies for the food supply chain necessary to cater to staff and guests at properties, especially in remote locations. Heating, cooling, lighting and ventilating hotel buildings requires large amounts of energy, often sourced from non-renewable production. To make matters more complicated and as Nicolas Dubrocard affirms in the *Hotel Yearbook Special Edition on Sustainability in Hospitality, 2018*: "In certain hotels, the vertical structure in place with out-of-date standard operating procedures (SOPs) allows for little room (if any) for innovation. Individual support and open dialogue on how to operate more efficiently is not present" (Dubrocard, 2017, p. 29). Finally, it is worth highlighting the human exploitation that occurs in the industry, which involves labour rights, human trafficking and other human rights. Human rights are a very important issue to tackle when discussing sustainable development and the hotel industry. These issues have long been ignored by the industry, where a real preference has been given to establishing yearly reports focusing on saving or reducing the use of water or energy. The hospitality industry has been historically criticised for being harmful and neglectful about issues such as the environment and culture. Through the pressures exerted by different sectors, hospitality companies had to integrate socio-environmental issues as a key part of the business model, going beyond philanthropic and ethical aspects. This integration requires political and social engagement with stakeholders for actions to be legitimate, transparent, continuous and possible (Gardetti, 2005).

Sustainable development in the hospitality industry

Sustainability within the hotel industry as we know it today has come a long way and faces perhaps an even longer process for further improvement. To elaborate, this section presents a brief history of sustainable development in the hospitality industry, including some of its main drivers during the different stages of this evolutionary process. The focus on sustainability is growing considerably, since the term "has been one of the hospitality industry's biggest buzz words for years. Following increased market pressure, hotel groups have already taken to implementing and marketing sustainable initiatives across their portfolios" (Harms & Farrell, 2017, p. 34).

Tourism industry and sustainability

As Houdré and Singh (2012) state in the book *Hotel Sustainable Development*, the origin of environmentalism in the tourism industry can be traced back to the late 19th century, when many protected areas around the world were transformed based on the model of United States national parks. The creation of parks ensured the preservation of their natural state and protected them from exploitation. The authors explain that, in the post-World War II period, the hotel industry began to expand and a large number of tourists, especially Americans, began to choose destinations in the Caribbean, while Europeans were heading to places in Southeast Asia. This movement of people for tourism purposes started to raise concerns about the tourism and hospitality industry's environmental impact.

Sustainable development in the hospitality industry emerged from an environmental movement in the tourism sector broadly known as 'ecotourism' – which in turn developed from global corporate sustainability initiatives. Yet historically, the tourism industry has been quite slow to take positive action on sustainability (Honey, 2008). However, while the lodging industry does not have the same environmental impact as the extractive and manufacturing sectors, it is nonetheless a major contributor to environmental problems (Singh & Houdré, 2012).

Although tourism was once thought of as a 'smokeless' industry with few, if any, environmental impacts, there is growing recognition of its potential for adverse impacts. Tourism consists of the activities undertaken during travel from home or work for the pleasure and enjoyment of certain destinations, and the facilities that cater to the needs of the tourist (Mathieson & Wall, 1982; Power, 1996).

Environmental concerns linked to tourism contributed to the emergence of the 'cautionary platform,' which basically argued that unregulated tourism development eventually would result in unacceptably high environmental, economic and sociocultural costs for destinations and residents there (Weaver, 2006). According to Houdré and Singh, the US hotel industry began to consider environmental matters in different areas of hotel operations as early as the 1950s (Houdré & Singh, 2012). In fact, it was back in the 1960s that the lodging sector started to look at environmental issues such as air purification, natural resources usage, radiation, ventilation, waste management, water supply control and sound control methods. This coincided with the release of *Silent Spring* – a pioneering book published by Rachel Carlson in 1962 that laid the foundations for modern environmentalism. Al Gore wrote in the introduction for the 1994 edition "The publication of Silent Spring can properly be seen as the beginning of the modern environmental movement" (Al Gore, 1994, p. xviii). Carlson set the stage for a new wave of green-activist movements and a massive formation of environmental protection organisations in the United States and other developed countries. In addition, activists began to relate the destruction of the natural environment to the complex interface of new technologies and corporate, political and economic power in the late 1960s and early 1970s.

As individuals became more aware of environmental issues, society became increasingly demanding of institutions. Environmental initiatives emerged and expanded. With mounting pressure, changes were made in both legislative and administrative environmental regulations. In subsequent years, these 'environmental regulations' were later replaced by the categories of "environmental engineering" and "environmental law" (Houdré & Singh, 2012, p. 8). Five decades ago, McEwen and Eberhard in their paper "Hotels and water crisis" (1963) presented a case of ten Sheraton hotels in which water use dropped to reach an average seventy-two gallons per occupied room a day. Their research provided one of the first examples of existing environmental concerns associated with property building. The authors discussed hotel water supply and water pollution and treatment, listing a variety of potential pollutants including infectious agents, different organic chemicals and other mineral, chemical and radioactive substances. The article noted that those chemicals involved were relatively new and thus had a possible negative effect on human and animal health. The authors suggested that the industry should take up the cause of water conservation in a public spirit to gain favourable national publicity.

The hotel industry has experienced a relentless growth in supply over the past 50 years, correlated to increased demand and attractive real estate investments. However, as Houdré and Singh discuss:

> As the global community has recognized the environmental costs of tourism, the increasing ecological costs of rapid hotel development have also been noticed. Most resort developments were criticized for being unattractive and not well assimilated into the surrounding area. High-rise hotels along the coastal zones of Atlantic City and Miami, for example, were perceived by many as visual pollution. Hawaii was one of the first tourist destinations in the United States to experience this problem, prompting articles about it as early as 1969.
> (Houndré & Singh, 2012, p. 8)

In the 1970s, the advent of wide-bodied, high-speed airplanes fuelled growth in the number of global travellers. The subsequent boom in tourism industry development and its fast penetration into underdeveloped regions, as well as the growing political influence of the environmental movement, contributed to the emergence of the aforementioned cautionary platform. During that time, the amount of research and literature related to environmental protection and sustainability increased exponentially in volume and sophistication as the idea of 'sustainability' gained further recognition (Weaver, 2006).

With the growth of mass tourism and harmful physical and socio-cultural effects of destination stress, resulting from overdevelopment in the 1970s, the environmental awareness of tourism gained momentum. One of the consequences was the rise of the concept of 'alternative tourism,' which emerged as a possible route toward sustainability in the tourism industry. This concept came from the broader discourse on the idea of 'sustainable development,' which, according to Bramwell and Lane (1981), emerged in the early 1970s World Conservation Strategy (1980). Alternative tourism was thought of as the best means to attain conservation of natural areas in order to maintain resource sustainability, avoid environmental damage, maintain resource quality and bring means of economic development to local people. It was also related to benefits for local communities, educational value for tourists and attracting foreign exchange for struggling developing countries (Boo, 1992; Brandon, 1996; Singh & Houdré, 2012).

The 1997 Kyoto Protocol is an international agreement that sets binding targets for thirty-seven countries and the European community to fight against global warming by reducing GHG emissions. The Protocol came into force in early 2005. Under it, countries' actual emissions have to be monitored and precise records have to be kept of trades carried out (McIntosh & Goeldner, 1990, p. 10; UNFFC, 2014). Noteworthy is the absence of the United States' signature. (Houdré & Singh, 2012). However, the Kyoto Protocol was seen as an important first step towards a truly global emission reduction regime that will stabilise GHG emissions and that can provide the architecture for a future international agreement on climate change (UNFFC, 2014). Legrand et al. (2017) discuss some of the key developments and agreements post-Kyoto, whereby an international agreement (known as the Paris Agreement) on climate change was adopted by 195 countries and the European Union in December 2015 (during the 21st Conference of the Parties – COP21). The Paris Agreement was the result of six years of work since the 2009 COP in Copenhagen. The agreement provides a global framework towards "holding the increase in the global average temperature to well below 2 °C above preindustrial levels and pursuing efforts to limit the temperature increase to 1.5 °C."

These global initiatives resulted in a heightened awareness and discussion within the tourism and hospitality sectors. In anticipation of the growing importance of sustainable development for business, the leaders of several hotel companies formed the International Hotels Environment Initiative (IHEI) in 1992. The main aim of this organisation was to create a collaborative forum to improve sustainability standards for hotels and, later, tourism-related companies. After twelve years, the organisation changed its name to the International Tourism Partnership (ITP), in order to have a broader mandate and appeal. Its programs have a strong educational and informative focus to inspire and show companies how to develop and operate a sustainable enterprise.

For instance, to analyse the present challenges of the hospitality industry, the ITP explains that

> the hotel industry can be a force for good and make a positive contribution to the SDGs (Sustainable Development Goals) and the COP21 climate agreements, and by working together, hotel companies can drive change further and faster than by working on their own. ITP's vision for 2030 is for sustainable growth and fairer future for all. ITP's goals, launched in the International Year of Sustainable Tourism for Development, send a clear call to action to the wider industry about the critical importance of use the SDGs as a focal point to drive responsible business in hospitality. For 25 years, the hotel industry under ITP's leadership has advanced sustainable tourism, developing tools and resources for hotels and lodgings around the world, sharing knowledge and working together for a more responsible future.
> (Hughes, 2018, p. 9)

The industry's increasing globalisation might be one factor contributing to the development of environmental activities.

In response to the recognition that a growing segment of travellers values conservation and preservation, another important organisation was launched that provided further impetus to hospitality organisations to increase their sustainability quotient.

The United Nations World Tourism Organization (UNWTO) considers ecotourism the fastest-growing market in the industry. The sustainability discussion and dialogue sought to merge economic development with a social agenda. In the late 1990s, initiatives looked at employment, training, the elimination of poverty and eradication of sexual exploitation and human trafficking. As the environmental movement evolved from preservation and conservation to incorporate a broader agenda of sustainable development, some leading hotel companies were quick to adopt a similar view. The term 'corporate social responsibility,' better known by its acronym 'CSR,' became an integrated part of the hotel industry terminology and strategy.

Triple bottom line & hospitality industry initiatives

According to Legrand et al. (2017, p. 394),

> Stricter governmental regulations, combined with increased public interest (and scrutiny) in environmental affairs and claims, have acted as a push factor for the steady development of ecolabels in various types of industries. Ecolabelling programmes started in Europe and their use has spread across the globe. This rapid development is also due to the fact that businesses have recognised that environmental concerns can be translated into a market advantage. Although in practice, consumers are still largely unaware of the differences between the many labels or simply confused.

For many years, companies have applied sustainable development principles to different extents, without labelling them as such. Some companies, following their corporate leadership agenda, have focused more on environmental issues, while others have focused on social responsibility issues. Some have developed activities around these two issues, but rarely have companies incorporated both issues into programs as an integral part of their strategy. Very few executives understood that it could become not only a part of their company's strategy, but actually the foundation of it. John Elkington presented the sustainable development concept as a tangible business model. In his book *Cannibals with Forks*, Elkington discusses the triple bottom line (TBL) paradigm. The foundation of TBL is a holistic approach to developing business through a strategy based on three pillars, sometimes called 'the 3Ps' – profit, people and planet:

- **Economic prosperity (profit):** Businesses are meant to make a profit and improve their bottom lines year after year, but they should conduct their operations with total transparency toward all stakeholders and do so ethically.
- **Social responsibility (people):** While conducting business, companies must take care of surrounding communities, starting, obviously, with their own employees, followed by the local community, the national community and the international community.

- **Environmental protection (planet):** The *impact* that any business has on the environment must be assessed and reduced as much as possible. This will have two positive immediate consequences – it will reduce the carbon footprint of the company and, by measuring and improving energy expenses, it will improve the economic bottom line (Elkington, 1997).

Twenty-five years later, Elkington wrote that he needed to do a 'strategic recall' to do some fine tuning (Elkington, 2018). In the interim twenty-five years of TBL, a global climate emergency has been declared, carbon emissions are in no way under control, biodiversity collapse has been observed across various ecosystems and the world is facing multiple tipping points. Business as usual, including efforts to incorporate TBL in form of voluntary CSR strategies reported extensively, has brought minimal gains. Why is it so? Elkington argues that "the TBL wasn't designed to be just an accounting tool" (2018, p. 8), happily sold by consultants. The TBL has not provoked a deeper thinking about capitalism and its future, as it should have (Elkington, 2018).

Sustainable development, and TBL, demands not merely a few programs labelled as 'green,' but a paradigm shift in the culture of business.

Hotels that practice sustainable development can accrue benefits including cost containment, revenue enhancement and a positive public image, not to mention employee satisfaction. All evidence indicates that sustainable development is here to stay, if not by choice, possibly by force, due to mounting climate change challenges and collapsing biodiversity. An increasing number of industry stakeholders are now more committed than ever before to sustainable development. For hoteliers around the world and the hospitality industry in general, a TBL strategy is not just an opportunity, but also a true responsibility. In various ways, business leaders are trying to signal their growing concern about the potential future impact of energy, climate and water security issues – and their interest in the solutions-based markets that will evolve as a result. "The market, even if patchily, is switching on" (Elkington, 2012, p. x).

And while much is left to do, the hospitality sector has experienced a transformation since Hailes and Elkington published their book *Holidays That Don't Cost the Earth* in 1992, following the 1988 publication of *The Green Consumer Guide*. At the time, even leading hotel groups had not adopted environmental audits – whereas today the best of them talk comfortably about energy efficiency, water footprints and food waste reduction, to mention a few.

Some cities have recognised the opportunity this presents. For example, towns located near some of the busiest tourist areas in Spain, such as Begur, Pals and Bigastro, have been able to differentiate themselves from the mass tourism and offer a much more relaxed atmosphere and authentic alternative, betting on the slow movement philosophy. Applicants must meet a number of requirements, including, among others:

> The importance of the slow movement lies not only in the business opportunities it presents, but also in the way that it can restate the existing tourism and urban development models, in line with current and important concepts for the touristic industry such as sustainable tourism or sensations tourism. In this sense, the present study was a descriptive introduction that opens the door to future work with quantitative or qualitative methods to explore different aspects of "slow tourism." Eventually, this concept will have to strengthen and social, environmental, or economic profitability can be explored.
> (Miretpastor, Peiró-Signes, Segarra-Oña, & Mondéjar-Jiménez, 2015, p. 324)

If the movement initially focused on food, today it includes aspects as diverse as tourism and urban planning.

> The slow tourism would be framed in these new forms of tourism that are not trying to move from the current model but to break dramatically with the traditional concept of tourism. The slow tourism aims for tourists to be a part of local life and to connect with the destination, its people and culture.
> (Miretpastor et al., 2015, p. 322)

The purpose of a trip is not to visit a city, but to discover it. Slow tourism and slow city concepts, as they share the same philosophy, may address urban development and tourism growth from the same perspective and seek common goals (Miretpastor et al., 2015).

To conclude, while the hospitality industry has made some advances towards sustainable development over the past few decades, it needs to show strong resiliency as it faces the multiple environmental and social challenges ahead.

CHAPTER CASE 1.1

Role and responsibility of the hospitality industry towards global challenges[5]

How is the hospitality industry approaching the Sustainable Development Goals (SDGs) through their management policies and practices?

Sustainable development goals

In 2015, the United Nations launched its 2030 Agenda for Sustainable Development, a new plan of action for people, planet, and prosperity. The Agenda comprises seventeen SDGs with 169 specific targets for all countries to aim for by 2030. The SDGs include eliminating poverty, ensuring equality, reducing environmental impact and creating economic prosperity and jobs. The travel and tourism industry is explicitly identified in three of the 169 targets (8, 12, 14), but its potential contribution to this new Agenda is much wider and the sector can play a role in each of the seventeen SDGs. The World Travel and Tourism Council (WTTC) endeavours to highlight this role throughout its activities, ensuring that the social benefits of the sector, as they relate to the SDGs, are identified and understood (WTTC, 2016, p. 7).

Gloria Guevara, President and CEO of the WTTC, established that

> recent research with WTTC Members highlighted sustainability as a top priority for the sector. Sustainability reporting, which is on the rise across Travel & Tourism, is a mechanism for companies to monitor progress and share best practices. Our aim with this guidance is to support companies, large and small, as they take this journey; and provide them with the mechanism to communicate their progress. As a sector which accounts for 10% of the world's GDP and generates 292 million jobs, we have a responsibility to ensure that growth is sustainable.
>
> (O'Neill, 2017)

The SDGs and the hospitality industry approach is discussed below:

Sustainable development goals for the 2030 global agenda

1. End the poverty in all its forms everywhere
2. End hunger, achieve food security and improve nutrition and promote sustainable agriculture
3. Ensure healthy lives and promote well-being for all at all ages
4. Ensure inclusive and equitable quality education and promote lifelong learning opportunities for all
5. Achieve gender equality and empower women and girls
6. Ensure availability and sustainable management of water and sanitation for all
7. Ensure access to affordable, reliable, sustainable and modern energy for all

8. Promote sustained, inclusive and sustainable economic growth, full and productive employment and decent work for all
9. Build resilient infrastructure, promote inclusive and sustainable industrialisation and foster innovation
10. Reduce inequity within and among countries
11. Make cities and human settlements inclusive, safe, resilient and sustainable
12. Ensure sustainable consumption and production patterns
13. Take urgent action to combat climate change and its impacts (acknowledging that the United Nations Framework Convention on Climate Change is the primary international, intergovernmental forum for negotiating the global response to climate change
14. Conserve and sustainably use the oceans, seas and marine resources for sustainable development
15. Protect, restore and promote sustainable use of terrestrial ecosystems, sustainably manage forests, combat desertification and halt and reverse land degradation and halt biodiversity loss
16. Promote peaceful and inclusive societies for sustainable development, provide access to justice for all and build effective, accountable and inclusive institutions at all levels
17. Strengthen the means of implementation and revitalise the global partnership for sustainable development.

As Siobhan O'Neill mentioned in an article published on the Green Hotelier website, "The WTTC report covers latest trend in sustainability reporting, including which governments and stock exchanges are mandating such reports, and how companies are refining the reports to be more engaging for audiences" (O'Neill, 2017). Thus, according to Nicolas Dubrocard "the use of sustainability reports is strongly advisable as it brings light to areas where savings can be made" (2017, p. 29). Applying the SDGs means thinking in the long term, while acting in the short term. There are plenty of cases about investments and the return on those investments also published.

Hospitality practices

First of all, the efforts of **Hotel Verde** as shown in an article written by Sarah Farrell (2017) for *The Hotel Yearbook Special Edition – Sustainable Hospitality 2018* can be noted. The Hotel Verde is a four-star hotel located in South Africa that integrated sustainability solutions into its business. It mainly focuses on resource efficiency through passive design strategies for optimised efficiency, as well as implementing active technologies to further increase efficiency. Hotel Verde has also instituted a policy of transparency and education for water and energy use. For instance, during tours for industry peers and public, the team explains what has and has not worked in terms of better water and energy management.

Soneva also provides a great example of sustainability management in the hotel industry. Soneva was the first resort in the Maldives. Founded by Eva and Sonu Shivdasani in 1995, on a then-deserted island, they created a villa with an environmental and social mission bridging sustainability and luxury experience. Quoting Chairman and CEO Sonu Shivdasani:

> I believe that all companies, hotel businesses included, must have a purpose beyond profit. They must play a greater role in the world beyond just enriching their shareholders. I don't believe that this has to run counter to a successful business model – in fact it can be central to it.
>
> (Shivdasani, 2016, p. 144)

Soneva demonstrates that business sustainability includes long term targets and starting with a step-by-step approach in the present and building alliances with stakeholder organisations. Shivdasani points out,

> There are two key areas to focus on climate change and the nitrogen phosphorus cycle. This means switching to renewable energy and food that does not require excessive use of fertilizers. At **Soneva** we are committed to leading the fight against climate change within the hospitality sector. In 2008, we took the simple step of adding a mandatory 2% carbon levy to our guests' bills, to offset their travel emissions. It was a small change, and relatively small charge, which we found our guests more than happy to accept. We have invested the funds through the Soneva Foundation in carbon mitigation projects, such as planting half a million trees in Thailand, funding a wind turbine in India, and providing nearly 200,000 people with energy efficient cook stoves in Darfur and Myanmar. We have a strong focus on moving over to renewable energy. Our aim is to make a difference. We strive to be the best employer. We aim to produce attractive returns to our investors, demonstrating that sustainability is good for business.
>
> (Shivdasani, 2017, p. 37)

Inge Huijbretchs, Global Vice President, Responsible Business and Safety & Security at **Radisson Hotel Group**, stated that by 2030 it is estimated that half the world's population will be living under profound water stress. She also argues that everything that we use, eat, buy or wear requires water to produce it. Thus, "the main hospitality companies are now looking at water beyond the borders of the hotel room" (2017, p. 40). At the Radisson Hotel Group, one of the world's largest hotel companies, this is done along with raising guest awareness of the importance of water in the Blue Planet Program, where mindfulness is part of the customer experience. Safeguarding water use involves innovative solutions, such as showers that filter water in a high-quality fresh cycle.

As a last case, let's consider **Inkaterra**, founded in 1975 by José Koechlin. This is a Peruvian pioneering project in ecotourism and sustainable development. From a holistic approach, Inkaterra creates knowledge and scientific research to lay the groundwork for enriching environmental conservation, while providing education and welfare to local communities. For the past thirty years, Inkaterra has supported the major inventories of flora and fauna. Also,

> since late 2016, this eco-lodge with a design inspired by the Ese'Eja culture and built with native materials, is the training centre for **Inkaterra** Explorer Guides – most of them are born and raised in local communities. It offers a knowledgeable experience for scientists, students, volunteers and eco-conscious travellers, welcoming guests to be part of diverse research and conservation projects overseen by NGO Inkaterra Association. Thus, given the current situation in Madre de Dios, Inkaterra aims to replicate these initiatives throughout the region, educating the local communities in biodiversity conservation and the sustainable use of natural resources through eco-friendly entrepreneurship.
>
> (Koechlin & Meseth, 2017, p. 53)

Tackling challenges

As shown by the above examples, entrepreneurs in the hospitality industry are taking action towards meeting the SDGs, considering them foundational values and as a business model transformation. While tackling all seventeen objectives at the same time may pose a great challenge, a responsible hotel industry can be achieved with awareness and tenacity. As is pointed out by the WTTC,

> Responsible tourism is not an isolated, niche market – travellers, companies, and governments all have to play a part to create a sustainable tourism industry for our collective futures. It is the cumulative effort and emphasis that will affect positive change.
>
> (WTTC, 2016, p. 21)

EXERCISES

Group discussion

Take some time to read Ehrenfeld definition:

> Sustainability is a possible way of living, of being in which individuals, firms, governments, and other institutions are responsible for taking care of the future as if it belonged to them today, for equitably sharing the ecological resources on which the survival of human and other species depends, and for assuring that all who live today and, in the future, will be able to satisfy their needs and human aspirations.
> (Ehrenfeld, 1999, p. 230)

Within the seventeen Sustainable Development Goals (SDGs), 'equality' is one of the fundamental issues that society has to tackle in order to achieve a more sustainable world.

1. How should the hospitality sector respond or act on the issue of equality?
2. Is the hospitality sector more (or less) responsible than other industry sectors for achieving sustainability?
3. What are ways hospitality can generate a change?

Individual research

Research and analyse the cases presented: Inkaterra, Soneva, and Hotel Verde.

Take some time to visit the websites and read the yearly sustainability reports, if available (e.g., the Soneva Total Impact Assessment report available here: https://sonevachangemakers.com/)

In relation to the seventeen SDGs and from the perspective of system thinking and systemic change needed to ground sustainability, provide possible answers to the following questions.

1. Which of the three hotel cases presents the most sustainable business model?
2. How did you derive your conclusion? Based on what factors?
3. How could your chosen hotel expand its sustainable strategy?
4. Do you have other examples of hotels that you would consider leading with best practices in regards to the SDGs and sustainability in general?

Group research/group discussion

Take some time to research the following topics and answer the questions presented at the end of each. Be ready to share your thoughts in a group discussion:

Climate emergency and the hospitality industry: Are we on track?

(Source: Legrand (2019a); originally published on *HospitalityNet World Panel on Sustainability in Hospitality*)

The hotel industry must reduce its GHG emissions per room per year by 66% by 2030 and 90% by 2050 (see ITP, 2017) to stay within the Paris Agreement target. However, looking at ten of the largest hotel companies, only one sets a goal in line with science-based targets. Decarbonisation has long been an integral part of risk assessment in other industries. Considering the current growth in hotel supply, the industry has already committed future carbon dioxide emissions via (often) poorly designed and air-conditioning hungry new properties.

1. What drives the lack of commitment in the hospitality industry?
2. What keeps developers and investors away from building a carbon-neutral future?
3. What are the main obstacles ahead?

Who makes hospitality sustainability happen: Governments, industry, consumers?

(Source: Legrand (2019b); originally published on *HospitalityNet World Panel on Sustainability in Hospitality*)

What (or who) helps hospitality companies improve faster? Consumer-led campaigns on plastic straws have pushed many hospitality companies to consider alternatives or simply ban single-use plastics. So far, however, the vast majority of guests still choose their hotels mainly based on location and price. Using levers such as taxation or legislation, governments are also increasing pressure. Recent examples include the European Union's ban on a series of single-use plastics such as cutlery, straws, and stirrers by 2021. Many states across the US are implementing similar bans. Beyond plastics, carbon pricing initiatives are in place or are planned in more than forty-five countries. The EU's Energy Performance of Buildings Directive requires all new buildings to be nearly zero-energy (NZEB) by the end of 2020 and existing buildings to transition towards NZEB by 2050. Finally, the hospitality industry's self-regulation and voluntary codes of conduct are considered popular approaches in dealing with sustainability challenges, but at times are met with limited success.

1. Facing mounting environmental issues, are all three parties (governments, consumers and industry) playing an equally important role?
2. Do consumers have the foresight to act as a useful lever of change? Taxes and legislation are in the pipeline across the globe, so what needs to be done today to minimise the risk of getting hit?
3. And how about driving consumer behaviour change through inspiring guest experiences?

Sustainable Development Goals (SDGs)

Take some time to visit the Sustainable Development Goals Knowledge Platform (https://sustainabledevelopment.un.org/index.html).

1. Choose one of the SDGs you are particularly interested in and find out the exact targets set to achieve the goal.
2. Now, check the progress made on that goal; any highlights to share?
3. How should the hotel industry operationalise those SDGs?

Notes

1 World Commission on Environment and Development (WCED): Our Common Future, Oxford University Press, 1987.
2 As referred to in the paper "The Politics of the Environment – Ideas, Activism, Policy," by Neil Carter (2001, p. 195), this concept was conceived from the World Conservation Strategy, integrated by three international NGOs (IUCN, UNEP and WWF). This document from 1980 was related to the ecological sustainability or the conservation of living resources and was less focused on political, economic or social aspects.
3 This club, created in 1968, is an NGO composed of scientists, economists, businessmen and state leaders, who contributed to a better understanding of global problems.
4 Social justice theories generally refer to the distribution of rights, opportunities and resources among human beings. There are many competing justice accounts, where distribution is based on principles such as needs, abandonment, legitimacy, public services and equity (Carter, 2001, p. 59). Moreover, one of the principles of environmental justice adopted by The First Nation of People of Color Environmental Leadership Summit (Washington, DC, 1991) is that environmental justice mandates a balanced and ethical use of resources for the development of a sustainable planet for human beings and all living beings (Bowers, 2001, p. 209).
5 This section shows the objectives for sustainable development of the UN's 2030 Global Agenda. However, the goals for each objective are not stated.

References

Agyeman, J., Bullard, R. D., & Evans, B. (2003). *Just Sustainabilities: Development in an Unequal World*. Cambridge, MA: MIT Press.

Allen, P., Bonazzi, C., & Gee, D. (2001). Sustainable development. In P. Allen, C. Bonazzi, and D. Gee (Eds.), *Metaphors for Change – Partnership, Tools and Civic Action for Sustainability* (pp. 9–10). Sheffield: Greenleaf Publishing Limited.

Barney, G., Director. (1981). *Global 2000 Report to the President*. New York: Penguin.

Boo, E. (1992). *The Ecotourism Boom: Planning for Development and Management*, Wild Lands and Human Needs Technical Paper Series. Washington, DC: World Wildlife Fund.

Bowers, C. A. (2001). *Educating for Eco-Justice and Community*. Athens: The University of Georgia Press.

Brack, D. (1998). *Trade and Environment: Conflict or Compatibility?* London: RIIA and Earthscan.

Bramwell, B., & Lane, B. (1993). Sustainable tourism: An evolving global approach. *Journal of Sustainable Tourism, 1*(1), 1–5.

Brandon, K. (1996). Ecotourism and conservation: A review of key issues. *Environmental Department Working Papers, No. 3 Biodiversity Series*. Washington, DC: The World Bank.

Carley, M., & Christie, I. (1992). *Managing Sustainable Development*. London: Earthscan.

Carter, N. (2001). *The Politics of the Environment – Ideas, Activism, Policy*. Cambridge: Cambridge University Press.

Costanza, R., & Daly, H. E. (1992). Natural Capital and Sustainable Development. *Conservation Biology, 6*(1), 37–46.

Cronon, W. (2008). *Foreword to DDT Silent Spring, and the Rise of Environmentalism: Classic Texts*. Seattle: University of Washington Press.

Daly, H. E. (2000). *Beyond Growth: The Economics of Sustainable Development*. Boston, MA: Beacon.

Dobson, A. (1996). Environment sustainabilities: An analysis and a typology. *Environmental Politics, 5*(3), 401–428.

Dobson, A. (1998). *Dimensions of Social Justice: Conceptions of Environmental Sustainability*. Oxford: Oxford University Press.

Dresner, S. (2002). *The Principles of Sustainability*. London: Earthscan.

Dubrocard, N. (2017). Sustainability. Really? Not yet. In W. Legrand, W. Wade, & H. Roelings (Eds.), *Hotel Yearbook 2018, Special Edition on Sustainable Hospitality* (pp. 28–29). Switzerland: Hsyndicate, and International University of Applied Science Bad Honnef. Grandvaux.

Durning, A. (1992). *How Much is Enough? The Consumer Society and the Future of the Earth*. London: W. W. Norton & Company.

Dyllick, T., & Hockerts, K. (2002). Beyond the business case for corporate sustainability. *John Wiley & Sons, Business Strategy and the Environment Journal, 11*(2), 130–141

Eder, K. (1996). The institutionalization of environmentalism: Ecological discourse and the second transformation of the public sphere. In S. Lash, B. Szerszynski, & B. Wymie (Eds.), *Risk, Environment and Modernity: Towards a New Ecology* (pp. 203–221). London: Sage.

Edwards, J. (2017). On social sustainability: An alarming global trend and how to disrupt it. In W. Legrand, W. Wade, & H. Roelings (Eds.), *Hotel Yearbook 2018, Special Edition on Sustainable Hospitality* (pp. 74–75). Switzerland: Hsyndicate, and International University of Applied Science Bad Honnef. Grandvaux.

Ehrenfeld, J. R. (1999). Cultural structure and the challenge of sustainability. In K. Sexton, A. A. Marcus, K. W. Easter, & T. D. Burkhardt (Eds.), *Better Environmental Decisions – Strategies for Governments, Businesses, and Communities*. Washington, DC: Island Press.

Elkington, J. (1997). *Cannibals with Forks: The Triple Bottom Line of 21st Century Business*. Oxford: Capstone Publishing Limited.

Elkington, J. (2012). Foreword: Treating Earth as if we intended to say. In A. J. Singh & H. Houdré (Eds.), *Hotel Sustainable Development. Principles & Best Practices* (p. ix–xi). Lansing, MI: American Hotel and Lodging Educational Institute.

Elkington, J. (2018). 25 Years Ago I Coined the Phrase "Triple Bottom Line." Here's Why It's Time to Rethink It. *Harvard Business Review*. Retrieved June 25, 2018, from https://hbr.org/2018/06/25-years-ago-i-coined-the-phrase-triple-bottom-line-heres-why-im-giving-up-on-it

Elliot, J. (1999). *An introduction to Sustainable Development*. New York: Roudledge.

Esty, D. C. (1994). *Greening the GATT Trade, Environment, and the Future*. Washington, DC: PIIE.

Faber, D., & O'Connor, J. (1989). The struggle for nature: Environmental crisis and the crisis of environmentalism in the United States. *Capitalism, Nature, Socialism, 1*(2), 12–39.

Farrell, S. (2017). Hotel Verde, Africa's Greenes hotel. In W. Legrand, W. Wade, & H. Roelings (Eds.), *Hotel Yearbook 2018, Special Edition on Sustainable Hospitality* (pp. 30–31). Grandvaux: Woody Wade, Wade & Company SA.

Foucault, M. (1972). *The Archaeology of Knowledge*. London: Tavistock.

Frankel, C. (1998). *In Earth's Company*. Gabriola Island: New Society Publishers.

Gardetti, M. A. (2005). *Textos en Sustentabilidad Empresarial. Integrando las consideraciones sociales, ambientales y económicas en el corto y largo plazo*. Buenos Aires: Dunken.

Gilding, P. (2000). Sustainability-doing. In D. Dunphy, J. Benveniste, A. Griffiths, & P. Sutton (Eds.), *Sustainability – The Corporate Challenge of the 21st Century*. St. Leonards: Allen & Unwin.

Goodman, D., & Redclift, M. (1991). *Environment and Development in Latin America*. Manchester: Manchester University Press.

Gore, A. (1994). Introduction. In R. Carlson (Ed.), *Silent Spring*. New York: Library of Congress.

Harms, A., & Farrell, S. (2017). Seven future trends in hotel sustainability in Africa. In W. Legrand, W. Wade, & H. Roelings (Eds.), *Hotel Yearbook 2018, Special Edition on Sustainable Hospitality* (pp. 34–35). Switzerland: Hsyndicate, and International University of Applied Science Bad Honnef. Grandvaux.

Helliwell, J. F., Layard, R., Sachs, J., & De Neve, J.-E. (2020). *World Happiness Report 2020*. New York: Sustainable Development Solutions Network.

Hobsbawm, E. J. (1988). *En torno a los orígenes de la revolución industrial*. Madrid: Siglo XXI de España.

Hobson, K. (2002). Competing discourses of sustainable consumption: Does the 'rationalization of lifestyles' make sense? *Environmental Politics, 11*(2), 95–120.

Honey, M. (2008). *Ecotourism and Sustainable Development: Who Owns Paradise?* (2nd ed.). Washington, DC: Island Press.

Hughes, F. (2017). The hotel sector, reporting and the sustainable development goals. In W. Legrand, W. Wade, & H. Roelings (Eds.), *Hotel Yearbook 2018, Special Edition on Sustainable Hospitality* (pp. 8–9). Switzerland: Hsyndicate, and International University of Applied Science Bad Honnef. Grandvaux.

Huijbrechts, I. (2017). Water mindfulness and the future of hotel supply chains. In W. Legrand, W. Wade, & H. Roelings (Eds.), *Hotel yearbook 2018, Special Edition on Sustainable Hospitality* (pp. 40–41). Switzerland: Hsyndicate, and International University of Applied Science Bad Honnef. Grandvaux.

Hvidberg, P. (2017). Moving towards sustainability: Future proofing in the hospitality sector. In W. Legrand, W. Wade, & H. Roelings (Eds.), *Hotel Yearbook 2018, Special*

Edition on Sustainable Hospitality (pp. 10-13). Switzerland: Hsyndicate, and International University of Applied Science Bad Honnef. Grandvaux.

International Union for Conservation of Nature (IUCN), United Nations Environment Programme (UNEP), and World Wildlife Fund (WWF). (1980). *The World Conservation Strategy: Living Resource Conservation for Sustainable Development.* Gland.

ITP. (2017). *Hotel Decarbonisation Report: Aligning the sector with the Paris Climate Agreement towards 2030 and 2050.* International Tourism Partnership, November. https://www.tourismpartnership.org/download/2053/

Jackson, T. (2005). Live better by consuming less? Is there a 'double dividend' in sustainable consumption? *Journal of Industrial Ecology,* 9(1-2), 19-36.

Jacobs, M. (1991). *The Green Economy: Environment, Sustainable Development and the Politics of the Future.* London: Pluto Press.

Jacobs, M. (1996). *The Politics of the Real World: Meeting the New Century.* London: Earthscan.

Koechlin, J., & Meseth, G. (2017). Peru's Inkaterra: Helping save the Amazon through sustainable landscape corridors while pushing the boundaries of eco-friendly luxury hotels. In W. Legrand, W. Wade, & H. Roelings (Eds.), *Hotel Yearbook 2018, Special Edition on Sustainable Hospitality* (pp. 52-55). Switzerland: Hsyndicate, and International University of Applied Science Bad Honnef. Grandvaux.

Lang, T., & Hines, C. (1993). *The New Protectionism: Protecting the Future against Free Trade.* London: Earthscan.

Legrand, W. (2019a). Climate emergency and the hospitality industry: Are we on track?. HospitalityNet World Panel Sustainability in Hospitality, Sept 24, 2019. https://www.hospitalitynet.org/panel/125000020.html

Legrand, W. (2019b). Who makes hospitality sustainability happen: Governments, industry, consumers?. HospitalityNet World Panel Sustainability in Hospitality, Oct 29, 2019. https://www.hospitalitynet.org/panel/125000024.html

Legrand, W., Sloan, P., & Chen, J. S. (2017). *Sustainability in the Hospitality Industry: Principles of Sustainable Operations* (3rd ed) London: Routledge.

Marcuse, H. (1964). *One-Dimensional Man: Studies in the Ideology cg' Advanced Industrial Society.* London: Routledge and Kegan Paul.

Martinez-Alier, J. (2003). *The Environmentalism of the Poor: A Study of Ecological Conflicts and Valuation.* Cheltenham: Edward Elgar Publishing.

Mathieson, A., & Wall, G. (1982). *Tourism: Economic, Physical and Social Impacts.* New York: Longman House.

McEwen, L., & Eberhard, I. P. (1963). Hotels and the Water Crisis. *Cornell Hotel and Restaurant Administration Quarterly,* 4(2), 43-57.

McIntosh, R. W., & Goeldner, C. R. (1990). *Tourism: Principles, Practices, Philosophies.* New York: John Wiley and Sons.

Merchant, C. (1980). *The Death of Nature: Women, Ecology and the Scientific Revolution.* London: Wfldwood House.

Miretpastor, L., Peiró-Signes, A., Segarra-Oña, M., & Mondéjar-Jiménez, J. (2015). The slow tourism: An indirect way to protect the environment. In H. G. Parsa (Ed.), *Sustainability, Social Responsibility and Innovations in Tourism and Hospitality* (pp. 71-90). Oakville: Apple Academic Press Inc.

Naciones Unidas – CEPAL. (2016). *Agenda 2030 y los Objetivos de Desarrollo Sostenible. Una Oportunidad para América Latina y el Caribe.* Santiago: Naciones Unidas – CEPAL.

O'Neill, S. (2017). Hotels need to report on sustainability using the Global Goals says WTTC. Retrieved January 29, 2018, from http://www.greenhotelier.org/our-themes/

policy-certification-business/hotels-need-to-report-on-sustainability-using-the-global-goals-says-wttc/print/

Power, T. M. (1996). *Lost Landscapes and Failed Economies: The Search for a Value of Place*. Washington, DC: Island Press.

Redclift, M. (1996). *Wasted: Counting the Costs of Global Consumption*. London: Earthscan.

Redclift, M., & Springett, D. (2015). Sustainable development: History and evolution of the concept. In M. Redclift & D. Springett (Eds.), *Roudledge International Handbook of Sustainable Development* (pp. 3–39) Oxon: Roudledge.

Reid, D. (1995). *Sustainable Development: An Introductory Guide*. London: Earthscan.

Rockström, J., Steffen, W., Noone, K., Persson, A., Chapin, F. S. et al. (2009a). A safe operating space for humanity. *Nature, 461*, 472–475. doi: 10.1038/461472a.

Rockström, J., Steffen, W., Noone, K., Persson, A., Chapin, F. S. et al. (2009b). Planetary boundaries: Exploring the safe operating space for humanity. *Ecology and Society, 14*(2), 32. http://www.ecologyandsociety.org/vol14/iss2/art32/

Schaltegger, S., Burritt, R., & Petersen, H. (2003). *An Introduction to Corporate Environmental Management – Striving for Sustainability*. Sheffield: Greenleaf Publishing Limited.

Seyfang, G. (2005). Shopping for sustainability: Can sustainable consumption promote ecological citizenship? *Environmental Politics, 14*(2), 290–306.

Shivdasani, S. (2016). Soneva, Thailand. In M. A. Gardetti & M. E. Girón (Eds.), *Sustainable Luxury and Social Entrepreneurship Volume II. More Stories from the Pioneers* (pp. 139:158). Sheffield: Greenleaf.

Shivdasani, S. (2017). Leading the fight against climate change within the hospitality sector. In W. Legrand, W. Wade, & H. Roelings (Eds.), *Hotel Yearbook 2018, Special Edition on Sustainable Hospitality* (pp. 36:37). Grandvaux: Woody Wade, Wade & Company SA.

Singh, A. J., & Houdré, H. (2012). The evolution of sustainable development in the hotel industry: Drivers shaping the sustainability agenda. In A. J. Singh & H. Houdré (Eds.), *Hotel Sustainable Development. Principles & Best Practices* (pp. 3–16). Lansing, MI: American Hotel and Lodging Educational Institute.

Spretnak, C., & Capra, F. (1985). *Green Politics: The Global Promise*. London: Paladin.

Springett, D. V. (2013). Critical perspectives on sustainable development. *Sustainable Development, 21*(3), 73–83.

Stern, N. (2007). *The Economics of Climate Change: The Stern Review*. New York: Cambridge University Press.

Stipanuk, D. M. (1996). The U.S. Lodging Industry and the Environment: An Historical View, *Cornell Hotel and Restaurant Administration Quarterly, 37*(5), 39–45.

Stockholm Resilience Centre. (n.d.). The nine planetary boundaries. https://www.stockholmresilience.org/research/planetary-boundaries/planetary-boundaries/about-the-research/the-nine-planetary-boundaries.html

The Ecologist. (1993). *Whose Common Future?* London: Earthscan.

United Nations Framework Convention on Climate Change. Retrieved January 29, 2018, from http://unfccc.int/kyoto_protocol/items/2830.php

Warhurst, A. (2001, Spring). *Corporate Citizenship and Corporate Social Investment: Drivers of Tri-Sector Partnership*. Sheffield: Greenleaf Publishing Limited. *The Journal of Corporate Citizenship*.

Weaver, D. (2006). *Sustainable Tourism: Theory and Practice*. Burlington, MA: Butter-Worth-Heinemann.

Welford, R. (2000). *Corporate Environmental Management – Towards Sustainable Development 3*. London: Earthscan Publications Limited.

WHO. (2020). Ultraviolet radiation and the INTERSUN Programme. World Health Organization. https://www.who.int/uv/faq/whatisuv/en/index2.html

World Commission on Environment and Development (WCED). (1987). *Our Common Future*. Oxford: Oxford University Press.

World Travel & Tourism Council (2016). Environmental, Social & Governance Reporting in Travel & Tourism: 3. Sustainability Reporting in Travel & Tourism. World Travel & Tourism Council, United Kingdom.

World Travel & Tourism Council. (2016). *Mission & Advocacy* in Progress and Priorities 2016, pp. 6–7.

Chapter 2

From entrepreneurship to social entrepreneurship

This chapter introduces key theories linked to the entrepreneurship phenomenon and reviews traditional approaches for generating entrepreneurial opportunities. It also examines the links between entrepreneurship, market instability, corporate social responsibility and social entrepreneurship. A discussion on the limitations and gaps associated with traditional entrepreneurship as well as market inefficiencies is provided. The chapter introduces various definitions and descriptions of social entrepreneurship.

The chapter concludes with a short case and corresponding exercises related to social entrepreneurship, with the example of entrepreneur Muhammad Yunus, Grameen Bank and the establishment of microfinancing. A set of additional exercises is provided at the end of the chapter, which are based on individual or group research and discussions.

The origin of entrepreneurship

Paul Hawken, entrepreneur and environmentalist, wrote that "the promise of business is to increase the general well-being of humankind through service, creative invention and ethical philosophy" (1993, p. 1) – a description that goes beyond certain views that businesses exist for the sole purpose of financial gains. However, it is not to say that the economic angle should be ignored in tracing a history of entrepreneurship.

The origin of the idea of entrepreneurship can be traced to the economist Richard Cantillon (1680s–1734). He was the first economist to analyze the entrepreneur's status in the economy. Cantillon in his book *Essay on the Nature of Trade in General*, published in 1755, described the entrepreneur as a person who takes risks and who is an important contributor to balance the economy. Cantillon saw the primary risk as being financial, recognizing that the entrepreneur is an individual willing "to buy at a certain price and sell at an uncertain price" (Cantillon in Swedberg, 2000, p. 19). It could be argued that Cantillon may have understood the entrepreneur as being a 'disruptor' in establishing business structures, a description later associated with the idea of being an 'entrepreneur'. Another economist who emphasized the role and function of entrepreneurs in the pre-classic economy was Jean-Baptiste Say (1767–1832), who described the entrepreneur as a person who "shifts economic resources out of an area of lower and into an area of higher productivity and greater yield" (Say in Drucker, 1999, p. 19).

Entrepreneurship and innovation

Cantillon's and Say's contribution was that they both described the entrepreneur's role in the economic system and laid the foundations for later studies of entrepreneurship. The economist and researcher Joseph Alois Schumpeter (1883–1950), regarded an authoritative figure of literature on entrepreneurship and innovation, is one of the most cited researchers through the ages concerning these two subjects. According to Schumpeter, entrepreneurs are key actors of economic development. Through their entrepreneurial activities and innovations, they can create instability and disturbances in the market – factors that move the market in a new direction, as well as key drivers of economic growth and prosperity (Schumpeter [1934] in Swedberg, 2000). According to Schumpeter, the innovative-minded entrepreneur creates 'new combinations', the ability to combine something existing with something new or to combine something already existing in new ways (Schumpeter, 2002). It is the development of new combinations, regardless of whether it is a new product, a new technology, a production method, the opening of a new market or a new economic organization, that change the terms of the company in a given market (Schumpeter [1934] in Swedberg, 2000). Thus, according to Schumpeter, new combinations evoke 'creative destructions', where the existing is destroyed (for example companies or industries) and replaced by something new and qualitatively different that matches the demand or unformulated needs of consumers (Schumpeter, [1944] 2003). Schumpeter calls the dynamic process within capitalism itself the 'perennial gale of creative destruction', which transforms the economic conditions for doing business in a certain industry and might convert, more or less, the rest of society into a new shape or direction (Schumpeter, [1944] 2003).

The entrepreneurial identity

Recent and prominent examples of entrepreneurial innovators include Steve Jobs' development of Apple; Bill Gates' establishment of Microsoft; Mark Zuckerberg's Facebook and Elon Musk's creation of Tesla Motors. These entrepreneurs have been able to establish successful companies, manufacturing innovative products or services. The innovation in each of those sectors changed market conditions and tapped into consumer needs on a global scale. The above-mentioned entrepreneurs, have been able to make creative destructions, in their own respective fields, through the development of new combinations that have both solved problems and also added new value for consumers and users. According to Schumpeter, the entrepreneur is characterized by being a 'Man of Action', which means a personality who has the will and capability to swim against the stream, instead of passively following it (Schumpeter (1911) in Swedberg, 2006). In Schumpeter's early writings, which had not previously been subjected to a closer examination, the idea of 'Man of Action' *(Mann der Tat)* is central to understanding the entrepreneurial personality or identity (Swedberg, 2006), which is dynamic in nature. The entrepreneurial identity is not subject to inner resistance to changes, which less entrepreneurship-orientated personalities might respond to. The entrepreneurial identity (or personality) moves out of the market equilibrium in an attempt to develop new solutions. This is opposed to a non-entrepreneurial personality, which seeks constancy in stable equilibrium relations in the market (Schumpeter (1911) in Swedberg, 2006). Schumpeter's distinction between Man of Action and the non-entrepreneurial person may seem too bold, however, and subject to generalization when faced with today's more complex market situations. In addition, Schumpeter's description of the entrepreneur has been criticized throughout the years for making the entrepreneurial personality a hero, not considering the complexity and the many gray areas between the two types of personalities that are pitted against each other.

Along the same lines as Schumpeter, Israel M. Kirzner argued that the entrepreneur is not a passive operating figure in a given world, but someone who creates a world different from that which he finds (Kirzner, 1973; Kirzner, 2009). Entrepreneurial activity may consist of developing significantly new products or services on the market or acting as a pioneer in creating revolutionary production methods for the benefit of customers and businesses, as Schumpeter suggested. The point is that an entrepreneurship-thinking person uses her or his creativity and ingenuity to challenge existing market conditions and create individual advantages from changes (Kirzner, 2009; Schumpeter [1934] in Swedberg 2000). The entrepreneur disrupts the serene market and puts it into a state of disequilibrium and reconstruction, which he or she benefits from (2009Foss & Klein, 2012; Kirzner, 2009).

Entrepreneurs and market instability

In fact, Schumpeter was one of the first economists to argue that instability (rather than equilibrium) between supply and demand is a main driver in economic progress. His argument was that neoclassical economists such as León Walras (1834–1910) relied blindly on market equilibrium but ignored the entrepreneur's central importance to the development of the economy (Schumpeter, [1944] 2005). While Walras in *Elements of Pure Economics* (Walras, [1874] 1954) perceived development in economic life as a passive cycle in balance, Schumpeter arrived at the opposite conclusion. Schumpeter criticized the Walrasian equilibrium argument for overlooking the dynamics and productive unpredictability that entrepreneurs create for the economy as well as for society in general. As Foss and Klein formulate, entrepreneurship is the exploration of and the reaction to the profit opportunities that exist in an imperfect world (Foss & Klein, 2012).

Entrepreneurs, profit and corporate social responsibility

An entrepreneurial discovery of profit potentials combined with a constant alertness towards understanding customer demands and attitudes are, according to Kirzner, the most important factors behind successful innovative entrepreneurial performance among pioneers within a dynamic market (Kirzner, 1997; Kirzner, 2009). Baumol (1922–2017) argues that there is a close link between a competitive free market on one hand and innovative power on the other. He further points out that a market under the right institutional conditions (understood as a deregulated market) is to be regarded an innovation machine (Baumol, 2002). This argument supports Schumpeter's perspectives on entrepreneurship, wherein the profit motive in a capitalistic market economy is the central engine that powers entrepreneurial endeavor (Schumpeter, [1934] 2003). The argument is that the entrepreneur – socially oriented or not, but pursuing selfish ends – creates social prosperity and welfare through generating new jobs, developing markets or launching new technology (Venkataraman, 1997).

The desire for profit and financial gains is supported or facilitated by free market competition. The idea of the benefits of free or deregulated markets has been addressed by economists belonging to the 'monetarist' or so-called 'neoclassical' tradition, represented by Milton Friedman (1912–2006) and the Austrian economic school personalized by Friedrich Hayek (1899–1992). The main message portrayed here is that centralized, defined, bureaucratic rules and tight business legislation create obstacles for entrepreneurship and innovation, which harm value creation within businesses (Friedman, 2002; Hayek, [1973] 2003). Friedman supported the idea that companies should not deal with social responsibility since the only responsibility they have is to satisfy their shareholders' desire for profit maximization (Friedman, 1970). Friedman's reasoning was that the only form of social responsibility that exists in a market economy is creating new jobs through economic growth. Therefore, businesses that may focus on social responsibility, instead of primarily satisfying their shareholders' needs, move into areas in which they do not possess in-depth knowledge. However, the current zeitgeist in regards to corporate social responsibility is different compared to arguments put forward by Friedman back in the 1970s. Arguably, shareholders are now particularly aware that businesses are expected to assume a social responsibility role that goes beyond legal requirements.

In 1984, Freeman presented a qualified counterargument to Friedman's narrow view of social responsibility in a business context. Freeman argued that businesses should involve stakeholders in the development of the company (Freeman, 1984). Freeman's idea of corporate social responsibility (CSR) has since become the dominant way for companies to engage in sustainability. The CSR movement has, so to speak, won the battle of ideas, as most leading international companies take their social responsibility into account and incorporate it into their respective policies, as they consider CSR an integral part of doing business (Crook, 2005). However, one must keep in mind that the outcome of decades of CSR work is rather mediocre in light of the climate emergency, biodiversity collapse and raising global inequalities.

Entrepreneurship and market competition

Leading economists in the field of entrepreneurship have, over the years, argued for the presence of a close link between entrepreneurship as an individual or social phenomenon and the market (Baumol, 2002; Kirzner, 1973; Kirzner, 2009). They observe the market as the place where entrepreneurial entity obtains an opportunity to meet its customers and test the quality of innovative products or services. Additionally, a market is an arena where competition between innovators and established companies takes place to the benefit of consumers. The rationale is that if competition between players in a given market functions efficiently, with equal access to information and knowledge, it can help to sort out the number of innovative solutions launched on the market, thereby enhancing the quality of entrepreneurs' ideas and products, which in turn has a derivative spillover effect in the form of wealth gains for society as a whole (Baumol, 2002; Hayek, [1973] 2003; Kirzner, 1997; Kirzner, 2009).

Self-organizing markets & entrepreneurs' interests

For example, Hayek was enthusiastic about the market, regardless of its built-in flaws. Despite the risks involved in overheating the economy and subsequent significant stock corrections or, in the worst case, financial collapse as experienced during the financial crisis of 2007–2008, Hayek would argue that the market has a unique ability to distribute knowledge between people. In that respect, the market represents a sum of individuals who, in a complex interplay, make better decisions for themselves, compared to what a more centrally controlled economic policy could ever achieve (Hayek, 1945; Hayek, [1973] 2003). The only coordinating element on the market is the price. Price is a result of the relationship between supply and demand, and works as a mechanism to help coordinate the various forms of knowledge and individual patterns of action of market players at a decentralized level (Hayek, 1945). In this respect, the market can be seen as an example of a 'social mind', which creates spontaneous coordination between people, buyers and sellers with common, but also competing, interests. It is a well-known phenomenon that sellers' mutual competition for customer favor in most cases causes prices to fall, while buyers' competition to secure access to certain goods increases price (Hayek, 1937).

As highlighted by Hayek, Friedman, Baumol and Kirzner, the market functions without the need for a central coordinating authority that regulates the price levels of goods and services. Instead, the market regulates itself through individuals' and companies' spontaneous interactions. Its self-organizing status is a result of people and businesses acting in their own interest and with the desire to provide for their own needs. Hayek often refers to the market as a 'spontaneous order' and as the optimal mechanism for distributing resources. Based on the thoughts put forward by Adam Smith (1723–1790), Hayek draws a direct parallel between the 'invisible hand' of the free market and the spontaneous order emerging through decentralized and deregulated coordination between a jumble of local interests and needs. Smith presented the idea and links between the invisible hand and the entrepreneur whereby the latter

> intends only his own gain, and he is in this, as in my other cases, led by and invisible hand to promote an end which is no part of his intention. Nor is it always the worse of the society that it has no part of it. By pursuing his own interest, he frequently promotes that of the society more effectively than when he really intends to promote it.
> (Smith, [1776] 2008, pp. 291–292)

According to Smith's classic example, a merchant is guided by an invisible hand in pursuit of his own interests. His actions will unintentionally benefit the greater interests of society, even without that being part of his original intent. The point that Smith puts forward, which has resonated significantly among subscribers to the concept of the free market, is that when entrepreneurs follow selfish motives they create a better society than if they had actually set our to solve a specific societal problem themselves. In this point of view, it would thus be inappropriate for companies to conduct CSR activities, including social entrepreneurship (which is discussed in subsequent chapters). The argument is that the derived social welfare and prosperity effects of traditional business operations (e.g., in the form of job creation) should obviously be greater than the use of resources by a social entrepreneur working to solve a specific problem (e.g., solving long-term unemployment, poverty or disease control). Friedman's argument that companies should not deal with social responsibility is based on Smith's reasoning about business owners promoting the interests of society more effectively when he follows his own interests.

Social welfare and markets

What seems to be overlooked by Smith, as well as by today's advocates for solely market-based models, is that many entrepreneurs are capable of successfully leading businesses dedicated to creating quantitative as well as qualitative social growth among citizens and communities at large. It is this not of interest for such entrepreneurs to passively wait for the non-intentional benefits of traditional business, rather they actively seek to directly create benefits for individuals or communities. A market can nevertheless be considered a societal value-creating phenomenon, leading to economic development and prosperity. However, a market's partial inability to distribute wealth and, in particular, its insufficient capacity to distribute resources to the neediest within a society is a challenge. Indeed, the darker side of the complex market mechanism is the creation of social imbalances, significant economic inequality and the inherent capability to bring global socio-economic crises in its wake. However, markets have also proven themselves to be competitive forms of social organization since those forms of exchange systems can be traced back to ancient times. In fact, markets are an integral part of the history of human civilization. And, as highlighted in this chapter, market competition is a source of entrepreneurship, ingenuity and innovation (Temin, 2013).

Market failures and negative externalities

Markets can be considered effective for distributing resources and serving as support for creating entrepreneurship and developing new products. Often, markets are perceived to function as motors of prosperity and development in society. However, they also have a fundamental problem in that they are not intended to tackle specific problems nor to be a guide towards the fulfilment of specific purposes. Thus, it may be foolish to rely on markets to provide a set of specific solutions that contribute to solving the socioeconomic and environmental challenges faced by large sections of the world population. Markets are not necessarily developed with the goal of poverty reduction or coping with climate change in mind. In many cases, these tasks fall into the hands of governments. Indeed, governments are given the task of repairing the maladies of market mechanisms by, among other things, ensuring that the poorest in society have the opportunity to have dignified lives. However, a government's interventions are far from sufficient to tackle a given problem. Social entrepreneurship as one of the remedial factors may be a valuable proposition. In this case, innovative solutions are developed from entrepreneurial market players who choose social responsibility as the main driver or motivation for being in business in the first place.

As described, markets are subject to a number of failures. These can be the monopoly structures that may arise in certain competitive situations where a few companies or a single one control a particular market. Market failures can also be about the presence of asymmetric information that keeps one or more participants unaware of key issues in the competition. Last, but not least, market competition involves negative externalities, for both prosperity and welfare of a society. Negative externalities are the dark side of market competition. Pollution is a classic example of this as Ronald Coase (1910–2013) presented in his article *The problem of social cost* (Coase, 1960). Pollution has a detrimental effect on the ecological system that is unwittingly passed on to a third party who has no stake in the trade between the two other parties. Similarly, anthropogenic climate change is a negative externality, a result of industry, agriculture and transport over a number of years emitting greenhouse gases on a scale that has destroyed the climatic balance of the earth. In terms of pollution and climate change, a number of negative externalities have emerged in the form of global damage, which the community must pay at the expense of the industry, agriculture or transport sector's profit maximization. It is important to emphasize that externalities can be both negative and positive. A positive externality is a derived unpaid benefit that accrues to a third party who has not otherwise been involved in an economic activity.

Overall, a negative externality equates to a "private cost being lower than the cost to society as a whole while a positive externality equates to a private return being lower than the return to society as a whole" (Legrand, Sloan, & Chen, 2017, p. 466). Coase's proposals to deal with the emergence of externalities, have them reduced and, at best, eliminated, consist of establishing local negotiations between the offender and the victim, to decide a financial compensation for the cost (Coase, 1960). On the other hand, inequality in economic resources and political power can risk benefitting the polluter (e.g., a large industrial company) and harm the local environment that is suffering from the pollution (e.g., neighbors of the company). Coase's perspective is based on the idea that a self-organizing exchange of property rights often will create solutions and solve negative externalities better than governmental intervention in form of legal sanctions (Coase, 1960). However, despite its great influence as a conceptual bid for resolving negative externalities, Coase's argument of the advantage of decentralized bargaining on property rights have not significantly reduced the environmental or human consequences of climate change. Negative externalities are 'negative' in that they create social costs and welfare losses for the society affected by them. On the other hand, negative externalities such as climate change and pollution are a source of innovation (to deal with those problems) and social entrepreneurship, which helps mitigate the social costs or welfare losses that a community is exposed to.

Social entrepreneurship: the man of social action

There is no comprehensive and widely recognized definition of social entrepreneurship. Instead, there are a number of different definitions describing the social entrepreneurship phenomenon. Alvord, Brown and Letts describe social entrepreneurship as "a process that creates innovative solutions to immediate social problems and mobilizes the ideas, capabilities, resources, and social arrangement required for sustainable social transformation" (Alvord, Brown, & Letts, 2004, p. 262). Alvord et al. describe three different types of social entrepreneurial initiatives: (1) transformational, (2) economic and (3) political. A **transformational** initiative focuses on building up local capacities in order to create resilience when challenges that threaten local cohesion arise (Alvord et al., 2004). An **economic** initiative enhances productivity by developing new tools and resources (Alvord et al., 2004). A **political** initiative is about activating local movements, including the resources found in civil society (Alvord et al., 2002). Dees suggested another definition of social entrepreneurship: "Adopting a mission to create and sustain social value (not just private value) [and] [r]ecognizing and relentlessly pursuing new opportunities to serve that mission" (Dees, 2001, p. 4). In short, social entrepreneurship is entrepreneurship with a social mission (Dees, 2001). When social entrepreneurship operates in the marketplace, the approach is to solve social problems by using market forces from a strategic point of view (Legrand et al., 2017). Mair and Marti define social entrepreneurship as "a process involving the innovative use and combination of resources to pursue opportunities to catalyze social change" (Mair & Marti, 2004, p. 3). In this context, social entrepreneurship is understood as creating social values by combining resources in new ways, regardless of whether social entrepreneurship is unfolding on market terms or is an activity without a profit perspective.

A common denominator of the above-mentioned definitions is the link between entrepreneurial power of innovation and a socially dedicated effort by the contractor to solving social or environmental challenges. Unlike the traditional entrepreneur who is oriented towards the development of new products or production methods, the social entrepreneur is primarily engaged in developing innovative solutions that can address social imbalances. In other words, and considering Schumpeter's approach, the entrepreneur has a predominant aim of creating profitability of innovation projects, while the social entrepreneur develops innovation projects with the greatest possible social impact in mind.

The man of social action

Borrowing from Schumpeter's idea of Man of Action, the social entrepreneur is a 'Man of Social Action'. He is a socially dedicated entrepreneur who generates creative social construction or reconstruction rather than creative destruction (Schumpeter (1911) in Swedberg, 2006). Social entrepreneurs show dedication towards raising individuals or communities above the challenges and struggles faced. Nevertheless, the concept of creative destruction is relevant to social entrepreneurship to the extent that the latter covers a wide range of specific practices that may lead to the dissolution of existing structures that otherwise have influenced how a market or community has worked so far. (Schumpeter, [1944] 2003). Likewise, the idea of 'new combinations' is meaningful, as social entrepreneurs, similarly to traditional ones, must be able to develop new combinations that create social value (Schumpeter, 2002).

Similarly, parts of Kirzner's entrepreneurial understanding can be incorporated into the analysis and understanding of social entrepreneurship. The same conditions apply to social entrepreneurs acting within a specific economic market as to market-based entrepreneurs. Social entrepreneurs have to be alert to interpret the needs of the socially vulnerable or take on initiatives to cope with environmental challenges while considering the profitability needs of innovation. Social entrepreneurs operating in markets are often part of a harsh competition process similar to any other entrepreneurial ventures. Social entrepreneurs compete with each other for donations or attracting volunteers to support their social mission, and use their energy to convince potential stakeholders about their cause (Dees, 2001).

Overall, social entrepreneurship creates social value by combing resources in new ways, thereby tackling issues faced by large sections of society. Those issues or challenges may take the shape of longtime unemployment, homelessness, poverty, sickness or social marginalization. We can conclude that social entrepreneurship is either an individual's, group's, or a corporate attempt to shape the social foundations of the present and/or future society.

CHAPTER CASE 2.1

Social entrepreneurship classic: Muhammad Yunus and Grameen bank

Developing microfinancing

Nobel Peace Prize laureate Muhammad Yunus is a classic example of social entrepreneurship. Yunus established the Grameen Bank and developed so-called 'micro-credit' aimed at the poor part of the population in Bangladesh. Grameen Bank provides micro loans for villagers, especially women. Women are perceived to be the most responsible borrowers due to their experience in handling small households and the skills acquired for being responsible for the well-being of children in otherwise very difficult conditions in one of the world's poorest countries (Bornstein, 1996; Counts, 1996). Ninety-nine percent of the loans have been repaid. The rate of repayment differs from customers' repayment ability in traditional banks. One of the reasons for this is the principle of group solidarity between borrowers, as they jointly guarantee the individual repayment of the loans (Stix, 1997). In that respect, microfinance is a loan combined with elements of an insurance policy, where borrowers share the financial risk if one or more of them is unable to repay their loans. Yunus and his concept of micro-credit have become a textbook example of social entrepreneurship that has been imitated by many other microfinance companies around the world. Yunus can be seen as a Man of Social Action who is able to create new combinations of resources in a novel way, while pursuing transformational social change in order to eradicate poverty in Bangladesh.

Rethinking entrepreneurship

By combining the idea of cheap small loans with joint liability reminiscent of group insurance solutions, Yunus developed new combinatorics that opened up a market for microfinance products. His entrepreneurial efforts are in line with Schumpeter's definition of an innovative entrepreneur. Yunus is the core example of a social entrepreneur who enacted creative destruction on the market of finance by building up Grameen Bank in 1976. As Foss and Klein describe it: "entrepreneurship is the act of discovering, or being alert to, information and opportunities that others fail to perceive" (Foss & Klein, 2012, p. 57). Yunus was able to capitalize on financial opportunities by inventing a concept addressed at the very poor – a relatively large group of potential customers that traditional financial institutions had ignored.

EXERCISES

Group discussion

Take some time to review Chapter Case 2: Social Entrepreneurship Classic: Muhammad Yunus and Grameen Bank

1. Discuss whether Muhammad Yunus' idea on micro-credit can be used within the hospitality context, for example in form of establishing bed & breakfasts or small hostels.

2. In light of the 2020 COVID-19 crisis, consider whether micro-credit can be a valuable financial tool and solution for tourism and hospitality resiliency.

Group discussion

On one hand, the existence of social entrepreneurship is considered a consequence of government, agencies and businesses that have failed to help the disadvantaged in society. On the other hand, it is argued that it is a sign of a failure in market economies, which has led to permanent oversupply of labor. As a result, social entrepreneurs must innovate in order to restore and strengthen the cohesion of society.

1. In groups, discuss the similarities and differences between traditional entrepreneurship and social entrepreneurship – give examples for both.

2. Debate the need of society for social entrepreneurship. Take into consideration whether social entrepreneurship stems from a lack of government initiatives, market failures or a combination of the two.

Individual research

Write an essay about community challenges, entrepreneurship and social entrepreneurship, taking an example from your own community. Consider the following questions:

1. What tells you there is a problem in the community (i.e., what are the specific indicators of the problem and what is the size of the problem)?

2. Which organization tackles the problem (if at all)? (e.g., governmental agencies; not-for-profit organizations; local businesses)

3. Can entrepreneurship in general, and social entrepreneurship specifically, help mitigate the impact and find solutions to the challenge? If so, how?

Reference

Alvord, S. H., Brown, L. D., & Letts, C. C. (2002). *Social Entrepreneurship – Leadership That Facilitates Societal Transformation: An Exploratory Study*. Working paper No 5. Center for Public Leadership, John F. Kennedy School of Government, Harvard University.

Alvord, S. H., Brown, L. D., & Letts, C. C. (2004). Social entrepreneurship and societal transformation: An exploratory study. *Journal of Applied Behavioral Science*, 40(3), 260–282.

Baumol, W. J. (2002). *The Free-Market Innovation Machine: Analyzing the Growth Miracle of Capitalism*. Princeton, NJ: Princeton University Press.

Bornstein, D. (1996). *The Story of Grameen Bank and the Idea That Is Helping the Poor to Change Their Lives*. New York: Simon and Schuster.

Coase, R. H. (1960). The Problem of Social Cost. *The Journal of Law & Economics*, III, 1–44.

Counts, A. (1996). *Give Us Credit*. New York: Times Books.

Crook, C. (2005). Special Report on Corporate Social Responsibility. *The Economist*.

Dees, J. G. (2001). *The Meaning of 'Social Entrepreneurship*. Reformatted and revised, May 30, 200. https://entrepreneurship.duke.edu/news-item/the-meaning-of-social-entrepreneurship/

Drucker, P. F. (1999). *Innovation and Entrepreneurship*. Oxford: Butterworth-Heinemann.

Foss, N. J., & Klein, P. G. (2012). *Organizing Entrepreneurial Judgment*. Cambridge: Cambridge University Press.

Freeman, R. E. (1984). *Strategic Management: A Stakeholder Approach*. Boston, MA: Pitman.

Friedman, M. (1970). The Social Responsibility of Business Is to Increase its Profits. *New York Times Magazine*, 126.

Friedman, M. (2002). *Capitalism and Freedom*. Chicago, IL: University of Chicago.

Hackett, S. C. (2015). *Environmental and Natural Resource Economics. Theory, Policy, and the Sustainable Society* (4th ed.). London: Routledge.

Hawken, P. (1993). *The Ecology of Commerce*. New York: HarperBusiness.

Hayek, F. A. (1937). Economics and Knowledge. *Economica*, 4(13), 33–54.

Hayek, F. A. ([1973] 2003). *Law, Legislation and Liberty. Volume 1. Rules and Order*. London: Routledge

Kirzner, I. M. (1973). *Competition and Entrepreneurship*. Chicago, IL: University of Chicago Press.

Kirzner, I. M. (1997). Entrepreneurial Discovery and the Competitive Market Process: An Austrian Approach. *Journal of Economic Literature*, XXXV, 60–85.

Kirzner, I. M. (2008). The Alert and Creative Entrepreneur: A Clarification. *Small Business Economics*, 32, 145–152.

Legrand, W., Sloan, P., & Chen, J. S. (2017). *Sustainability in the Hospitality Industry. Principles of Sustainable Operations* (3rd ed.). London: Routledge.

Mair, J., & Marti, I. (2004). Social entrepreneurship research: A source of explanation, prediction, and delight. WP No 546, March, IESE Business School – University of Navarra.

Schumpeter, J. A. (1934). *Entrepreneurship as Innovation*, extract from, *Theory of Economic Development*, in Swedberg, R. (Ed.). (2000). *Entrepreneurship. The Social Science View*. Oxford: Oxford University Press.

Schumpeter, J. A. (2002). Theorie der wirtschaftlichen Enwicklung (Becker, M. and Knudsen, T., Trans.). *American Journal of Economics and Sociology*, 61(2), 405–548.

Schumpeter, J. A. ([1944] 2003). *Capitalism, Socialism and Democracy*. London: Routledge.

Smith, A. ([1776]2008). *An Inquiry into the Nature and Causes of the Wealth of Nation*. Oxford: Oxford University Press.

Stix, G. (1997). Small (Lending) is Beautiful. *Scientific American*, 276, 16–20.

Swedberg, R. (2000). The social science view of entrepreneurship: Introduction and practical application: In R. Swedberg (Ed.), *Entrepreneurship. The Social Science View*. Oxford: Oxford University Press.

Swedberg, R. (2006). Social entrepreneurship: The view of the young Schumpeter. In C. Steyaert & D. Hjorth (Eds.), *Entrepreneurship as Social Change. A Third Movement in Entrepreneurship* (pp. 21–35). Cheltenham, UK: Edward Elgar.

Termin, P. (2013). *The Roman Market Economy*. Princeton, NJ: Princeton University Press.

Venkataraman, S. (1997). The distinct domain of entrepreneurial research. In J. Katz & R. Brockhaus (Eds.), *Advances in Entrepreneurship, Firm Emergence, and Growth* (Vol. 3, pp. 119–138). Stamford, CT: JAI Press.

Walras, L. ([1874] 1954). *Elements of Pure Economics or The Theory of Social Wealth*. London George Allen and Unwin.

Chapter **3**

Social entrepreneurship: definitions and concepts

This chapter explores the origins and development of the field of social entrepreneurship. It examines the definitions and boundaries of social entrepreneurship, including social entrepreneurs, social entrepreneurship, sustainable entrepreneurship and 'ecopreneurs'. The chapter also discusses perspectives on studying social entrepreneurship and provides an overview of the research areas addressed by articles.

The chapter concludes with two case studies on (1) olive oil production in Turkey and the company Hiç and (2) the Chumbe Island Coral Park Ltd. (CHICOP) and lessons learned from setting up the first private marine protected area. A set of additional exercises are provided at the end of the chapter, based on individual or group research and discussions.

Origins and developments

A delicate balance exists in the natural world based on continuous cycles of endless replenishment. Disturbing this balance leads to unintended consequences: "When the last tree is cut down, the last fish eaten, and the last stream poisoned, you will realize that you cannot eat money" (Native American saying, in Speake, 2015, p. 176).

Bill Drayton is often credited with inventing the term 'social entrepreneur' in the 1980s. Recent research, however, traces the source to three decades before Drayton (in 1954) in a reference to a form of social entrepreneurship in the mining industry in Germany, by an economic historian, W. N. Parker:

> To the individual German in the mining industry all three types of activity appeared as outlets for enterprise and ambition. The first is obviously "economic entrepreneurship" and contributed clearly to the functioning of the economy and, under other favorable conditions, to its growth. The individual's interest in the second (which may be called "social entrepreneurship") depended on the fluidity of the German social structure, the standards of advancement, and the individuals own restlessness.
> (1954, p. 400 in Sassmannshausen & Volkmann 2018, p. 254)

Here 'social entrepreneurship' to Parker was the possibility of increasing social mobility for the working class and better paid employment through entrepreneurial conduct. The actual origins of social entrepreneurship may be traced to two different sources:

1. Social entrepreneurship shares the same organizational determinations as entrepreneurship. Dees (1998) makes the point that social entrepreneurs are a species of the genus 'entrepreneur'. Classically, there are several characteristics of entrepreneurship that may be derived from leading writers and thinkers. Dees (1998), in a comprehensive review, found that entrepreneurs are involved in value creation, innovation, opportunities and resourcefulness. Thornton argues that "the supply-side school examines entrepreneurship by focusing on the individual characteristics of entrepreneurs, specifying potential mechanisms for agency and change, whereas the demand-side emphasizes the push and pull of context [such as social environmental needs]" (1999, p. 21). In other words, agency theory is applicable to the social entrepreneur's role of being both the principal and the agent of change in meeting a social or environmental need for specific stakeholders.

2. Social entrepreneurship is concerned with income generation by a non-profit venture, along with a more general interpretation that defines it as a process that involves identifying, addressing and solving societal problems (Desa, 2007).

Interest in the field has grown exponentially over the past twenty years (Kraus, Filser, O'Dwyer, & Shaw, 2014; Sassmannshausen & Volkmann, 2018).

Sassmannshausen and Volkmann (2018) give a comprehensive, scientific overview of the state of the social entrepreneurship field, from the first use of the term to the first academic paper, covering the number of references to the term, citations and the development of the field along with its current state.

Growth in the interest in social entrepreneurship is evident in several areas: firstly, the number of publications and the rise of publication frequency.

Sassmannshausen and Volkmann (2018) report that "in 1985 the research topic was picked up by two publications, one from the US, and one from the Netherlands" (p. 7), however, entering the new millennium, publications containing the words 'social entrepreneurship' grew rapidly with more than 2300 publications in 2011 only and over 6000 for the year 2019 alone (Google Scholar). A similar trend is noted in regards to peer-reviewed journal articles pertaining to social entrepreneurship (Sassmannshausen & Volkmann, 2018). Thus, both sets of figures from the Google Scholar and EBSCO academic databases show an exponential growth in the literature on this subject. The authors question whether social entrepreneurship is a fad with a short-term increase in the literature, or whether there are more deep-rooted examples of solid, independent research and academia.

They point to an institutionalization of social entrepreneurship in academia, evidenced in the creation of specific journals, edited volumes, conferences, teaching materials, integration of topics in curricula and the acceptance of social entrepreneurship by leading journals. They list sixteen different dedicated centers to social entrepreneurship, distributed as follows: seven in the USA (focused in California and New York); three in Germany; two in Switzerland and then one in each of France, the UK, New Zealand and Canada (Sassmannshausen & Volkmann, 2018).

Definitions and terms

Social entrepreneurs

As mentioned in the previous section, the origins of social entrepreneurship may be traced to two sources: that of revenue generation by a not-for-profit venture, and a more general interpretation that defines it as a process that involves identifying, addressing and solving societal problems (Desa, 2007).

Dees (1998) in his influential work traces the roots of social entrepreneurship to the genus 'entrepreneur'. He found that entrepreneurs are involved in creating value, innovation, opportunities and resources.

As with many areas of academic research, and perhaps due to the increase in interest in social entrepreneurship as a theme, there is not a clear consensus on what a social entrepreneur is.

As mentioned previously, Bill Drayton has been credited with inventing the term in the 1980s and for creating the Ashoka Foundation, the first organization to support social entrepreneurship at a global level. Drayton was categorical that social entrepreneurs are concerned with "large-scale systemic social change" (Light, 2008, p. 4). "Social entrepreneurs are the essential corrective force. They are system-changing entrepreneurs. And from deep within they, and therefore their work, are committed to the good of all" (Ashoka, n.d., para 2).

WHAT IS SOCIAL ENTREPRENEURSHIP?

This idea of enacting major societal change is reflected by Light (2008), who states that "the job of the social entrepreneur is to recognize when a part of society is not working and to solve the problem by changing the system, spreading solutions and persuading entire societies to take new leaps" (p. 4). Similarly, to Ashoka, the Skoll Foundation (along with the Skoll Centre for Social Entrepreneurship based in the SAID Business School at the University of Oxford, England), also stresses the 'big picture' approach. The Skoll Foundation's definition further emphasizes the transformational nature of social entrepreneurship whereby "social entrepreneurs both take direct action and seek to transform the existing systems. They seek to go beyond better, to bring about a transformed, stable new system that is fundamentally different than the world that preceded it" (Skoll, n.d., para 2).

All of these definitions point to the need to disrupt the status quo and to change current systems.

A definition that seems to be based on common-sense is given by Smith, Barr, Barbosa and Kickul (2008): "The social entrepreneur tackles opportunities in the domain of social problems (such as hunger or poverty) and measures achievement in terms of accomplishment of social value". Using innovation and resourcefulness, the social entrepreneur ultimately seeks to better the human condition (Dees, Emerson and Economy, 2001 quoted in Smith et al., 2008, p. 341).

Desa (2007) evaluates twelve different definitions categorized into four themes of non-profit entrepreneur, non-profit innovation, social entrepreneur and a subset of business entrepreneurship. Oncer and Yildiz (2010) list eighteen different definitions of social entrepreneurship, with many stressing social needs, playing the role of change agent, emphasizing the benefits to the marginalized and the poor and employment of innovation. They assert that it is necessary to understand the motivations of the entrepreneurs who undertake these new business ventures and organizations (with all the inherent risks and work involved) in the creation of "sustainable value for society" (Oncer & Yildiz, 2010, p. 223).

Another perspective developed by New York University (NYU) identifies three types of social entrepreneurs and their intentions:

1. Those who have a plan to develop an innovative idea to address a specific social problem in a pattern-breaking, sustainable and scalable way
2. Those that will work in and/or build the infrastructure needed for social entrepreneurial work to take root
3. Those who will bring action-oriented awareness on a national and/or global scale to particular problems. (de Lange & Dodds, 2016)

The fundamental point is that the major outcome of social entrepreneurship is for social impact to take place (Dees, 1996) and, when developing a product or service, a social entrepreneur will aim to attack the root causes of a problem rather than its symptoms (Chahine, 2016, p. 9). Miric et al. (2019) are more specific: "Social entrepreneurs focus on transforming systems and practices that are the causes of poverty, marginalization, and environmental deterioration" (Miric et al., 2016, p. 129).

Social entrepreneurship

Social entrepreneurship is the recognition of a social problem and the subsequent use of entrepreneurship principles to organize, create and manage a local venture to achieve a desired change within the communities where such initiatives operate (from Peredo & Wurzelmann, 2015).

Social entrepreneurship may be used as a vehicle for companies to introduce and apply various forms of their Corporate Social Responsibility (CSR) initiatives (Benn & Bolton, 2011). The compelling force for social entrepreneurship is market failures (Sigala, 2016, p. 1246), as discussed in the previous chapter.

Light (2008) streamlines social entrepreneurship into four basic categories: entrepreneurs, ideas, opportunities and organizations. Any organization may inspire entrepreneurial activity, but the difficulty is in replicating and continuing that activity and sustaining a culture of social entrepreneurship, which involves management: a critical aspect that visionary social entrepreneurs may overlook (Light, 2008). The author makes the point that although social entrepreneurship's objective is often focused on large-scale change, this may take many forms. An objective could be poverty reduction, dealing with access to food and water or trying to alleviate disease, the choices may come in a variety of forms.

Zahra, Gedajlovic, Neubaum and Shulman (2009) offer a very comprehensive view of social entrepreneurship encompassing "the activities and processes undertaken to discover, define and exploit opportunities in order to enhance social wealth by creating new ventures or managing existing organizations in an innovative manner" (Zahra et al., 2009, p. 523). Bacq et al. (2013) have a very straightforward definition of social entrepreneurship: "Individuals, organizations or initiatives engaged in entrepreneurial activities with a social goal" (p. 42).

Although financial viability and sustainability are necessary objectives for the longevity of the project, financial success in social entrepreneurship is considered a means to an end, not the end in itself. The final objective and "the only bottom line of a social venture is its social impact" (Chahine, 2016, p. 9)

Mair and Marti (2004) have a broad definition, where they define social entrepreneurship as "the innovative use of resources to explore and exploit opportunities that meet a social need in a sustainable manner" (p. 3).

This latter definition also ties in with the merging of entrepreneurship and sustainable development literature, producing a new stream of research titles in sustainability entrepreneurship (Tilley & Parrish, 2006), such as, 'ecopreneurs' – those who combine environmental awareness with business objectives to ensure environmentally friendly activities (Gibbs, 2006, p. 65). Shane (2000) argues that "most research on entrepreneurship investigates the entrepreneurial process after opportunities have been discovered" (p. 448). For example, research has shown that ecopreneurial motives necessarily intersect with economic and social constructs, rather than acting in a vacuum of strictly environmental corrections and solutions. For example, ecopreneurs are change agents who are motivated to be innovative in product and services, have a keen interest in ethical practices towards stakeholder networks and identify with a profit-driven purpose to perpetuate their visions (Gibbs, 2006, p. 72). Stakeholder networks are the backbone of an entrepreneurial milieu focused on the value of meeting socioeconomic and eco-friendly economic ends. In other words, "sustainability-driven entrepreneurs pursue economic as well as non-economic values" (Schlange, 2006, p. 14).

Sustainability entrepreneurship is seen to be a transformative model, not merely bolting on a social conscience to the standard entrepreneurship model. In other words, this construct is transformative in that socioeconomic innovation is a core driver of the development of environmental impacts, mitigation and value creation for communities that an entrepreneurial enterprise seeks to disentangle (O'Neill, Hershauer & Golden, 2006). On a micro level, the sustainability entrepreneur disaggregates the eco- and socio-efficiencies and effectiveness as sources of opportunities for a variety of enterprise endeavors, including those in manufacturing supply chains, healthcare delivery systems and hospitality and tourism services. Moreover, sustainability entrepreneurial approaches utilize a 'holistic value proposition' (HVP) to drive market opportunities that intersect with stakeholders and capital (O'Neill et al., 2006, p. 36). Sustainability-driven entrepreneurs see their enterprises in terms of a larger context, contributing to an overall improvement in social conditions, with a future-oriented perspective (Schlange, 2006).

More recently, Chahine (2016) offers a pragmatic definition of social entrepreneurship as "the process by which effective, innovative, and sustainable solutions are pioneered to meet social and environmental challenges" (Cahine, 2016, p. 2). Social entrepreneurship may be used as a vehicle for companies to introduce and apply various forms of their CSR initiatives (Benn & Bolton, 2011). Often the compelling force for social entrepreneurship is market failures (Sigala, 2016). Sanzo-Perez, Álvarez-González and Rey-García (2015) differentiate between social entrepreneurship and social innovation, whereas the traditional view of social entrepreneurship is that of an individual striving to do the right thing to fix the ills of society, social innovation relies more on teamwork and a collective approach by different actors working collaboratively. Considered especially important to the development of social innovation are human resource policies that facilitated an 'internal market orientation', and competencies in information and communication technologies. They defined four different types of social innovations:

1. Innovations in the type of activities, projects or programs provided by the organization –the 'what' that the organization supplies that could be, inter alia, 'new to the world' and would meet a specific social need.

2. Innovations in the planning, implementation and delivery process of those activities – this is 'how' the organization supplies the service and could include co-creation with customers or other stakeholders.

3. Marketing innovations – this is how the organization uses new forms of communication and relationship management with stakeholders.

4. Organizational innovations – this includes new forms of governance and practices.

Examples could include new products (car sharing), new organizational forms (social franchise), new processes of social production (co-creation), marketing innovations (social sponsorship) and organizational innovations (micro-financing) (Sigala, 2016)

There are obvious links between social entrepreneurship and sustainability entrepreneurship. Social entrepreneurs have anchored sustainability as a fundamental value.

Sustainability entrepreneurship

Tilley and Young (2006) stated that an important perspective of viewing sustainability entrepreneurs is that of a shift to a broader view of wealth creation, with an eight-point model that encompasses the three pillars of sustainability (environmental, economic and social) in interaction with a fourth pillar labelled 'sustainable entrepreneurship'.

The four pillars and eight points include

I. environmental entrepreneurship (1 – environmental stability, 2 – eco-effectiveness);

II. economic entrepreneurship (3 – eco-efficiency, 4 – socio-efficiency);

III. social entrepreneurship (5 – socio-effectiveness and 6 – social responsibility); and

IV. sustainability entrepreneurship (7 – environmental sustainability and 8 – futurity). Also included in the interaction between pillars are ecological equity, economic equity and inter-generational equity and sufficiency. The main argument is that to be truly considered 'sustainable', all of the elements of the model have to be pursued, rather than focusing on the social or environmental aspects only. A final point is that Tilley and Young see sustainability entrepreneurs as *the* major source of wealth generation for the future.

Perspectives on studying social entrepreneurship

Sigala (2016) examined many generic and tourism-specific studies on social entrepreneurship and proposed that there are three major research themes (RT):

RT1: Social entrepreneurship research that examines the entrepreneurial *behavior* and *goals* of social enterprises

RT2: Research on the *personality, distinctive traits* and *competencies* of social venture founders

RT3: Research concentrating on the *tangible outcomes* of social entrepreneurship

In respect to *entrepreneurial behavior* and *goals* (RT1), the different roles that social entrepreneurs play in society were identified by Dees (1998). According to Dees, who was a seminal figure in the literature, social entrepreneurs play the role of change agents in society by fulfilling the following five behaviors:

1. Adapting a mission to create and sustain social value not just private value;
2. Recognizing and relentlessly pursuing new operations to serve that mission;
3. Engaging in a process of continuous innovation, adaptation and learning;
4. Acting boldly without being limited by the resources currently at hand and
5. Exhibiting a heightened sense of accountability to the constituencies served and for outcomes created.

In regards to *personality, distinctive traits* and *competencies* of the social venture founder (RT2), the personality, traits and competencies were analyzed by Abu-Saifan's (2012) evaluation of differing characteristics of social entrepreneurs compared to 'regular' or traditional entrepreneurs (see Table 3.1). Characteristics and motivations of social entrepreneurs are discussed in greater length in Chapter 4 as well.

In regards to *tangible outcomes* of social entrepreneurship (RT3), researchers are debating the intended social impact and the measurement of its success. Additionally, there are questions about the value of measurement in itself. For example, the produced desired change may (or may not) be a result of the social entrepreneur's interventions. It could also be due to other factors independent of those.

Another perspective may be to approach social entrepreneurship from a structural lens by analyzing the five pivotal dimensions of social mission, social innovation, social change, entrepreneurial spirit and personality (Praszkier & Nowak, 2012, quoted in Sheldon & Danielle, 2017).

Table 3.1 Abu-Saifan's unique and common characteristics of profit-oriented entrepreneurs and social entrepreneurs.

Unique Characteristics of Profit-Oriented Entrepreneurs	Characteristics Common to Both Type	Unique Characteristics of Social Entrepreneurs
High achiever	Innovator	Mission leader
Risk bearer	Dedicated	Emotionally charged
Organizer	Initiative taker	Change agent
Strategic thinker	Leader	Opinion leader
Value creator	Opportunity alert	Social value creator
Holistic	Persistent	Socially alert
Arbitrageur	Committed	Manager
		Visionary
		Highly accountable

Source: Abu-Saifan (2012, p. 25).

A similar method is proposed by Volkmann, Tokarski and Ernst (2012), wherein four factors may be analyzed when defining social entrepreneurs:

1. The scope of the activity;
2. Their characteristics;
3. Their primary mission and outcome and
4. The processes and resources used (as quoted in Sheldon & Danielle, 2017).

Desa identified four major themes for research:

1. definitions;
2. resource-constrained environments;
3. governance regulations; and
4. performance metrics (Desa, 2007).

Based on a bibliometric citation analysis of 129 core papers and 5,228 cited references, Kraus et al. defined five topic clusters: (1) Definitions and conceptual approaches, (2) Impetus, (3) Personality, (4) Impact and performance and (5) Future research agendas. This was extended to fifteen by Sassmannshausen and Volkmann (2018) (see Table 3.2).

Peredo and Wurzelmann extended and applied social entrepreneurship to local indigenous entrepreneurs. The authors argued that the most significant effect of the social entrepreneur's persistent occupation with an environmental, economic or health issue is the resulting impact on disadvantaged groups, thereby delivering

Table 3.2 Research areas addressed by articles on social entrepreneurship (in percent).

#	Research Areas Addressed by Social Entrepreneurship Articles	Frequency (Percent)
1	Definitions, theoretical constructs or frameworks for social entrepreneurship, description or understanding of phenomena, typologies, taxonomies	59.5
2	Measuring social impact, special value creation, performance and other consequences of social entrepreneurship	29.1
3	Resources, supporting and financing social entrepreneurship, and decision making by social investors	26.6
4	Networks, and communities in social entrepreneurship	20.3
5	Social enterprises from an organizational theory perspective	20.2
6	Processes in social entrepreneurship	17.7
7	Social entrepreneurs and their motives, methods and psychology	17.3
8	Reviews on social entrepreneurship research	11.4
9	Reports and narratives or interviews on (single) projects in social entrepreneurship	10.1
10	Social opportunity recognition and development	8.9
11	Social entrepreneurship education	6.3
12	Social innovation	5.1
13	(Single) book reviews	2.5
14	Interviews, forum contributions, comments, and notes (no original scientific research, but expression of opinion, mind teasers, and so on)	1.3
15	Other	5.1

Source: Sassmannshausen and Volkmann (2018, p. 260).

"sustainable new social value" (2015, p. 4). They also make the point that although indigenous entrepreneurs may be behind standards in the global tourism industry, this may be compensated for by blending innovation, inventiveness and opportunity to work on the required change in the local community.

Sigala (2016) maintains, however, that there are many shortcomings to the existing methods of studying social entrepreneurship, and that most existing studies have analyzed the why of social entrepreneurship. However, although these approaches (of the market) highlight the importance of structural capitalism supporting social value creation and transformation, there is still no research investigating *how* social entrepreneurs may develop and exploit structural capital for identifying and exploiting (new) market opportunities (p. 1265). This particular aspect is discussed in subsequent chapters.

Conclusions

It may be seen from the relatively recent interest in social entrepreneurship as a phenomenon in the 1980s that there is evidence that social entrepreneurship has become accepted as a serious field of study, both generically and also in the hospitality and tourism industries in particular (Sassmannshausen & Volkmann, 2018; Sigala, 2016). The increase in the volume of academic references, studies and centers for social entrepreneurship, and the establishment of social entrepreneurship in many business schools curricula throughout the world is one particular indicator of the interest in the topic. This is in direct combination with many social entrepreneurship projects that are directly improving people's lives, especially in the developing world. Examples presented in Chapter 2 such as the much publicized Grameen bank in Bangladesh but also the much smaller, but no less significant, project for local stakeholders of the Nema foundation, based at the Gulado Beach Lodge hotel resort in Mozambique, Africa (Altinay, Sigala & Waligo, 2016) that was, tragically, devastated by the cyclone 'Kenneth' in 2019.

Although there is no consensus on defining social entrepreneurs and social entrepreneurship, the former has been analyzed according to different perspectives (See Chapter 4 for further material on social entrepreneurs' individual characteristics and motivations):

1. Personal behaviors and characteristics perspective;
2. An organizational setting perspective – social entrepreneurs, sustainable entrepreneurs;
3. Motivations and types of activity perspective, including social bricoleurs, social constructionists and social engineers.

It is acknowledged that all the definitions have certain things in common (focusing on the social good and social impact of the venture). However, much of the research has been qualitative in nature and there is a need for more quantitative studies that do not test just the impact or financing of social projects but also develop a scale that can test social entrepreneurship *itself* (Sassmannshausen & Volkmann, 2018, p. 261). Sigala (2016) reinforces the need for a more general understanding of the way that social value is created and the need to expand the conceptualization of markets from mainly an economic to a broader social outlook.

CHAPTER CASE 3.1

The Hiç Olive Company, Urla, Turkey

Background information

Hiç is an olive oil company and an agriculture and gastronomy tourism platform established in Urla, Turkey by a woman entrepreneur in 2012 (www.hicoliveoil.com and https://www.hicoliveoilstore.com). The company produces many items, including olive oil and specialty food products, and even offers a restaurant and cooking class. The main concept of the company includes maintaining purity in their products and following the motto, "Less is more". Running a 2400 acre natural farm they acquired from the Ministry of Forestry in 2010, the company not only exemplifies sustainable practices for the region but also displays best practices related to social entrepreneurship in creating social transformation (Figure 3.1).

Figure 3.1 Hiç entrepreneur Ms. Duygu Ozerson at the olive farm. (Photo credit: Hiç).

Contribution to the region

Hiç's holistic approach is based on sustainability principles. They created a circular economy and help the community by preserving nature and providing additional value-added benefits including improvements to the agricultural economy, promoting gastronomy tourism and integrating a platform that contributes to the well-being of the society. Olive farming and olive oil production in the Urla region has been considered a 'cultural heritage' activity for the last 2600 years. Through Hiç's movement, the local economy is positively affected. The harvesting team of the company is carefully selected from local homemakers in need of additional income. The company not only provides employment in the region but also connects new generations with their cultural roots, in order to continue this ancient tradition of olive farming and olive oil production dating back to the 6th century BC. This also helps create for the region an identity that combines culture and rich traditions, which in turn leads to increased domestic and international tourism.

WHAT IS SOCIAL ENTREPRENEURSHIP?

Making a difference

The Hiç Restaurant and Cooking Classes are also a great example of 'forest to fork' practices. After a long renovation period, the restaurant was established in a 160-year-old building. Its all-organic products are grown and foraged in the edible 'Organic Hic Forest' and exemplify local flavors known as 'New Urla Cuisine', while also using high-tech kitchen equipment and minimum pre-packaged ingredients. In addition to olive oil tasting panels and workshops, the restaurant also provides employment for the region.

Economic impact

The company also has a busy events calendar, which contributes to the tourism of the region year-round. These include wine tastings, alternative tastings with local and unique producers, educational workshops, 'Food & Design Weekends', tasty movie nights and different seasonal harvest tours of plants such as olives, edible greens and wild lavenders. They also make their own ceramics and pottery, exemplifying local heritage, which are then all used at the restaurant and are found for sale at the atelier. All products, including the olive oil, olive, honey, bread, sauces, vinegars and ceramics, are sold at a corner in the restaurant and online.

CHAPTER CASE 3.2

Chumbe Island Coral Park Ltd. (CHICOP): Lessons learned from setting up the first private Marine Protected Area

(Source: The Long Run, Chumbe Island Coral Park Ltd.)

CHUMBE ISLAND
CORAL PARK
Zanzibar Tanzania

Synopsis

This case study outlines the process that the Chumbe Island Coral Park Ltd. (CHICOP) carried out to establish a privately governed Marine Protected Area (MPA) in order to address the challenges of overexploitation, lack of environmental awareness and poor marine governance by the government in Zanzibar, which threatened the island's biodiversity and the local coral reefs.

The Chumbe MPA, set up by Sibylle Riedmiller, became the first private MPA in the world, paving the way for others. Key ingredients of the starting-up success included the establishment of an ecotourism business to sustain the MPA financially, engaging the community actively, establishing a robust baseline with scientific data and creating a clear management plan for the area.

About CHICOP

CHICOP is an award-winning private nature reserve established in 1991 for the conservation and sustainable management of Chumbe Island, Zanzibar – one of the last pristine coral islands in the region.

The aim of CHICOP is to create a financially and ecologically sustainable model, where ecotourism supports conservation, research and environmental education, as well as providing benefits for local people (Figure 3.2).

Figure 3.2 Areal view of Chumbe Island.
(Photo credit: Markus Meissl).

Challenges

The rich biodiversity and delicate coral reefs in Zanzibar were threatened by overexploitation, lack of environmental conservation awareness and, at the time, an absence of any policies and legislation for establishing marine parks owned by the government.

When Riedmiller arrived in Zanzibar in 1991, local people considered the corals 'rocks and stones', as their language Kiswahili had no word for corals. The corals were smashed by the destructive fishing techniques used to chase fish into nets or were extracted to be burned into plaster sold at the market. There was little awareness about the role coral reefs played in local ecosystems, livelihoods and, ultimately, in people's wellbeing.

In addition, the rapidly growing population, lack of employment opportunities in the region, easy availability of explosives in villages and poor governance of the fisheries sector had encouraged people to resort to illegal fishing techniques to survive, such as using dynamite fishing.

There were neither an awareness of the need for nor legislation and mechanisms (such as public MPAs) available to protect the marine environment in the early 1990s. Once established, in later years these were often poorly managed. Such 'paper MPAs' lacked on-site management or, in mainland Tanzania, were sometimes managed by government employees who were not from coastal areas and had little understanding of the local social and cultural context and fishing practices. This, and the lack of sharing and transparency in the use of proceeds from coastal tourism, resulted in poor relationships between the government and fishermen, making it very difficult to protect the environment and educate local communities.

Solutions

In order to address the challenges and protect the marine and coastal environment of Zanzibar, Riedmiller set out to develop a privately managed MPA. However, this was not done overnight. Her first proposal to establish a small educational marine park in collaboration with the government, funded by ecotourism, was ignored. As a result, she started the process of creating the first-ever private MPA in the world. Steps she took included:

SELECTION OF A SUITABLE SITE

After two months of joining fishers and snorkeling around Zanzibar's coral reefs, Riedmiller identified the uninhabited Chumbe Island as most suitable area for the MPA because:

- The reef conditions were ideal. The western fringing coral reef of the island was highly diverse and shallow enough to be used for environmental educational programs.
- The island was uninhabited; thus no local stakeholders would be displaced.
- The waters surrounding the island were part of a military zone where the army conducted shooting range exercises from the adjacent coast. In addition, fishing was already restricted to avoid small fishing boats obstructing vessels plying the adjacent shipping channel to Dar-es-Salaam.

WHAT IS SOCIAL ENTREPRENEURSHIP?

- At the time, few fishers could afford outboard engines to reach areas distant from the markets of Zanzibar Stonetown. However, fishermen had started to move towards Chumbe in search of new fishing grounds as stocks had been depleted in many areas due to overfishing. Therefore, the timing of establishing the MPA at Chumbe Island was ideal to avoid further exploitation and development and to conserve the still relatively intact reef, though engaging fishers in the protection of the reef would also be essential.

- The above conditions meant that the creation of the MPA would rely more on collaboration with local fishers rather than through government enforcement.

NEGOTIATIONS

Negotiations of the investment proposal with the semi-autonomous government of Zanzibar to successfully gazette Chumbe Island as an MPA took nearly four years. It included liaising with seven departments of the Government of Zanzibar.

In order to ensure the long-term security of land tenure and protection, Riedmiller managed to obtain a lease on 2.44 ha of the island for a period of thirty-three years for the development of the ecolodge and a management agreement for the conservation of the forest covering the rest of Chumbe Island for the same duration. Furthermore, the management of the MPA was assigned to CHICOP for a renewable period of ten years, which has been renewed twice since then (Figure 3.3).

Figure 3.3 Chumbe eco-bungalows: living in the open with a near-zero environmental impact.
(Photo credit: Peter Bennett).

SCIENCE-INFORMED DECISION-MAKING AND CAPACITY BUILDING

At the start of the process, baseline social, physical and biological surveys were carried out by professional volunteers to acquire reliable scientific information to help determine the conservation value and boundaries of the MPA, as well as to help set its objectives.

- Marine biologists were employed as conservation coordinators in 1992 for training park rangers and overseeing all research and monitoring programs.
- Projects were initiated to build cross-institutional capacity both within the Chumbe MPA and with partner institutions and emerging coastal conservation programs across the region.
- Partnerships with local and regional organizations were created and maintained to ensure the facilitation of training opportunities beyond Chumbe.

COMMUNITY INVOLVEMENT AND BENEFITS

From the beginning, Chumbe ensured that local communities were fully involved in the MPA and that its stakeholders (e.g., fishermen and nearest communities on Zanzibar) directly or indirectly continued to benefit from the MPA, in order to offset the impacts of restricting or modifying access to traditional resources (Figures 3.4 and 3.5). The participation of local communities was ensured through the following:

- Creating employment opportunities for the community, especially fishermen, as park rangers and later tourist guides, and giving preference to villagers for other jobs;
- Involving village leaders in the development of management plans and participation in Advisory Committee meetings;
- Conducting continuous outreach programs and consultations in six adjacent villages before and during the development of the MPA;
- Sustaining clear and positive communications with all stakeholders at all times;
- Providing wider income opportunities for local communities and women's groups, such as supplying agricultural products for the restaurant of the ecolodge, building materials and handicrafts, outsourcing road and boat transport and craftsmen services during maintenance;
- Communicating and effectively delivering project benefits to local communities through the protection of valuable biodiversity and restocking depleted fishing grounds and degraded coral reefs;

Figure 3.4 Chumbe's head ranger, Omari Nyange, on boat patrol. (Photo credit: Viktor and Nora Jelinek).

Figure 3.5 Chumbe's environmental education (EE) program takes local school children snorkeling in the protected reef. Most of the children don't know how to swim and need life jackets and training before exploring the coral reef.
(Photo credit: CHICOP).

- Providing emergency services to local fishermen in distress in the absence of a marine rescue service in Tanzania;
- Respecting local culture and incorporating traditional practices (such as cuisine, art, etc.) into hospitality operations and
- Maintaining a high level of accountability and transparency.

FINANCIAL SUSTAINABILITY

CHICOP identified ecotourism as a means to generate revenue to cover all of the MPA's operational costs, as well as its conservation, research and education activities. Although the company's objectives are not-for-profit, it follows commercial principles in order to maximize revenue and promote cost-effectiveness to sustain its activities. In order to design a financial sustainable tourism business, CHICOP:

- Invested a total of $1.2 million in the pre-operational phase (1991–1998). Of this, 50% was funded with private capital from Riedmiller for start-up and development costs; small donor funds contributed another 25% for non-commercial components such as baseline surveys, the visitor center, ranger training and boats, forest nature trails and education programs. The remaining 25% came from volunteer work from individuals and agencies.
- Worked with committed professional volunteers to support activities such as carrying out baseline surveys and designing monitoring schemes, training local fishermen as park rangers in patrolling, monitoring and guidance skills, teaching English, designing nature trials and educational materials, designing the ecolodge and installing and maintaining technical equipment.
- Financed costs through ecotourism profits. The minimum management costs of CHICOP are nearly US $250,000 per year. By 1997, 52% of the investment accounted for conservation costs, 39% for tourism infrastructure and 9% for educational infrastructure.

EFFECTIVE MPA MANAGEMENT AND ENFORCEMENT

Following the gazettement of the MPA by the Government of Zanzibar in 1994 and the entrustment of the management of the MPA to CHICOP, they ensured effective management by:

- Developing management plans from 1995 onwards, which defined the objectives, activities, research regulations and "dos and don'ts" both for visitors and staff. These were agreed upon by the government and CHICOP and were developed with wide stakeholder participation.

WHAT IS SOCIAL ENTREPRENEURSHIP? 65

- Allowing only non-consumptive and non-exploitative activities, with 100% of the reef sanctuary protected as a 'No-Take Zone'.
- Limiting research to non-extractive studies, prohibiting fishing and non-authorized anchoring in the MPA. For conservation purposes, scuba diving is only permitted for researchers and documentary film crews.
- Using strict state-of-the-art eco-technologies in building the ecolodge and visitors' center (rainwater catchment, composting toilets, vegetative grey water filtration and sun and photovoltaics for all energy needs) and all operations.
- Restricting the number of visitors per day and allowing only boats arranged by Chumbe to take visitors to the MPA.
- Using demarcation buoys to highlight the boundaries of the MPA.
- Strengthening enforcement capacity by providing on-going training to rangers in basic coral reef ecology, monitoring and surveillance techniques and processes for promoting and ensuring MPA compliance. Patrols are carried out by boat, on foot and from the top of the lighthouse. The rangers are unarmed and utilize educative techniques, persuading fishers and raising awareness.
- Sharing monitoring methods and reports with the Department of Fisheries Development in Zanzibar to raise awareness and highlight compliance (Figures 3.6 and 3.7).

Figure 3.6 Chumbe Reef Sanctuary – a protected coral garden of high biodiversity value.
(Photo credit: Markus Meissl).

66 WHAT IS SOCIAL ENTREPRENEURSHIP?

Figure 3.7 The closed forest reserve on Chumbe Island is home to a large population of coconut crabs (*Birgus latro*), the largest terrestrial crab in the world.
(Photo credit: Markus Meissl).

Impacts

- Developed the first self-sustaining privately owned and managed MPA in the world, funded by ecotourism. The ecolodge reached up to 86% annual occupancy within ten years of operation, while the minimum average occupancy rate needed to cover management costs (40%) was met after three years of opening commercial operations.

- There has been increasing revenue, reaching US$500,000 per year, of which about 40% is destined for general operations, salaries, administration and running the ecolodge; 30% is spent on taxes, leases and permits for operations; and the remaining 30% goes to conservation and education services, such as education programs, research, monitoring, etc.

- Became a leading example for marine and coastal developers and managers, sharing experiences and lessons learned to help develop policies for conservation.

- It is recognized as an effectively managed MPA based on biophysical, social and governance criteria and scientific knowledge.

- Helped improve fishing grounds adjacent to the MPA, positively impacting the livelihoods of local communities. Ninety-four percent of artisanal fishers interviewed believe their yields adjacent to the MPA have increased through the spillover effect, with fish stock from inside the MPA travelling to nearby fishing grounds. Similarly, research has shown that Chumbe has a greater biomass of commercially important fish species than other protected areas without No-Take Zones.

- Ninety-three percent of CHICOP's employees are local, providing jobs to forty-five people, each with an average of twelve dependents, which promotes social resilience.
- Created access to sponsored education and financial credit schemes. Since 1996, 8189 students, 1363 teachers and 1311 community members and government officials have participated in Chumbe's Environmental Education program (up to March 2020). Meanwhile, almost all employees at Chumbe have benefited from extensive on-the-job training and credit access.
- Created markets for local products and handicrafts.

Lessons learned

- Ecotourism is a financially viable mechanism to sustain an MPA
- The selection of the place to set up an MPA has to take into consideration both the conservation goals and the tourist market potential to make the ecotourism project commercially viable.
- Chumbe's remoteness, relatively small size and the commitment of the staff have been crucial to effectively support enforcement and decrease poaching. "If you want a park to function, start small and start private", according to Sibylle Riedmiller.
- A mixture of private capital and small donor grants were needed in order to fund the MPA. Having experience with the application and accounting processes of aids schemes is beneficial to successfully access donor grants.
- Long-term thinking is needed both from conservation and financial perspectives. Long-term security of land tenure is needed, as well as investors' understanding that the project has a future payback, if any.
- Similarly, a long-term management commitment and strong leadership determined to overcome challenges is crucial for successfully developing an MPA.
- When evaluating the commercial viability of a project, additional costs to fund conservation, environmental technologies and the employment of operational staff for park management and education programs must be taken into account, since it can impact competitiveness. This is particularly the case in places where, as in Tanzania,

no tax incentives are available for Privately Protected Areas, which are only now beginning to be recognized internationally for their contribution to biodiversity conservation, e.g., by the Resolution 36 of the IUCN, approved in the World Parks Congress in Hawaii in 2016.

- Volunteers have been crucial for developing and sustaining CHICOP.
- Strong community engagement and support is required. In order to gain this, the benefits of the project must be felt in the community, political challenges need to be minimized and both formal and informal meetings are needed in order to build trust with local communities. Inconsistent communication and political challenges, particularly during election campaigns, can result in temporal confusion, anger and mistrust amongst local fishers, as in Chumbe during the early stages.
- Providing equitable jobs and opportunities to local communities to benefit from the project enhances support and involvement.
- Understanding the local peoples' culture, traditions and religion facilitates negotiations with communities because actions that go in line with the community's ways of life will be more easily accepted and implemented.
- Recruiting and training local community members who have limited formal education and skills requires considerable time and investment, but it increases environmental awareness and provides a sense of ownership, team spirit and motivation to protect the monitored habitats.
- The effectiveness of MPA management can only be assessed if long-term monitoring data is collected in order to verify compliance with established goals (Figure 3.8).

Figure 3.8 Zanzibari students learning about marine ecology on Chumbe Island.
(Photo credit: Markus Meissl).

An effective participatory planning phase was a crucial aspect of the success of Chumbe's MPA. However, adequate and adaptive management is required to sustain it in the long run. Key factors for success include:

- Daily patrols, surveillance, presence of rangers (24/7) and compliance monitoring.
- Comprehensive specialist ranger training on how to approach and engage fishers positively (using educative, non-confrontational techniques to promote compliance).
- Keeping daily records to identify causes of any infringements in order to implement acceptable and practicable mitigating measures.
- In-house ranger skills-building on coral reef, forest ecology and survey techniques to undertake long-term biophysical monitoring (supported by expert external parties) to document change and enable reactive real-time measures to be implemented based on observations.
- Long-term community engagement, outreach and transparent communications.
- Dedicated staff from key community areas and secure employment opportunities effectively create a cadre of skilled educators.
- Positive and open communications with wider stakeholder groups (government, NGOs, etc.).
- Willingness and flexibility to implement real-time adaptive management under ranging scenarios.
- Commitment to excellence and strong leadership.

EXERCISES

Group discussion

Take some time to review Chapter case 3.1: The Hic Olive Company, Urla, Turkey and visit the company's website (https://www.hicoliveoilstore.com/pages/about-us).

1. Discuss the contribution of 'Hic' to the community.
2. What else would you recommend the company to dedicate time and resources to?

Group discussion

Take some time to review Chapter case 3.2: Chumbe Island Coral Park ltd. (CHICOP): Lessons Learned from Setting Up the First Private Marine Protected Area and visit the company's website (https://chumbeisland.com/)

1. Review the many initiatives started by the team at Chumbe Island Coral Park; which one impresses you the most? Discuss your decision.
2. What are guests staying in bungalows saying about Chumbe Island Coral Park? Take some time to read reviews on major review sites. What recommendations would you make to Chumbe Island Coral Park?
3. Discuss the model used by Chumbe Island Coral Park to create a financially and ecologically sustainable park management, where ecotourism supports conservation, research and educational programs; can this model be replicated? And if so under what conditions?

Individual research

Write an essay about ecotourism and social entrepreneurship. Consider answering the following questions:

1. Reviewing the principles of ecotourism (Quebec Declaration on Ecotourism) as well as the Global Code of Ethics for Tourism (UNWTO), to what extent is social entrepreneurship compatible with tourism in general and alternative forms of tourism?
2. In which way can social entrepreneurship bring about greater sustainability in tourism development?

References

Abu-Saifan, S. (2012). Social entrepreneurship: Definition and boundaries. *Technology Innovation Management Review*, 2(2): 22–27. 10.22215/timreview/523

Altinay, L., Sigala, M., & Waligo, V. (2016). Social value creation through tourism enterprise. *Tourism Management*, 54, 404–417.

Ashoka. (n.d.). *Social Entrepreneurship*. https://www.ashoka.org/en/focus/social-entrepreneurship

Bacq, S., Hartog, C., & Hoogendoorn, B. (2013). A quantitative comparison of social and commercial entrepreneurship: Toward a more nuanced understanding of social entrepreneurship organizations in context. *Journal of Social Entrepreneurship*, 4(1), 40–68.

Benn, S., & Bolton, D. (2011). *Key Concepts in Corporate Social Responsibility*. London, UK: Sage.

Chahine, T. (2016). *Introduction to Social Entrepreneurship*. Cleveland, OH: CRC Press.

de Lange, D. & Dods, R. (2017). Increasing sustainable through social entrepreneurship *International Journal of Contemporary Hospitality Management, 29*(7), 1977–2002.

Dees, G. (1998). *The Meaning of Social Entrepreneurship, Stanford Center for Social Entrepreneurship.* http://www.fntc.info/files/documents/The%20meaning%20of%20Social%20 Entreneurship.pdf

Desa, G. (2007). Social Entrepreneurship: Snapshots of a research field in emergence. *The 3rd International Social Entrepreneurship Research Conference*, Copenhagen.

Gibbs, D. (2006). Sustainability entrepreneurs, ecopreneurs and the development of a sustainable society. *Greener Management International,* Autumn, 63–78.

Kraus, S., Filser, M., O'Dwyer, M., & Shaw, E. (2014). Social entrepreneurship: An exploratory citation analysis. *Review of Managerial Science, 8*(2), 275–292. doi: 10.1007/s11846-013-0104-6

Light, P. (2008). *The Search for Social Entrepreneurship.* Washington, DC: Brookings Institution Press.

Mair, J., & Marti, I. (2006). Social Entrepreneurship research: A source of explanation, prediction and delight. *Journal of World Business, 41(1),* 36–44.

Oncer, A. Z., & Yildiz, M. L, (2010). Creating sustainable value for society: Social entrepreneurship. *The Business Review, 14*(2), 222–228.

O'Neill, G. D., Hershauer, J. C., & Golden, J. S. (2006). The cultural context of sustainability entrepreneurship. *Greener Management International, 55*(Autumn), 33–46.

Parker, W. N. (1954). Entrepreneurship, industrial organization, and economic growth: A German example. *Journal of Economic History, 14*(4), 380–400.

Peredo, B., & Wuzelmann, S., (2015). Indigenous tourism and social entrepreneurship in the Bolivian Amazon: Lessons from San Miguel del Bala. *The International Indigenous Policy Journal, 6*(4), 1–26. doi: 10.18584/iipj.2015.6.4.5

Sanzo-Perez, M. J., Álvarez-González, L. I., & Rey-García, M. (2015). How to encourage social innovations: A resource-based approach. *Service Industries Journal, 35*(7–8), 430–447. doi: https://doi-org.jpllnet.sfsu.edu/10.1080/02642069.2015.1015517

Sassmannshausen, S. P., & Volkmann, C. (2018). The Scientometrics of social entrpreneurship and its establishment as an academic field. *Journal of Small Business Management, 56*(2), 251–273.

Schlange, L. E. (2006). Stakeholder identification in sustainability entrepreneurship. *Greener Management International, 55*(Autumn), 13–31.

Seidman, I. (2006). *Interviewing as Qualitative Research a Guide for Researchers in Education and the Social Sciences.* New York and London: Teachers College Press, Columbia University,

Shane, S. (2000). Prior knowledge and the discovery of entrepreneurial opportunities. *Organization Science, 11*(4), 448–469.

Sheldon, P. J., & Danielle, R. (2017). *Social Entrepreneurship and Tourism: Philosophy and Practices.* Cham, Switzerland: Springer Publications.

Sigala, M. (2016). Learning with the market: A market approach and framework for developing social entrepreneurship in tourism and hospitality. *International Journal of Contemporary Hospitality Management, 28*(6), 1245–1286.

Skoll. (n.d.). Approach. http://skoll.org/about/approach/

Smith, B. R., Barr, T. F., Barbosa, S. D., & Kickul, J. R. (2008). Social entrepreneurship: A grounded learning approach to social value creation. *Journal of Enterprising Culture, 16*(4), 339–362.

Speake, J. (Ed.). (2015). *The Oxford Dictionary of Proverbs* (6th ed.). Oxford: Oxford University Press.

Thornton, P. H. (1999). The sociology of entrepreneurship. *Annual Review of Sociology, 25,* 19–46.

Tilley, F., & Parrish, B. D. (2006). Introduction. *Greener Management International, 55*(Autumn), 5–12.

Tilley, F., & Young, W. (2006). Sustainability entrepreneurs: Could they be the true wealth generators of the future?. *Greener Management International, 55*(Autumn), 79–92.

Zahra, S. A, Gedajlovic, E., Neubaum, D. O., & Shulman, J. M. (2009). A typology of social entrepreneurs: Motives, search processes and ethical challenges. *Journal of Business Venturing, 24*(5), 519–532.

Chapter 4

Social entrepreneurs: characteristics and motivations

This chapter explores the key attributes or characteristics of social entrepreneurs and the reasons or motivations why some individuals decide to invest in social entrepreneurship ventures. 'Push' and 'pull' motives as well as the concepts of 'necessity' and 'opportunity' entrepreneurship are reviewed. A well-established typology of social entrepreneurs is presented. The chapter concludes with a discussion of the role of social entrepreneurs in being 'change agents' towards building a better world.

The chapter presents the case of Inkaterra, a hospitality company dedicated to pushing the boundaries of eco-friendly luxury hotels by being actively involved in rainforest preservation and marine biodiversity protection in Peru. A set of additional exercises is provided at the end of the chapter, which are based on individual or group research and discussions.

Why become a social entrepreneur?

"Social entrepreneurs are not content just to give a fish or teach how to fish. They will not rest until they have revolutionized the fishing industry" (Bill Drayton, in Bessant & Tidd, 2007, p. 299). The above quote from Bill Drayton, founder of the Ashoka Foundation, an organization dedicated to promoting and facilitating social entrepreneurship, summarizes the frame of mind of many, if not all, social entrepreneurs. Some entrepreneurs have created structures in affordable housing; developed innovations in the field of health and wellbeing; found ways to restore the natural environment or proposed business models to support the integration of refugees. All those entrepreneurs have different backgrounds and unique profiles. However, all chose to do business differently. What unites them is the drive to take action and change the status quo.

In a very connected and globalized world, social entrepreneurs thrive by finding opportunities in the imperfection of the uniform market logic of the predominant economic system. Planetary and societal challenges and needs are colossal and constantly changing. Social entrepreneurs must therefore constantly devise new ways to tackle those challenges by developing new concepts and ideas and putting them into practice. In short, innovation is essential.

Similar to a traditional entrepreneur, the social entrepreneur also works hard to ensure projects, products or services see the light of day. Unlike traditional entrepreneurship, however, the goal of social entrepreneurship does not reside in ownership, hierarchical achievement or corporate titles, but in thinking and implementing responses to societal problems. The pursuit of personal enrichment and the logic of profit, associated with more classic entrepreneurship values, therefore appear to be secondary here (Zahra, Gedajlovic, Neubaum, & Shulman, 2009). The common denominator across social entrepreneurs is the desire to move the lines and bend the norms to achieve net positive change. The social entrepreneur's prime satisfaction is derived from the merits of the action undertaken. However, it is not excluded that traditional entrepreneurs, having reached a certain level of financial success with their endeavors, may in time decide to attach a greater value to societal and environmental actions via corporate social responsibility programs or donations. Academic researchers have looked into the topic of social entrepreneurship for the past few decades as discussed in Chapter 3. In regards to the motivations driving social entrepreneurs, four main ones have been identified: (1) the desire to create social wealth; (2) the need to contribute to overall wealth, including economic (3) the need for social justice and (4) the need to solve certain social problems (Zahra et al., 2009). This may be a partial answer to the question, 'Why become a social entrepreneur?' Zahra et al., in an article published in the *Journal of Business Venturing*, mentioned that "defining social entrepreneurship requires appreciating the motivations of individuals and groups who take the risks associated with conceiving, building, launching and sustaining new organizations and business models" (2009, p. 522). The authors discuss that various types of social entrepreneurs exist and operate, each "addressing specific social problems in their own ways and within their own realms" (Zahra et al., 2009, p. 523). Nevertheless, as discussed above, the commonality amongst them is the "ability to inspire, marshal and mobilize the efforts of commercial and non-commercial partners, donors, volunteers and employees in the pursuit of social wealth" (Zahra et al., 2009, p. 523).

The 'push' or 'pull' entrepreneur

The concept of 'push' and 'pull' motives in entrepreneurship has been discussed widely. The work from Amit and Muller, published in the *Journal of Small Business & Entrepreneurship*, provides an excellent starting point, wherein the authors investigate the individual motives for becoming an entrepreneur (1995). The authors' inquiry results in two type of entrepreneurs: 'push' and 'pull' entrepreneurs. Along the same line, researchers have coined the terms 'opportunity entrepreneurship' and 'necessity entrepreneurship' (e.g., Bergmann & Sternberg, 2007; Calderon, Iacovone, & Juarez, 2017; Dawson & Henley, 2012; Fairlie & Fossen, 2018; Fossen & Buettner, 2013; Kautonen & Palmroos, 2010; Thurik, Carree, Van Stel, & Audretsch, 2008; Van der Zwang, Thurik, Verheul, & Hessels, 2016; Van Stel, Storey, & Thurik, 2007; Wennekers, van Stel, Thurik, & Reynolds, 2007). The basic distinction between the two is that "some entrepreneurs create businesses when they see a business opportunity whereas other entrepreneurs are forced into starting a business out of necessity because of the lack of other options in the labour market" (Fairlie & Fossen, 2018, p. 1).

'Push' entrepreneurs, 'necessity entrepreneurship'

'Push' entrepreneurs refer to individuals who engage in entrepreneurship not because of entrepreneurial skills but rather because they may be in a situation forcing them to do so (Amit & Muller, 1995). This can be due to the fact that those individuals may have no other possibility of finding adequate work or are highly dissatisfied with their current status. The most common causes are dismissal, unemployment, job insecurity, dissatisfaction and frustration (Thurik et al., 2008). More recently, the concept has also been described as 'necessity entrepreneurship'. Although there are variations in the definition, a starting point could be employment status, as discussed by Fairlie and Fossen (2018). The basic idea is that "individuals who are initially unemployed before starting businesses are defined as 'necessity' entrepreneurs" (Fairle & Fossen, 2018, p. 2).

'Pull' entrepreneurs, 'opportunity entrepreneurship'

'Pull' entrepreneurs, on the other hand, are motivated by the venture itself as well as the potential personal and professional gains and the overall attractiveness associated with the idea (Amit & Muller, 1995). The concept is also defined as 'opportunity entrepreneurship' wherein an individual voluntarily pursues an entrepreneurial opportunity (Fairly & Fossen, 2018). Motivations may be multifaceted, whether it be financial gains, increased work satisfaction, the desire for more autonomy and independence, achieving a certain social status or greater recognition in the community the entrepreneur operates in, for example (Carter, Gartner, Shaver, & Gatewood, 2003; McMullen, Bagby, & Palich, 2008).

The dichotomy

It becomes clear that a dichotomy exists in the concepts of 'necessity' versus 'opportunity' entrepreneurship. Dawson and Henley looked into whether individuals choose to become self-employed based on push or pull motivations in an article published in the *International Journal of Entrepreneurial Behaviour & Research* (2012). Multiple factors, categorized in 'push' or 'pull' terms, were used to identify why men and women chose self-employment. The authors identify two dimensions framing the factors. Third-party constraints or enablers are identified as 'external factors' while personal goals and objective or self-perceptions are labelled as 'internal factors' (Table 4.1). Ultimately, 'push' motivation accounted for half the overall factors towards self-employment, with 'independence' the most common (Dawson & Henley, 2012).

However, it is worth mentioning that motivational factors pertaining to 'necessity' and 'opportunity' entrepreneurship have been investigated predominantly from the perspective of classical, traditional views on business entrepreneurship. However, unlike traditional entrepreneurs, social entrepreneurs may show a broader range of motivations.

Table 4.1 Summary of 'pull' and 'push' factors.

	External Factors	Internal Factors
'Push' factors	Lack of alternative opportunity (e.g., no (other) jobs available)	Job dissatisfaction (e.g., to have a low to no motivation)
	Redundancy (e.g., loss of work)	Family constraints (e.g., to want to work at home)
Combined 'push' and 'pull' factors	Resources (e.g., access to capital, equipment, space etc.)	Financial (e.g., to want more money)
'Pull' factors	Market opportunity (e.g., identify a demand or a market)	Autonomy (e.g., to be independent)
	Innovation (e.g., identify an opportunity)	Challenge (e.g., to join the family business)
		Perceived self-efficacy (e.g., to control one's environment)

Source: Based on Dawson and Henley (2012).

Becoming a social entrepreneur: two basic motives

Gabarret, Vedel and Decaillon (2017) explored the motivation of social entrepreneurs by applying the 'push' and 'pull' approach as discussed above. The authors shared their results in an article published in the *International Journal of Entrepreneurship and Small Business*. While the results of Gabarret et al. are considered exploratory in nature, they indicate that the motivations of 'necessity' and 'opportunity' for social entrepreneurs are broad and that "motivation is a composition of push factors (dissatisfaction) and pull factors (social opportunity and independence)" (2017, p. 14). However, it is interesting to point out that within the construct of 'push' and 'pull' motives, "social entrepreneurs are motivated principally by non-economic factors" (Gabarret et al., 2017, p. 14). Additionally, and contrary to the basic dichotomy of 'push' and 'pull' motives, the authors, and several other researchers discuss the concept of a 'push/pull continuum', which explains the motivations of social entrepreneurs (e.g., Gabarret et al., 2017; Hughes, 2003; Kirkwood, 2009). More fluid, the continuum allows researchers to explore the multifaceted motivations of social entrepreneurs rather than squaring individual decisions as being 'pushed' or 'pulled' into entrepreneurship. An entrepreneur may move from a 'necessity' phase underpinned by numerous external reasons into an 'opportunity' phase accompanied by numerous individual reasons. For example, Gabarret et al. (2017) discovered that social entrepreneurs made the conscious decision to resign from work commitments specially to establish the social enterprise with the full knowledge that this would entail reduced financial earnings (compared to staying at the job). They write that social entrepreneurs "are confident in their employability; they know that they could find a job if the project were to fail" (2017, p. 14). As such, the sole economic concern is the pressure to 'make a living' and be able to continue developing the entrepreneurial project. Table 4.2 provides a summary of factors of motivation of social entrepreneurs.

Table 4.2 Summary of factors of motivation of social entrepreneurs

	Level of Motivation	
	Socio-Economic (Macro)	Individual (Micro)
'Push' factors	Out of necessity (e.g., dissatisfaction with society)	Dissatisfaction with current state
Social Entrepreneurship 'Pull' factors	Identifying an opportunity (e.g., social, environmental)	Acquiring independence

Source: Based on Gabarret et al. (2017)

It is important to understand that motivation factors, entrepreneurial behavior and the larger context of operations are often interlinked. For example, an individual may be a casualty of the socioeconomic system, which, in one way or another, excludes him or her (e.g., loss of job). That individual turns around and under a set of socioeconomic push factors (out of necessity) decides to establish a social enterprise. The likely outcome is a strong desire to 'fix' the imbalances of that same socioeconomic context through the enterprise. The motivation and outcome are linked, in this particular case by the desire to create social wealth. As discussed at the start of this chapter Zahra et al. (2009) identified four main motivations of social entrepreneurs and, additionally, discussed the diversity of social entrepreneurs and provided a description of three distinct types.

Typology of social entrepreneurs

Independent from the motivation factors, social entrepreneurs share a drive and passion for pursuing social issues. One of the essential factors is that social entrepreneurship is equally about problem finding as it is about problem solving (Zahra et al., 2009). However, Zahra et al. argue that "major differences exist among them in how they discover social needs (i.e., search processes), pursue social opportunities, and impact the broader social system" (2009, p. 523). Some social entrepreneurs have identified global problems to confront, which may necessitate a large network of collaborators and supporters (Zahra et al., 2009). Others may establish an organization to accomplish the same task (Zahra et al., 2009). Finally, some may decide to act regionally or locally, identifying the community challenges to be tackled (Zahra et al., 2009). Consequently, Zahra et al. (2009) propose three types of social entrepreneurs (also briefly introduced in Chapter 3): social bricoleurs, social constructionists and social engineers.

Social bricoleurs

Social bricoleurs have the expertise and resources to address a local social need. Their actions remain small in terms of scale but still have a significant impact in regards to local social harmony (Zahra et al., 2009). Often, social bricoleurs "act from being in the right place at the right time" (Zahra et al., 2009, p. 524). For example, social entrepreneurs collecting used soaps from hotels to supply refugee camps or communities in need.

Social constructionists

Social constructionists generate substitute or alternative structures to provide services or products addressing a social need. They tackle problems that governments or other businesses have failed to address (Zahra et al., 2009). They can create structures that operate on a small or large scale, locally or globally. Similarly, to social bricoleurs, they "mend the social fabric where it is torn, address acute social needs within existing broader social structures, and help maintain social harmony" (Zahra et al., 2009, p. 524). The case of entrepreneur Muhammad Yunus,

Grameen Bank and the establishment of microfinancing discussed in Chapter 2 would be a prominent example of this.

Social engineers

Social engineers create a "newer, more effective social systems designed to replace existing ones when they are ill-suited to address significant social needs" (Zahra et al., 2009, p. 524). By nature, the undertaking is often very large both in scale and scope. According to Zahra et al., social engineers "rip apart existing social structures and replace them with new ones" (2009, p. 524), fracturing the prevailing social equilibrium and with the goal of replacing it for a more socially just and efficient system (Zahra et al., 2009). Day and Mody (2017) identified businesses operating within the sharing economy aimed at positive social outcomes to be examples of social engineers. The authors also come to the conclusion that the scarcity of examples of "disruptive social enterprises in tourism has resulted in the apparent lack of attention to social entrepreneurs in the tourism sector" (Day & Mody, 2017, p. 66).

Characteristics of social entrepreneurs

According to Abu-Saifan, "Social entrepreneurs design their revenue-generating strategies to directly serve their mission to deliver social value" (2012, p. 24). He published a review of definitions and boundaries of social entrepreneurship in *Technology Innovation Management Review*. Ultimately, he proposed a definition of the social entrepreneur as "a mission-driven individual who uses a set of entrepreneurial behaviours to deliver a social value to the less privileged, all through an entrepreneurially oriented entity that is financially independent, self-sufficient, or sustainable" (Abu-Saifan, 2012, p. 25). Abu-Saifan proceeds to formulate the following four main pillars which distinguish social entrepreneurs from other types of entrepreneurs:

1. They are mission-oriented or mission-driven. They act in the context of the creation and transmission of social value to less privileged social groups.

2. They have the capacity to operate in an entrepreneurial manner within a set of predetermined characteristics that distinguish them from other entrepreneurs.

3. They act through entrepreneurship-oriented organizations that operate in a context that reinforces innovation and openness.

4. They operate within financially independent organizations, through which they design and apply strategies to generate income, while trying to provide a predetermined social value intended for under-served social groups. (Abu-Saifan, 2012, p. 25)

Table 4.3 summarizes unique and common characteristics of traditional and social entrepreneurs and indicates the inherent characteristics of for-profit entrepreneurs and social entrepreneurs, while identifying the most common characteristics for each type of entrepreneur separately.

Table 4.3 Summary unique and common characteristics of traditional and social entrepreneurs.

Unique Characteristics of the Profit-Oriented Entrepreneur	Characteristics Common to Both Types	Characteristics of the Social Entrepreneur
Desire to establish and grow a viable sustainable business or social enterprise		
Passion for a product or service	Innovator Dedicated	Passion for a cause
Pursue return on investment (ROI)	Initiative taker Leader	Seek social return on investment (SROI)a
High achiever	Opportunity alert	Mission leader
Risk bearer	Persistent	Emotionally charged
Organizer	Committed	Change agent
Strategic thinker		Opinion leader
Value creator		Social value creator
Holistic		Socially alert
Arbitrageur		Manager
		Visionary
		Highly accountable

Source: Adapted from Vega and Kidwell (2007) and Abu-Saifan (2012).
a Social Return on Investment (SROI) is discussed in details in Chapter 5.

Social entrepreneurs: being the change agent

Social entrepreneurship has become increasingly associated with a new generation of entrepreneurs who wish to use their potential to transform an industry, mend a societal problem or restore the environment, whether within a community or on a global scale. Far beyond volunteering at a local non-governmental organization for a good cause, social and environmental entrepreneurship is the idea that entrepreneurship can be used as a means to help others and improve the social or natural environment.

Arguably, new technologies and the internet have greatly helped this increased awareness of global challenges and equally have provided the necessary platform for social entrepreneurs to connect, share, grow and be part of a global 'awakening'. The internet has, to a certain extent, revolutionized social entrepreneurship, allowing an individual to launch an initiative, at times with modest or limited investment, all the while having the opportunity to interact with potential beneficiaries, partners or supporters from around the globe. The internet has democratized entrepreneurship to the extent that skills, knowledge and experience can be shared freely, working as 'push' factor for the co-creation of solutions to local or global problems without having to go through the prism of an established infrastructure, whether a professional or governmental agency, an employer or a consultant.

For some, social entrepreneurship has even become fashionable, 'hip' and in high demand. Whether social entrepreneurs are tackling ways to revolutionize the world of fashion (e.g., the Global Fashion Agenda, 2019) or providing alternative solutions for coffee-to-go cups (e.g., RECUP), they may also create, develop and sell products and services, but for a cause.

Changing status quo: effectual entrepreneurship

The driving force and motivation of a social entrepreneur, as discussed above, can be multifaceted. However, above all, there is a strong desire to solve a problem, tackle a challenge or change the world. Arguably, being a social entrepreneur means embodying the change he or she wants to see in this world. Dacin et. al. explain that "much of the social entrepreneurship literature focuses on individual social entrepreneurs and tends to characterize these individuals as heroic" (2011, p. 1205). Social entrepreneurs are portrayed as inspiring individuals, with powerful storylines that get noticed and celebrated (Dacin et al., 2011). Therefore, they argue, much of the literature is skewed with the following three biases; "(1) a bias against learning from failure, (2) a biased focus on the individual level of analysis, and (3) a bias in terms of the motives and mission of social entrepreneurs" (2011, p. 1205). Parris and McInnis-Bowers (2014) challenged the 'heroic' characterization of social entrepreneurs and discussed the 'effectual entrepreneurship' paradigm (this is discussed in detail in a publication by Saras D. Saravarthy in the *Academy of Management Review*, 2001). The authors discuss the causation process of social entrepreneurship, which, they argue, "starts with a given social problem and focuses on selecting between effective ways to positively impact the problem" (Parris & McInnis-Bowers, 2014, p. 360). The authors explain that the

> process follows the causation process of entrepreneurship that starts with search for an opportunity such as a solution for a market need or a new product that brings value to customers followed by marshalling of resources, financial and otherwise, resulting in the creation of a sustainable organization.
> (Parris & McInnis-Bowers, 2014, p. 360)

The effectual entrepreneurship paradigm, however, "begins the process of starting a new venture in the opposite direction of first exploring a set of means, or resources, available" (Parris & McInnis-Bowers, 2014, p. 361). Using the case of Clean the World, an organization that recycles hotel soap and hotel amenities to prevent diseases through soap distribution, Parris and McInnis-Bowers illustrate the path taken in two starting points "(i) questioning the status quo and (ii) focusing on existing or available resources first before identifying opportunities" (2014, p. 360). They argue that "not all social ventures start with the intention of creating social value" and that, at times, a business may enter the social entrepreneurship paradigm "by 'accident', while recognizing waste as a resource" (2014, p. 360).

Social entrepreneurs that view waste as a resource, question the status quo and are passionate about change may identify social, environmental and economic opportunities that are in line with solving societal problems.

82 WHO ARE SOCIAL ENTREPRENEURS?

Figure 4.1 Areas of opportunities for social entrepreneurs.

Socially active and useful

The social entrepreneur is often considered a 'change agent' but also assumes cross-functional roles. Despite the various obligations, a consensus seems to be established on the social utility targeted by the social entrepreneur through the business endeavor. The primary objective of the social entrepreneur is, a priori, to have a socially useful activity, often because a gap has been identified that neither the market nor the public sector satisfies. Figure 4.1 shows some areas of opportunities for social entrepreneurs that have received attention over the past decade. The 17 Sustainable Developments Goals (see: https://sustainabledevelopment.un.org/) discussed in Chapter 1 also provide a good framework to consider some of the global challenges where social entrepreneurs can identify new opportunities.

The goal – to engage in social entrepreneurship and be socially active and useful – is very topical when economic cycles are showing signs of weakness. This may be due to a 'push' factor as discussed previously, where an individual has been confronted with a specific problem, which has ultimately led to the creation of (a) business in an area where demand was identified. In that sense, social entrepreneurs start from the principle that any social or environmental problem has a solution.

Building a better world?

Whatever the driving forces behind social entrepreneurs, independent of the sector of activities, status or individual characteristics, ultimately, social entrepreneurs innovate in building a better world (Steinerowski, Jack, & Farmer, 2008).

In our globalized society, with herculean challenges in scale and scope (e.g., the climate emergency, pandemics, biodiversity collapse, pressuring inequalities, etc.), social entrepreneurs are at the forefront of an uncertain fight, which, for some, has already been lost in advance. Only few battles can be won, they argue. A certain degree of idealism carries social entrepreneurs; an ambition to create a system where everyone (and the ecosystem at large) can find a place.

CHAPTER CASE 4.1

Inkaterra pushing the boundaries of eco-friendly luxury hotels: from Amazon sustainable landscape corridors to a marine reserve in Peru

(Source: José Koechlin, Founder and CEO Inkaterra; Gabriel Mevseth, Head of Content, Inkaterra; HYB, 2018; Legrand, Sloan, & Chen, 2017; Inkaterra, https://www.inkaterra.com/)

> Ecotourism has allowed us to improve the quality of life of many living beings at all Inkaterra destinations, creating a harmonious relationship between man, flora and fauna through the encouragement of sustainable entrepreneurship.
>
> José Koechlin, Founder Inkaterra (Sustainability Leaders Project, 2019)

Synopsis

Inkaterra in Peru is a pioneer in combining hospitality services, nature conservation, education and local community involvement. Biodiversity and ecosystems are key mitigation tools but also directly affected by the climate emergency. Since its establishment four decades ago, Inkaterra's scientific initiatives and studies have helped uncover an abundant number of birds, butterflies, ants and mammal species. Inkaterra is also committed to mitigating the effect of deforestation in the Amazon rainforest through the preservation of Peru's first ecological concession, with more than 10,000 hectares of virgin rainforest allowing for carbon sequestration. The seven properties all contribute to sponsoring biodiversity inventories in natural areas where they are located.

Figure 4.2 Inkaterra Hacienda Concepcion: sheltered by the forest's canopy. (Photo Credit: Inkaterra).

Figure 4.3 Inkaterra Reserva Amazonica: 35 wooden cabanas inspired in the Ese'Eja culture. 540 bird species have been inventoried in hotel grounds, deep in the rainforest.
(Photo Credit: Inkaterra).

The founder

José Koechlin established Inkaterra in 1975, pioneering ecotourism and sustainable development in Peru. Koechlin has been close to the Amazon rainforest since his youth. He recalls: "At the age of ten, I volunteered on trips that took me to the Amazon, and a second one to Cusco, Puno, Arequipa and Nazca" (Sustainability Leaders Project, 2019, para 3). He was the co-producer of Werner Herzog's classic film *Aguirre, The Wrath of God* (1972), which sealed his passion to protect the Amazon and its vibrant biodiversity. In order to achieve that goal, he chose ecotourism as his path. Koechlin established Inkaterra within Peru's first land concession for ecotourism purposes (an area of 10,000 ha), in the Amazon rainforest of Madre de Dios. Nowadays, the company operates multiple properties in this region, considered one of the world's nature hotspots.

He has been honored with the 2017 LEC Award in the 'Large Enterprise' category; the first-ever HOLA Lifetime Achievement Award (2016) and the 2015 PURE Award for his contribution to experiential travel. Inkaterra is also recipient of the prestigious 2020 Global Vision Award given by Travel & Leisure (American Express Group). To promote travel experiences in Peru, Koechlin has sponsored various publications on nature and culture.

Figure 4.4 José Koechlin, social entrepreneur and founder of Inkaterra. (Photo Credit: Inkaterra)

WHO ARE SOCIAL ENTREPRENEURS?

The sustainability policy

Inkaterra's extensive sustainability policy under fourteen points is presented here:

1. Define and respect authentic cultural, social and environmental values.
2. Create professional development opportunities and encourage the recruitment and training of local staff.
3. Develop an ideal work environment providing better living conditions than those covered by labor laws.
4. Develop activities in accordance with current legislation, such as corporate, tax, labor and the concepts of sustainable development.
5. Provide experience in the formulation of standards and creation of protected areas.
6. Develop contingency plans for natural, social or financial disasters.
7. Continuously update analyzed financial statements in order to facilitate the decision making process and the decentralization of administrative actions. Raise awareness within partners, travelers and locals on the conservation of the environment, with activities and materials.
8. Encourage the development of local communities, taking into consideration their environment and culture.
9. Use environmentally friendly products and maintain good communication with suppliers.
10. Use energy and water efficiently, and provide adequate waste treatment.
11. Develop continuous improvement in our management and process controls by minimizing negative impacts.
12. Identify the positive and negative effects generated by human action.
13. Offset the greenhouse gas emissions generated by the organization's operations, in order to be carbon neutral.
14. Being a replicable business model of low initial cost and high positive impact on local populations.

This is then turned into seven themes for a responsible approach to travel:

I. Built-in Sustainability
II. Long Term Projects

III. Local Impact

IV. Positive Footprint

V. Sense of Place

VI. Engaging Experience

VII. Profitability

Two extensive projects are presented below.

Saving the Amazon through sustainable landscape corridors

To measure Inkaterra's long-term impact on biodiversity, the brand has sponsored major flora and fauna inventories for the past four decades, in natural areas where its hotels are located – the Amazon rainforest of Madre de Dios; the Machu Picchu cloud forest; the Sacred Valley of the Incas; the city of Cusco and the Cabo Blanco tropical ocean, desert and dry forest.

Experts have registered 903 bird species (equivalent to Costa Rica's total bird diversity) on Inkaterra grounds, as well as 362 ant species (a world record sponsored by Harvard biologist E. O. Wilson), 313 butterfly species, 100 mammal species and 1266 vascular plant species. Twenty-nine species new to science have been published – twenty orchids, five amphibians, one butterfly, two bromeliads and one tropical vine.

Inkaterra Guides Field Station is the most recent addition to the hotel collection. Since late 2016, this ecolodge, with a design inspired by the Ese'Eja culture and built with native materials, has been the training center for Inkaterra Explorer Guides – most of whom were born and raised in local communities. It offers a knowledgeable experience for scientists, students, volunteers and eco-conscious travelers, welcoming guests to be part of diverse research and conservation projects overseen by the NGO Inkaterra Asociación.

Interactive excursions at Inkaterra Guides Field Station include a Palmetum walk with a most diverse sample of native palms; a bio-orchard nurtured with ancestral agroforestry techniques; one of the five bird-banding stations in Peru and a motion-sensitive camera trap system to study wildlife on hotel grounds, which has registered jaguars, giant armadillos, tapirs, peccaries and tamanduas.

Given the current situation in Madre de Dios, Inkaterra aims to replicate the aforementioned initiatives throughout the region, educating local communities in biodiversity conservation and the sustainable use of natural resources through eco-friendly entrepreneurship.

Since the construction of the interoceanic highway in 2010, the regional economy shifted to extractive industries such as livestock, logging, oil exploration and alluvial gold mining. Nowadays, it is estimated that forty-nine plant species are threatened due to the surface extension of livestock and mining areas, the latter having grown 916% in the past twenty years. Mostly illegal and unregulated, these extractive activities have devastating consequences over local biodiversity and human populations, including loss of ecosystem connectivity, migration of native cultures and mercury pollution.

Dr. Francisco Dallmeier, director of the Smithsonian Center for Conservation and Sustainability, uses the analogy of the brain and Alzheimer's disease to explain the loss of landscape connectivity. Information from the brain travels through the body via the nervous system. When someone suffers from Alzheimer's, the messages are no longer able to get through and become isolated in the brain. The same thing happens with a depredated forest: connections between ecosystems disappear and the biodiversity becomes isolated, piling up in small areas. Inevitably the biodiversity then begins to deteriorate and rapidly disappear.

In order to improve connectivity among landscapes and ecosystems in the Amazon region, as well as land management and the reduction of mercury levels in water, Inkaterra Asociación has proposed the creation of a 78,756 ha sustainable landscape corridor off the Tambopata National Reserve, from the city of Puerto Maldonado along the Madre de Dios River, up to the Peru-Bolivia border.

Relying on strategic alliances with the U.S. Department of State, the Smithsonian Center for Conservation and Sustainability, the Development Bank of Latin America (CAF), Fondo de las Américas (FONDAM) and other influential organizations, Inkaterra Asociación's new project will stabilize fluctuations in wildlife and assist in repairing habitat fragmentation. Sustainable landscape corridors will link two or more larger blocks of habitable land, which will allow for the safe movement of wildlife, protecting them from the effects of mining and logging.

According to U.S. Science Envoy, Dr. Thomas Lovejoy, the future of the Amazon depends on Madre de Dios. Underscoring that natural resources are capital goods and that conservation is not to be considered as an expense but as an investment, Inkaterra is encouraging ecotourism and other sustainable activities among local communities, in pursuit of their own long-term economic development. Through capacity building in local communities and the replication of conservation initiatives developed at Inkaterra Guides Field Station, sustainable landscape corridors seem to be the most effective way to save the Amazon.

Inkaterra 'ocean and forest' at Cabo Blanco

Inkaterra is working to restore the Peruvian tropical sea, where destructions was caused by destructive fishing practices such as bottom trawling, bycatch, the use of explosives and ghost fishing. Their plan for economic and social development in Cabo Blanco serves as a replicable model for other coastal communities.

The Cabo Blanco tropical sea is set on one of the seventeen most megadiverse countries in the world; Peru is among the signatory nations in the Convention on Biological Diversity. Inkaterra Asociación is dedicated to scientific research towards natural preservation. Scientific research is currently being performed to assess the current situation of Cabo Blanco's marine ecosystem. Daily reports on weather, sea conditions and fish counts are produced. It is valuable information for conservation strategies and for the sustainable use of natural resources.

Figure 4.5 Artisanal fishing.
(Photo Credit: Inkaterra).

The initiative aims to restore biodiversity, promoting the reproduction of commercial species, the creation of new fisheries for artisanal fishermen and the mitigation of illegal fishing in reproduction areas.

Inkaterra has signed agreements with local communities via El Alto Town Hall and the Artisanal Fishermen Guild, organizing workshops on sustainable fishing and fish management (including Japanese techniques for tuna processing) onboard Inkaterra's school-boat 'Analúa'. Inkaterra is also developing the 'Sea to Table' traceability certificate with the Peruvian Gastronomy Society (APEGA) to guarantee good practices and high product standards, creating added value for artisanal fishermen. On the other hand, the use of ancestral watercrafts such as raft and sail are being recovered to bring back to life Cabo Blanco's cultural heritage.

Local communities are also trained on hospitality and eco-friendly activities, such as marine life observation (especially humpback whales, green turtles and pelagic birds), surfing, sport fishing and artisanal fishing. Inkaterra is also creating tourism infrastructure with a positive social impact: running water service disrupted since the 1983 El Niño phenomenon has been recovered and the implementation of a new dock is currently in progress.

Inkaterra also supports the design of public policies for the conservation and sustainable use of marine resources, as well as to determine the application of techniques for sea managing and zoning, creating conservation corridors to recover priority areas. Public-private alliances with the Latin American Development Bank (CAF), Peru's Ministry of Environment, the National Fund of Fishing Development (FONDEPES), El Alto Town Hall and the Association of Artisanal Fishermen have been established to ensure the value of biodiversity.

The value of ecotourism

In the eyes of founder José Koechlin, public-private partnerships are key to achieving sustainability in Peru and "ecotourism might become a leading business model on a world scale, generating more income and better quality of life for local populations than many extractive industries today" (Sustainability Leaders Project, 2019).

EXERCISES

Group discussion

Take some time to review the Chapter 4 case study and visit Inkaterra's website (https://www.inkaterra.com/).

1. Discuss the extent to which luxury tourism and hospitality is compatible with biodiversity protection and preservation. Are there any frictions?

2. What are some strategies to overcome the potential frictions? How can a social entrepreneur mitigate potential negative impacts from business endeavors (especially environmental negative externalities)?

3. Inkaterra provides the tourism and hospitality industries at large with a set of best practices. Can you find other examples of companies that are equally successful (on all pillars of sustainability)?

Group research & discussion

What does it take to be a social entrepreneur? Conduct interview(s) with local social entrepreneurs and report back to the group for a discussion. Consider the following aspects:

1. What motivated the social entrepreneur to set up a venture in the first place?
2. How did the social entrepreneur go about establishing the social business?
3. What were and are the major hurdles?
4. How can the social entrepreneur measure the success of the social business?
5. What does it take to be a social entrepreneur (characteristics, skills etc.)

Individual research

Write an essay about luxury tourism and hospitality, social entrepreneurship and biodiversity protection and preservation. Consider the following questions in drafting your paper:

1. How is 'luxury tourism' or 'luxury hospitality' defined?
2. Is the concept of 'luxury' compatible with 'sustainability' in the tourism and hospitality industries?
3. What are some of the gaps in the market and socioeconomic or environmental challenges that a social entrepreneur can answer with an innovation?

References

Abu-Saifan, S. (2012). Social entrepreneurship: definition and boundaries. *Technology Innovation Management Review*, 22–27.

Amit, R., & Muller, E. (1995). Push and pull entrepreneurship. *Journal of Small Business and Entrepreneurship*, 12(4), 64–80.

Bergmann, H., & Sternberg, R. (2007). The changing face of entrepreneurship in Germany. *Small Business Economics*, 28(2–3), 205–221.

Bessant, J., & Tidd, J. (2007). *Innovation and Entrepreneurship*. Hoboken, NJ: John Wiley & Sons.

Calderon, G., Iacovone, L., & Juarez, L. (2017). Opportunity versus necessity: Understanding the heterogeneity of female micro-entrepreneurs. *World Bank Economic Review*, 30(Suppl. 1), 86–96.

Carter, N. M., Gartner, W. B., Shaver, K. G., & Gatewood, E. J. (2003). The career reasons of nascent entrepreneurs. *Journal of Business Venturing*, 18(1), 13–39.

Dacin, T., Dacin, P. A., & Tracey, P. (2011). Social entrepreneurship: A critique and future directions. *Organizational Science*, 22(5), 1203–1213.

Dawson, C., & Henley, A. (2012). 'Push' versus 'pull' entrepreneurship: An ambiguous distinction? *International Journal of Entrepreneurial Behaviour & Research*, 18(6), 697–671.

Day, J., & Mody, M. (2017). Social entrepreneurship typologies and tourism: Conceptual frameworks. In P. Sheldon & R. Daniele (Eds.), *Social Entrepreneurship and Tourism: Philosophy and Practice* (pp. 57–80). Cham, Switzerland: Springer.

Fairlie, R. W., & Fossen, F.M. (2018). *Opportunity versus Necessity Entrepreneurship: Two Components of Business Creation*. IZA Institute of Labor Economics. Discussion Paper 11258. http://ftp.iza.org/dp11258.pdf

Fossen, F. M., & Buettner, T. J. M. (2013). The returns to education for opportunity entrepreneurs, necessity entrepreneurs, and paid employees. *Economics of Education Review*, 37, 66–84.

Gabarret, I., Vedel, B., & Decaillon, J. (2017). A social affair: Identifying motivation of social entrepreneurs. *International Journal of Entrepreneurship and Small Business*, 31(3), 399.

Global Fashion Agenda. (2019). *Pulse of the Fashion Industry 2019 Update*. https://globalfashionagenda.com/pulse-2019-update/#

Hughes, K. (2003). 'Pushed or pulled? Women's entry into self-employment. *Gender Work and Organization*, 10(4), 433–454.

HYB. (2018). Peru's Inkaterra: Helping save the Amazon through sustainable landscape corridors while pushing the boundaries of eco-friendly luxury hotels. In W. Legrand (Ed.) *Hotel Yearbook 2018 Special Edition on Sustainable Hospitality* (pp. 53–53). https://www.hotel-yearbook.com/edition/37000021.html

Kautonen, T., & Palmroos, J. (2010). The impact of necessity-based start-up on subsequent entrepreneurial satisfaction. *International Entrepreneurship and Management Journal*, 6, 285–300.

Kirkwood, J. (2009). Motivational factors in a push-pull theory of entrepreneurship. *Gender in Management: An International Journal*, 2(5), 346–364.

Legrand, W., Sloan, P., & Chen, J. S. (2017). *Sustainability in the Hospitality Industry: Principles of Sustainable Operations* (3rd ed.). London: Routledge.

McMullen, J. S., Bagby, D., & Palich, L. E. (2008). Economy freedom and motivation to engage in entrepreneurial action. *Entrepreneurship Theory and Practice*, 32(5), 875–895.

Parris, D. L., & McInnis-Bowers, C. (2014). Social entrepreneurship questioning the status quo: Waste as a resource. *Journal of Economic Issues*, 48(2), 359–366. doi: 10.2753/JEI0021-3624480209

RECUP. (2018). *Weltverbrecher*. https://recup.de/ueber-uns

Sarasvathy, S. D. (2001). Causation and effectuation: Toward a theoretical shift from economic inevitability to entrepreneurial contingency. *The Academy of Management Review*, 26(2), 243–263.

Steinerowski, A., Jack, S. L., & Farmer, J. (2008). Who are the social 'entrepreneurs' and what do they actually do? *Babson College Entrepreneurship Research Conference (BCERC); Frontiers of Entrepreneurship Research 2008*. https://ssrn.com/abstract=1348129

Sustainability Leaders Project. (2019). *Interview with José Koechlin von Stein, Founder of Inkaterra Hotels in Peru.* April 24, 2019. https://sustainability-leaders.com/jose-koechlin-von-stein-inkaterra-interview/

Thurik, A. R., Carree, M. A., Van Stel, A., & Audretsch, D. B. (2008), Does self-employment reduce unemployment? *Journal of Business Venturing, 23*(6), 673–686.

Van der Zwang, P., Thurik, A. R., Verheul, I., & Hessels, J. (2016). Factors influencing the entrepreneurial engagement of opportunity and necessity entrepreneurs. *Eurasian Business Review, 6,* 273–295.

Van Stel, A., Storey, D. J., & Thurik, A. R. (2007). The effect of business regulation on nascent and young business entrepreneurship. *Small Business Economics, 28*(2–3), 171–186.

Vega, G., & Kidwell, R. E. (2007). Toward a typology of new venture creators: Similarities and contrasts between business and social entrepreneurs. *New England Journal of Entrepreneurship, 10*(2), 1–14.

Wennekers, S. A., van Stel, A., Thurik, A. R., & Reynolds, P. (2005). Nascent entrepreneurship and the level of economic development. *Small Business Economics, 24*(3), 293–309.

Zahra, S. A., Gedajlovic, E., Neubaum, D. O., & Shulman, J. M. (2009). A typology of social entrepreneurs: Motives, search processes and ethical challenges. *Journal of Business Venturing, 24*(5), 519–532.

Chapter 5

Social impact assessment, social return on investment and networks & certifications[1]

This chapter discusses the concept of social impacts, assessment methods and social return on investment. An overview of the existing global and regional networks of social entrepreneurs as well as existing certification systems is provided. The chapter also reviews tools to identify social entrepreneurs in tourism and hospitality.

The chapter concludes with two case studies on (1) Authenticitys – the first travel company in Europe to become a certified B Corp and (2) Caiman Ecological Refuge and reviving and celebrating local culture. A set of additional exercises is provided at the end of the chapter, which are based on individual or group research and discussions.

Identifying social entrepreneurs

Lester R. Brown, president of Earth Policy Institute, wrote in *Plan B: Mobilizing to Save Civilization* that "we now need to restructure the global economy, and quickly" 2009, p. 266) and that requires every section of society, especially entrepreneurs, to take an active role because "saving civilization is not a spectator sport" (Brown, 2009, p. 266).

In the previous chapter, the characteristics of the social entrepreneur were introduced (e.g., Table 4.1 in Chapter 4).

But, how do we know who is a social entrepreneur? Is it an individual, a company, a non-governmental organisation (NGO) or a social enterprise? And how do we know if they are *truly* social entrepreneurs?

Those questions are valid to the extent that once identified, social entrepreneurs may provide numerous opportunities for individuals or communities. These may include generating employment for the less privileged, contributing to educational endeavours or seeking positive outcomes for all stakeholders, including the natural environment and society at large. Operating under the umbrella of social entrepreneurship comes with challenges. Potential investors could discredit the business idea as an unprofitable concept for instance. Other stakeholders, including academia, might thoroughly investigate the background and reach the conclusion that 'greenwashing[2]' or 'social-entrepreneurial washing' is taking place. The latter could mean that the business 'only' follows the ideas of Corporate Social Responsibility (CSR) (as discussed in Chapter 2) and therefore does not place the societal mission and purpose above the monetary one, which is necessary in social entrepreneurship.

As discussed in Chapters 2, 3 and 4, social entrepreneurship proposes solutions for social problems while applying a market-based approach. The founders of enterprises (the entrepreneurs) where the purpose benefitting society is paramount are called social entrepreneurs. These people tackle societal challenges with innovative solutions by using entrepreneurial instruments, with the societal return valued more than the financial one. Social entrepreneurs may furthermore transform markets and create social value. The measurement of that social impact is a highly debated, controversial and complex topic. In short, it is of utmost importance that the social and/or environmental pillars, rather than the economic outcome, are considered in the performance judgment while assessing the overall impacts achieved by the activity executed by the social entrepreneur (see: Tilley & Young, 2006 on Sustainability Entrepreneurship in Chapter 3).

Social entrepreneurs and social impacts

The term social impact refers to "analysing, monitoring and managing the economic, social and environmental consequences of business activity, both positive and negative, independently of the intentionality of the activity" (Florman, Klingler-Vidra, & Facada, 2016, p. 5). At times, social impact is also referred to as 'social return' or 'social value creation' and is discussed not only amongst sociologists, impact investors and social entrepreneurs, but increasingly also on general strategic management levels of different types of companies and consequently by business, society and management literature (Maas, 2008). Another team of researchers defines impact in general as "the portion of the total outcome that happened as a result of the activity of the venture, above and beyond what would have happened anyway" (Long, Clark, Rosenzweig, & Olsen, 2004, p. 7), which could be applied in the same way to social impact.

While activities of social entrepreneurs vary greatly, it is generally recognised that there is a common need to further develop the measurement and reporting of their impacts (McLoughlin et al., 2009). This is particularly relevant to existing social entrepreneurs, but also new entrants, seeking to grow or manage scalability. It is, furthermore, of importance, as social investors and other donors may be strategic with their choice of social partners (Moody, Littlepage, & Marron, 2013).

Independent of the legal status – that is, being an NGO, for-profit company or hybrid social enterprise – it is important for all social entrepreneurs to assess their social impact as it represents a strategic role in analysing if the social mission has been accomplished (Grieco, Michelini, & Iasevoli, 2015). It is important to mention that the measurement and accounting of social impacts occurs in many different sectors and, contrary to public belief, is not specific to only one (Maas, 2008). The desire to be able to quantify social impact is not only the work of governmental institutions and NGOs, but increasingly a task undertaken by private or social enterprises. Beyond the measurement of impacts, social entrepreneurs show increased interest in participating in relevant assessment methods and/or certifications.

> **BOX CASE 5.1**
>
> **Categorisation of Impacts at Authenticitys**
>
> The full Authenticitys case is presented at the end of this chapter. However, parts of it are used here to highlight certain themes or concept. Authenticitys is an online platform that connects conscious travellers with local change-makers through city experiences and tours. Social impacts at Authenticitys are categorised into six areas:
>
> 1. Health
> 2. Education
> 3. Environment
> 4. Employability
> 5. Freedom and Equality
> 6. Happiness
>
> For example, results related to the Education category show that 90% of the travellers experience a learning process throughout the journey, whereas 80% of the experiences let travellers learn about culture, local people or hidden places. Under Employability, 100% of the people employed in the experiences have been selected in a fair and non-discriminatory manner. Furthermore, 60% of the travellers feel the high engagement of the guides within the experiences (Authenticitys, 2019).

For a regular business without a social mission at its core, the process of measuring its impacts or obtaining social impact certifications might not be of interest. And even if a certification is of interest, such a business enters a long, complex and costly processes with an uncertain end. Social entrepreneurs, on the other hand, already possess the necessary prerequisites, which result in quicker and easier certification, for example.

Holders of certificates and assessments

A first option to identify social entrepreneurs is to scan for holders of certificates or assessments, which is the most logical form of identification. Businesses aim to prove that they are making a positive economic and social impact (Florman et al., 2016; Long et al., 2004). This proof may be achieved through certifications and internal and/or external assessments. Third-party certification represents the most trustworthy, objective and rigid method of identification, which is based on the completion of specific set of standards and performance criteria. Maas and Grieco (2017) state that it is difficult to know if social entrepreneurs are actually measuring social impacts from the ventures. The researchers proceeded to analyse 3194 social entrepreneurs from the Global Entrepreneurship Monitor (GEM), concluding that only 33% of the sample actually measure their impacts. Since certification requires businesses to measure their impacts, it can be concluded that, beyond certification, other forms of identification need to be considered.

Affiliation to social entrepreneurship networks

A second option for identification is the affiliation with national or international networks and organisations, which also implies having a common denominator imposed by those bodies. Considering specific networks for social entrepreneurship, prominent examples would be the Global Social Entrepreneurship Network (GSEN) or national initiatives such as the Social Enterprise UK in the United Kingdom and the Social Entrepreneurship Netzwerk Deutschland (SEND) in Germany. Examples for organisations, on the other hand, could be the Ashoka Foundation as introduced in Chapter 3, which offers one of the most prominent fellowships in the world and is able to provide an extensive list of social and environmental entrepreneurs. Other stakeholders that could serve as a source for identifying social entrepreneurs can be specialised universities and academies, such as the Skoll Centre for Social Entrepreneurship of the Saïd Business School, as well as social impact investors such as Acumen. Table 5.1 shows examples of prominent stakeholders.

Marketing efforts

A third, and by far less objective method for the identification of social entrepreneurs, is to take into consideration individual initiatives recognised as being of

98 SOCIAL ENTREPRENEURSHIP AND IMPACT ASSESSMENT

Table 5.1 Prominent stakeholder of social entrepreneurship.

Stakeholders of Social Enterprises	Examples
Universities & academies	Skoll Centre for Social Entrepreneurship (Saïd Business School, University of Oxford)
Foundations and non-profit organisations	Schwab, Kellogg
Governments	States and/or Regions
Investors	Socially responsible investors (e.g., Triodos, Acumen)
Practitioners	NGOs; Social Enterprises (founded by social entrepreneurs); Individual social entrepreneurs and movements

social value by the market. This represents a more complicated approach. The entire value proposition, mission and vision may be social but within the realm of 'self-proclamation' it remains very subjective. For example, the corresponding use of hashtags may be a tool for identification of social entrepreneurs that are, however, neither certified, nor part of an association (as examples):

#socialentrepreneur;
#socialimpact;
#socialimpactinhospitality;
#hospitalitysocialentrepreneurship

A plausible reason for the missing networking elements could be the fact that the social entrepreneurship initiative is still at the very beginning of operations.

In summary, there are three main options to identify social entrepreneurs as summarised in Table 5.2.

Table 5.2 Methods for the identification of social entrepreneurs.

Methods of Identification of Social Entrepreneurs
1. Certifications and Assessment of Social Impacts
2. Networks (regional, national or international)
3. Marketing efforts (external and internal)

Certifications and assessments of social impact

Different models have been developed to measure social impact, generally referring to Social Impact Assessment (SIA), but a system to classify them is still lacking (Grieco et al., 2015). SIA is defined as an effort to estimate social consequences originating from policy or government actions (United Nations Public Administration Network – Centre for Good Governance, 2006). For private enterprises or organisations, it can be deduced that SIA may be related to measuring positive social consequences and results in society, stemming from the business activities.

Triple and quadruple bottom lines as a point of departure for social impact measurement

When a company wishes to be assessed on social impacts, it is probable that it has already been considering or following the triple or quadruple bottom line approach (TBL and QBL, respectively). Instead of only measuring the profit by means of profit and loss accounts, when using TBL, companies additionally take into consideration the people and the planet. According to The Economist (2009), "Only a company that produces a TBL is taking account of the full cost involved in business". Apart from TBL, the QBL adds 'purpose' to the bottom line mix (see Figure 5.1). This refers to company culture, spirituality and/or philanthropy (Sood et al., 2014; Zahringer, 2014).

Many different measurement and certification methods have been created, developed, analysed and renewed in the last twenty-five years. Private institutions, public institutions and scholars all gained increased interest, which resulted in the development of a broad set of possibilities for actors interested in obtaining certifications. Some methodologies have been developed for specific areas, whereas others may be considered generalised and applicable to all sectors and to whole

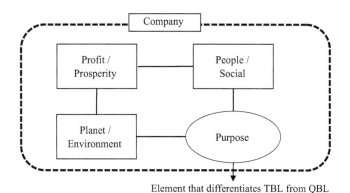

Figure 5.1 Differentiating TBL and QBL (adapted from Rachel, 2012; Bremser, 2014; Knowles, 2014, Sood et al., 2014; Zahringer, 2014).

companies (Florman et al., 2016). The current chapter only introduces 'all-rounder' social impact checks, which include economic, ethical, social, financing, educational and environmental factors. More importantly, only those assessment methods are taken into consideration that provide a generalised use for companies and not just for donors or investors, for example. Most decisively is that both internal (matters related directly to the company such as the treatment and compensation structure of workers, incentives, participatory schemes, transparency of salaries, etc.) as well as external social impacts should be measured. As such, three social impact assessment (SIA) methods out of the original list of eight put forward by Florman et al. (2016) are presented here.

Social return on investment (SROI)

Social return on investment (SROI) is an internationally recognised measurement tool for social enterprise (Millar & Hall, 2013). It dates back to 1997 when the Roberts Enterprise Development Fund (REDF) created this assessment method (Florman et al., 2016). It covers economic, social and environmental areas and is used by a broad range of companies. As the name already implies, it represents the ratio of SROI, including the monetisation of future outputs and outcomes (The Rockefeller Foundation, 2003). Monetisation in form of a real social return calculation represents the second last step of the analysis and may be regarded as a factor that distinguishes it from other assessments, which do not include this element. Consequently, SROI results are particularly useful to investors and governments.

The assessment methodology has undergone several changes over the years, although core principles have stayed the same. The umbrella organisation representing the assessment method is Social Value UK with 700 international members. This network is essential in order to continuously work on the evolution of the method (Millar & Hall, 2013). In the following paragraphs the latest European version from the UK Government's Office of the Third Sector is referred to (Nicholls, Lawlor, Neitzer, & Goodspeed, 2009), which developed and renewed formerly established guidelines to provide guidelines to those social entrepreneurs and enterprises applying for government grants.

The point of departure for this six-step assessment method is the definition of impact, which is "the difference between the outcome for participants, taking into account what would have happened anyway, the contribution of others and the length of time the outcomes last" (Nicholls et al., 2009, p. 14). The six steps are presented in Table 5.3.

Each step is described in further details here:

1. Step one is to identify the scope and identity of stakeholders, as well as take decisions on how to involve those stakeholders. Furthermore, the purpose of

Table 5.3 The six steps in SROI.

Steps in Social Return in Investment
1. Identification of stakeholder and establishment of scope
2. Establishment of the outcomes
3. Identification of outcomes and setting values
4. Establishment of the impact
5. Calculation of the SROI
6. Report, use and embedding

Source: Social value UK.

the analysis, the audience, resources available and/or allocated, time period, persons executing the SROI analysis and the concrete range of activities play key roles here.

2. Step two in the SROI assessment refers to the identification of inputs and outputs for each stakeholder group (including the internal stakeholder: the actual worker of the company). The outcomes are then considered as especially important in the following step.

3. Step three is when indicators must be developed to make outcomes measurable. An example within a social hotel could be the employment of refugees, who gain jobs as an outcome. An indicator could then relate to the continued work relation after twelve months.

4. Step four calculates the actual impact, including some important calculations on what would have happened anyway. Nicholls et al. (2009) call this the 'deadweight' and explain the term with examples such as reducing the unemployment rate and the percentage by which the unemployment rate has gone down anyway. Likewise, the participation of other stakeholders in the improvement process also needs to be accounted for, which is the so-called percentage of attribution (Social Value, 2013) and basically refers to others contributing to the outcomes. Once all these factors have been subtracted, the actual impact can be established and measured (Millar & Hall, 2013).

5. Step five provides the actual calculation of the ratio of social return to investment by projecting into the future and setting values for the inputs established, as well as financial values of the indicators for each time period. (Social Value, 2013).

6. Step six concerns reporting to stakeholders, the actual usage and embedding in the company under analysis (Nicholls et al., 2009). Acceptance plays a big role here, as this needs to be achieved not only amongst the external public, but especially also amongst internal stakeholders, such as employees. Embedding is key to success, meaning that all stakeholders should be sufficiently informed, willing to participate and used to transparency. Without this, the time-intensive elaboration of the SROI assessment lacks logic and usefulness.

Status of implementation and examples of the SROI assessment method

Noteworthy is the fact that the assessment method resulted in several spin-offs (adaptions and variations) such as the SROI Calculator, SROI Toolkit and SROI Analysis (Florman et al., 2016). It may therefore be deduced that the SROI is under constant review and continuous improvement. The main contention against SROI is the cost of operationalisation, which is at the same time seen as a burden to managers and other affected parties (Daye & Gill, 2017). A more intensive promotion of the various tools might furthermore reflect positively on the usage, which is not very high, especially in the tourism and hospitality industry. An actual complete database with contact data of all the companies that followed the assessment method that could serve as examples is not easily available. Yet, the website (see http://www.socialvalueuk.org) offers a resources section, which also includes a report database. One may filter by report type, topic, country and date of publication. No specific tourism or hospitality categories are identified, but the category closest (or most probable) that includes examples related to tourism and hospitality is 'Culture, Recreation and Sport' (with sixty-five entries). Other categories potentially containing tourism and hospitality examples are 'Business & Professional', 'Economic Development' and 'International Development'. Most categories are very specific (e.g., homelessness or health) and do not include examples related to the tourism and hospitality sectors.

The B Impact Assessment

The B Impact Assessment (also referred to as B Rating system) is one of the fastest growing assessment methods in terms of members (called 'certified B Corporations', henceforth 'B Corps'). It was founded by the non-profit B Lab institution in 2007 and quickly reached 500 B Corps by 2011. From 2012 onwards, businesses in Africa, India and Brazil started to use and apply the system in various ways: from measurement and comparison (pure assessment method), to undergoing the actual certifications process. In 2013, more than 15,000 companies used the free B Impact Assessment, with 5000 of actually completing it. In 2013, the percentage of international (outside the US) B Corps had risen to 25%. The year 2014 saw even a stronger internationalisation, when B Lab Australia was launched with forty-five Australian B Corps (B Lab, n.d.). Since then B Corps have spread over the globe, reaching 3131 certified B Corps at the time of writing (December 2019). In terms of eligibility, it is important to outline that any for-profit company may undergo the process, whereas NGOs are excluded. In that respect and within the B Lab framework, social entrepreneurship is understood as the idea that the provision of goods and services are not regarded as an end, but the means to achieve social objectives (Borzaga & Bodini, 2014; Maas & Grieco, 2017; Mair & Marti, 2006). The underlying statement is the focus on economic activity being an essential and a component that differentiates social enterprises from charities (Maas & Grieco, 2017). Considering functioning and process, B Lab does not only provide the actual certification process, but also free of charge best practise guides, comparative data and individualised improvement reports. Taking the B Impact Assessment (which situates the company and makes benchmarking possible) does not obligate the respective enterprise to become a certified B Corporation. Becoming a B Corporation results from paying an annual certification fee (Honeyman, 2014).

The current fee scheme builds up on two-year periods and annual sales volume and therefore tries to consider every company's needs and possibilities. Fees range from US$500 for businesses with annual sales until US$149,999 to $US50,000 or more for companies with an annual sale of over $1 billion. The score system presents a range of 0–200, with any positive score implying that the company in question is doing something beneficial for environment, society and workers. The majority of companies score between forty and sixty out of the maximum 200 points. Becoming B Corp-certified requires a minimum score of eighty. Certified B Corporations have to have passing scores in different areas as shown in Table 5.4 – B Impact Assessment.

The table shows fields addressed in the B Impact Assessment, which is the step before certification, it covers the same elements as the certification, but is free of charge. The report may help the business improve performance in certain impact areas before it opts for certification. It provides a maximum score of fifty-eight points. The summary and observations provided in Table 5.4, as well as the following explanations, are based on Honeyman (2014) and the official B Corp website.

Table 5.4 B Impact Assessment.

Worker Impact Assessment (max. score 15)	Community Impact Assessment (max. score 15)
Work environment (max. 6)	Job creation (max. 1)
Compensation, benefits & wages (max. 8)	Diversity (max. 3)
	Civic Engagement and Giving (max 6)
Work ownership (max. 1)	Local Involvement (max 4)
	Suppliers, Distributors & Product (max 1)
Long-term/governance impact assessment (max. score 12)	Environmental impact assessment (max. score 14)
Mission & engagement (max 6)	Land, Office and Plant (max. 10)
Transparency (max. 5)	Energy, Water and Materials (max. 1)
Corporate structure (max. 1)	Emissions and Waste (max. 2)
	Transport, Distribution & Suppliers (max. 1)
Core impact/business model assessment (two points sufficient for excellent – ten options Business model identificators	

Source: https://bimpactassessment.net/

The first area covers the 'Good for workers' aspect, identified as **worker impact assessment**. In a work environment, factors such as health and wellness programmes, the conduction of worker satisfaction surveys, the transparent collection of employee metrics in relation to retention, turnover and diversity and flexibility at workplace (e.g., allowing home offices) are assessed. Worker ownership regards any existing plan to transfer ownership of the company to full-time employees. Further elements covered are compensation structures, where the business must be able to present elements such as the relation between the highest-paid worker in comparison to the lowest-paid full-time worker.

The **community impact assessment** covers fifteen items to check the business' involvement with and impact on the community. Job creation refers not only to 'normal' qualified job creation, but more specifically long-term unemployed populations. Diversity is related to nationality and ethnic backgrounds, as well as women employed within the company, but also amongst suppliers. Civic engagement includes partnerships with local charities, incentives for employees to organise volunteering activities, set goals for the number of workers participating in volunteering activities, matching charitable contributions made by employees and the existence of a formulated community service policy. Local involvement covers the area of purchasing from local, minority-owned or women-owned businesses, the consideration of fair-trade standards when opting for a supplier, using the banking services of a local independent bank, credit union or in the best possible scenario (resulting in an extra point) using banking services of a bank that it also a certified B Corp.

Environmental impact is scored with a total of fourteen points, where the questions on land, office and plants may be considered the decisive ones. Some elements covered refer to the use of renewable energies, water-efficient systems, indoor air quality, energy-efficient lighting systems and the provision of incentives to workers to use alternative commuting options. Four more points may be collected by conducting life-cycle assessments of products, monitoring greenhouse gas emissions and having a recycling programme. Lastly, and in line with the other impact areas, one point may be collected for encouraging suppliers and distributors to start their own environmental audits.

Long-term impact is measured by a focus on mission and engagement; a maximum of six points may be obtained. Social and/or environmental commitment must be included in the corporate mission statement, followed by a compulsory training for all employees on the mission. Performance of employees should be measured including social and environmental targets and bonuses must be tied to that performance in order to get another point. Furthermore, written statements must be provided to external stakeholders. Stakeholders are able to comment on the company's social and environmental performance. A last element in this mission area is that the board of directors must include at least one independent outside member, in charge of reviewing the company's social and environmental performance.

The **core impact assessment** is designated as 'Good to the Core' and refers to the actual business model assessment by B Corp. Ten very specific and innovative aspects are considered, with two or more ticked boxes already representing excellence.

Examples would be at least 40% of a business being owned by its workers, a company being specifically created to rebuild the local community or practicing micro distribution. Social and environmental entrepreneurs would possibly achieve a high score in this specific area due to their embedded social business orientation.

Status of implementation and examples of the B Impact Assessment

The B Impact Assessment is considered to be user friendly and accessible for everyone (Florman et al., 2016). One of the most important aspects is the opportunity to complete the free online test as a first stage; another is the possibility of benchmarking. The B Impact Assessment can be considered an important tool for continuous improvement, even if a business opts out of the certification process. The impact assessment brings benefits, including recognition and free promotion. The actual application of the free assessment method, as well as the utilisation of the paid certification may be easily tracked on the official website of the organisation. As stated at the start of this chapter, there are 3100 businesses currently certified. One of the most prominent is the clothing company Patagonia. The relevant category of industries for the present research is determined to be 'Hospitality', which lists sixteen certified companies, of which eight are accommodation providers (e.g., Zoku in Amsterdam, Gladstone Hotel in Toronto), while the rest represent intermediaries such as tour operators or travel agents. The section 'Restaurants' registers thirty-one businesses, while 'Travel & Leisure' accounts for thirty-two companies (Source: https://bcorporation.net/directory).

Global social venture competition

The Global Social Venture Competition (GSVC) applies Social Impact Assessment as a requirement for the participation. The competition was founded at UC Berkeley's Haas School of Business in 1999 and has expanded into a global network. The main idea behind the competition is to help social entrepreneurs transform their ideas into business ventures that address root causes of systematic social or environmental challenges (Global Social Venture Competition, 2018).

Considered a generalised and complete assessment process by Florman et al. (2016), the GSVC expects all businesses participating to not only generate social impact, but also account for impacts along the various stages of the competition. The stages of the competition comprise of three parts labelled, 'Define', 'Quantify' and 'Track'. The purpose of the questions under those three parts is to assess whether the solution presented by the company and its business model achieves social impact (Global Social Venture Competition, n.d.). Although it is stated that governance and environmental aspects are covered, a strong focus is on the external social impacts. The explanation of the three main areas below is based on the 'Approach to Social Impact Summary', provided as supplemental guidance by the GSVC.

The **first part** covers the definition of the project, where the Impact Value Chain (IVC) and the corresponding theory of change need to be discussed. Four main questions with sub-questions (that are not compulsory) have to be answered in detail, as well as in the form of an executive summary. When commenting on the challenge to be solved, aspects such as the magnitude of the challenge need to be brought to attention by covering aspects such as breadth, immediacy and severity (see Table 5.5). 'Breadth' could be represented by a significantly wide spread of low wages in the hospitality sector, 'severity' by individuals not having enough money to eat and 'immediacy' by a situation being at risk of worsening should the challenge not be addressed soon. The solution presented needs to focus on the reduction of negative societal outcomes or the improvement of positive societal outcomes. Examples could include the reduction of discrimination at a workplace or the funding of an educational programme. The solution put forward by the entrepreneur must intentionally solve societal problems and thus, a concrete reflection in vision and mission statement must be provided. The entrepreneur must also explain why the proposed solution addresses the societal challenge with greater probability of success than what is proposed by other possible actors such as NGOs or governmental agencies. Positive social change should affect all involved stakeholders (distributors, suppliers, customers and employees). Future planning is taken into consideration in relation to revenue sources once the venture has potentially scaled. Lastly, the creation of behavioural and structural changes, as well as the company playing an active role in developing the marketplace, are considered important factors. Table 5.5 – Step

Table 5.5 Step one of the global social venture competition and social impact assessment.

Step 1: Define Challenge			
What is the challenge you are trying to solve?			
Breath	Severity		Immediacy
Why is the challenge important?			
Treatment of social injustice and loss of human dignity	Improvement of positive societal outcomes		Reduction of negative societal outcomes
How do you intend to solve the challenge?			
Way of bringing positive social change to all stakeholders	Solution addresses the challenge better than other possible actors	Intentionally solves societal problem & part of vision and mission	Social Impacts of solution in relation to concrete challenge
What is your vision for future beyond the challenge?			
Role in developing the marketplace	Creation of behavioural and structural changes		Consideration of revenue sources once venture has scaled

Source: Global social venture competition

one of the global social venture competition and social impact assessment – helps visualise the different elements considered in stage one of the competition and assessment, which is denominated the 'definition stage'.

The **second part** relates to concrete quantification. This part is only relevant to participants that have reached the semi-finals of the competition. Candidates need to select one or two key social metrics directly related to the mission, before choosing concrete sub-metrics. The chosen metrics need to quantify at least one out of the following four purposes: (1) improving operations; (2) tracking undesired outcomes; (3) highlighting how to achieve the ultimate goal or (4) serving as a proxy when the intended goal is hard to measure (e.g., when impact is known only after a long time).

The **third part** principally exists to discuss the follow-up process. It is also about understanding how social entrepreneurs plan to incorporate tracking and measurement into their ongoing business operations. The most important aspect is to be able to make data-driven decisions and to have a feasibility plan for continuous evaluation and improvement. It is crucial to track positive impact and changes, but also to provide monitoring on negative or unintended consequences of the respective business.

Advantages and disadvantages of social impact assessment methods

In the following paragraphs, possible benefits and drawbacks of SIA methods are reflected upon.

Advantages of SIA

As presented in Table 5.6 – Advantages and disadvantages of social impact assessment methods, one of the major benefit factors of undertaking a SIA is building

Table 5.6 Advantages and disadvantages of social impact assessment methods.

Advantages of SIAs	Disadvantages of SIAs
Building trust & credibility	Time investment
Creating a community & network	Associated costs
Generating business referrals	Complexity
Generating press coverage	Difficult to choose the matching assessment
Benchmarking	Embedding assessment in 'daily life' – Operational aspects (e.g., data collection)
Continuous assessment	Possibly existing need for outsourcing
Establishing a collective voice	Return on Investment
Attracting a highly motivated and aligned workforce	Long timespans

trust, which is linked to increased credibility. Ambiguous concepts such as 'being social' or 'going green' are now being 'measured' and have to be 'concrete'. Not only is transparency essential, but so is accountability in regard to the company's performance (Murray, 2012). The outcome of an assessment (the granting of a passed assessment, certificate or award), makes it easier for investors, policy makers and consumers to distinguish between a credible and trustworthy social company, and one that only provided sole marketing actions. When belonging to a network of other certified companies (or winning ventures such as the case in GSVC), benefits may include specialised networking events, increasing collaboration, the generation of business referrals and press reviews. Using the power of business to solve social and environmental problems is positive and compelling, and often a high level of media interest is generated (Honeyman, 2014). Additionally, socially responsible companies receive more positive and supportive news coverage (Cahan, Chen, Chen, & Nguyen, 2015).

Benchmarking and continuous performance improvement can be regarded as another benefit (Ebrahim & Rangan, 2014). Since impacts of the business on workers, the community and the environment are automatically measured, it creates a base towards continuous improvement.

Belonging to a certification network can also allow social entrepreneurs to amplify and organise a collective voice. Certification can serve as branding tool. The B Corp Certification is an example of this. Members may speak with one voice when inviting and talking to shareholders, investors, friends and family about using business as a force for good (Honeyman, 2014).

Finally, a social impact assessment may lead to attracting talent and engaging employees. The employer's social status plays an increasingly important role and may represent the last decisive factor to attract top talent in a very competitive market. Millennials search for places that can integrate work-and-life aspects, including the wish to do something they feel passionate about (Karakas, Manisaligil, & Sarigollu, 2015).

Disadvantages of SIA

Having commented on the benefits of SIAs, difficulties and challenges inevitably exist. One of the most important factors is the time invested and costs involved (Weinreb, 2018). As stated by Dichter, Adams, and Ebrahim (2016, p. 1), "For years, the complex and costly nature of impact measurement has kept many social enterprises from doing it – or from doing it well". Complexity is a third challenge and is not necessarily the same as time dedicated to SIAs. Continuous assessment is another inhibitor, as embedding it into a business' daily operations often represents an issue (McLoughlin et al., 2009). Similar outcomes have been identified by Murray (2012) whereas a full, long-term, implementation often represents a major obstacle. The alignment of assessment methods is another difficulty. A social entrepreneur, especially during the start-up years, may find it difficult to choose which assessment to opt for. In recent years, the tendency has been to opt for the B Impact Assessment. The B Impact Assessment has seen a steady increase in participating companies (B Lab, n.d.). Important challenges are related to operations such as the data collection process. This is sometimes outsourced and relates back to the cost problem. Additionally, long timeframes for measuring outcomes and impact and the fact that not all values can be measured offer another challenge. Lastly, there is significant diversity and complexities across and within each field or business sector (The Rockefeller Foundation, 2003). The tourism and hospitality sectors are highly heterogeneous and fragmented, which provides great opportunities for social entrepreneurs but also multiple challenges as discussed above.

Social entrepreneurship networks & institutions

There are social impact assessment and certification methods in place, as discussed in this chapter, that measure social impact. However, not all assessment methods take into account external as well as internal factors. Additionally, not all social and environmental entrepreneurs wish or opt to measure social impacts. Only half of the social entrepreneurs that participated in the largest comparative study of social entrepreneurship in the world have been found to put substantial effort into measuring the social and environmental impact of their respective venturing activities (Bosma, Schott, Terjesen, & Kew, 2015). Networking efforts can help social entrepreneurs discuss how best to estimate the impacts of their ventures. Indeed, networking efforts are considered to be of high importance for social entrepreneurship (Alkier, Milojica, & Roblek, 2017; Aquino, Lück, & Schänzel, 2018; OECD, 2009). Social entrepreneurs may learn and take advantage of the necessity of sharing synergies, experiences and marketing efforts through networking (as are any other 'regular' entrepreneurs). NGOs are also active in the social entrepreneurship field and oversee lobbying, networking and annual award ceremonies. The Schwab Foundation or the Skoll Centre for Social Entrepreneurship are interesting networking platform considered by social entrepreneurs. The same applies in regards to renowned institutions (e.g., the World Economic Forum) or consultancies such as Ernst & Young or the Boston Consulting Group, the latter which partners up with Yunus Social Business to offer a specific page for social impact careers (Boston Consulting Group, 2019). However, it may be important to distinguish between those institutions that focus only on social entrepreneurs and those organisations that understand social entrepreneurship as a 'side business'. Local or large-scale inter-governmental initiatives, such as the EU's Social Business Initiative (European Commission, 2011) are worth investigating for the social entrepreneur.

Identification of tourism and hospitality social entrepreneurs

When searching for inspiring social entrepreneurs in tourism or hospitality, it might help to divide it into specific fields as visualised in Figure 5.2.

There are various types and forms of social entrepreneurs and enterprises that could be operating in the highly diverse field of hospitality and tourism. Currently, a specific database of social entrepreneurs in tourism and hospitality does not exist. A method for to identify these social entrepreneurs has to rely on a mixed method approach. Searching for certificate holders and self-assessment holders as well as finalists and winners of competitions in relation to social entrepreneurship, social innovation and social impact are good ways to identify social entrepreneurship ventures in tourism. Searching the members of official networks is another good method. Although less objective in nature, one might also consider social entrepreneurship ventures that market themselves specifically as hospitality social entrepreneurship ventures. Proof of a clear social purpose being tackled should be available, as well as a clear reflection on the purpose of the social business in the form of a public mission statement. An example for the latter is Good Hotels. The mission statement appears on the homepage: "Premium Hospitality with a cause" and "Stay good, do good" (Source: Good Hotel Group website). Information is provided on the business values as well as concrete examples of social missions and impact.

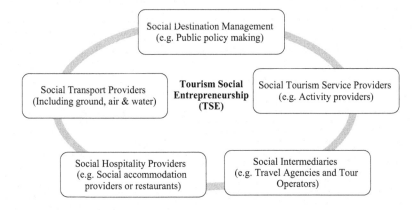

Figure 5.2 Hospitality social entrepreneurship within tourism social entrepreneurship.

BOX CASE 5.2

Good Hotels: premium hospitality with a cause

Good Hotels is part of the Good Group, a non-dividend company built on entrepreneurial spirit that believes businesses should give back to society.

> Good Hotels does so by training and employing long-term unemployed people in Antigua (Guatemala) and London (United Kingdom). For more information on the inspiring project, founded and directed by Marten Dresen, visit: https://www.goodhotellondon.com/ and https://www.good.community/

A search in specialised academic journals also points to interesting social entrepreneurship ventures in hospitality and tourism. Applying a set of specific and clear key words such as 'social entrepreneurship in tourism' and 'social entrepreneurship in hospitality' in databases can facilitate the search. Hospitality social entrepreneurship examples that can be extracted from academic articles applying the formerly mentioned key words are (categorised according to date of publication):

- Hotel con Corazón in Nicaragua (Franzidis, 2018)
- Green Planet Catering, Triangle Raw Foods & Angelina's Kitchen in the United States of America (Kline, Boluk, & Shah, 2017)
- Juha's Guesthouse in Israel (Stenvall, Laven, & Gelbman, 2017)
- Guludo Beach Lodge in Mozambique (Altinay, Sigala, & Waligo, 2016; Carter-James & Dowling, 2017)
- InOut Hostel in Spain (Alegre & Berbegal-Mirabent, 2016)
- Hotel Schani, Boutiquehotel Stadthalle, Steinschaler Naturhotel and Vila Vita Pannonia in Austria (Majer, Altenburger, Bachner, & Steckenbauer, 2015)
- Art&Woonhotel in the Netherlands, Embrace Hotels in Germany, Hotel Tritone in Italy, Rainforest Expedition Lodges in Peru, Periyar Tiger Reserve Lodges in India, Uakari Lodge in Brazil and The Ratcha Hotel in Thailand (Sloan, Legrand, & Simons-Kaufmann, 2014)
- Yachana Lodge in Ecuador, Guludo Beach Lodge in Mozambique and Misool Ecoresort in Indonesia (von der Weppen & Cochrane, 2012)

However, using the keywords in academic databases presents the drawback of leaving out examples that have formerly been categorised under 'sustainable tourism' or 'sustainable hospitality' rather than 'social entrepreneurship'.

Finally, the proposed described identification methods, ranging from certifications over networks and marketing approaches to academic literature, are by no means exclusive or the only correct options. Other tourism certifications or awards, such as the Responsible Tourism Awards, might be considered useful tools and should be explored in relation to tourism social entrepreneurship in the future.

CHAPTER CASE 5.1

Authenticitys – the first travel company in Europe to become a certified B Corp

Authenticitys, an online boutique platform founded in 2014 by Elena Rodriguez, offers over one hundred social impact experiences in forty different cities worldwide. Experiences range from "Paddle surf the beach clean" in Barcelona and "Streets & Saints" in Delhi to "Experience the contrasts" in São Paolo. The travel platform curates social impact experiences for people to travel, share and learn together. The main driver for the business is to solve real social issues. Elena and Authenticitys are an example of a tourism social entrepreneurship. Authenticitys was the first online travel platform to connect organisations that achieve social impact with conscious and responsible travellers and locals. Authenticitys' mission is to create meaningful employment opportunities for local communities through authentic city experiences, while providing experiential education to travellers and increasing environmental awareness. Authenticitys' impact is generally characterised into six categories: health, education, environment & resources, employability, freedom & equality and happiness. Currently, the company is able to measure three of those aspects, namely:

1. Employment (are the experiences creating employment opportunities for vulnerable groups?)
2. Education (are both travellers and local partners benefitting from educational activities? Travellers through experiential learning and partners, such as social enterprises and NGOs, through engagement in entrepreneurial activity or through expanding knowledge?)
3. Environment (does the experience create awareness about environmental challenges?)

The concrete measurement of social impact is not an easy task, yet Authenticitys decided to publish a Social Impact Report (in 2016) with their achievements, one year after their first year of operations. The 2018 edition shows concrete examples for those three measurable impacts, such as sharing cultural heritage stories in India or integrating homeless individuals into the labour market in Austria for employability. Authenticitys additionally decided to opt for B Corp Certification and was the first travel company in Europe to achieve certified B Corp status in 2016. Those businesses that have passed the certification process meet the highest standards of overall social and environmental performance, as well as accountability and transparency. Authenticitys opted for this instrument to show full transparency and take advantage of the benefits from joining a network of progressive companies. The results of the complete certification process are presented in Table 5.7 – Authenticitys' B Corp performance.

Table 5.7 Authenticitys' B Corp performance.

Assessment area	Points achieved
Community	50.9
Governance	15.2
Environment	9.7
Customers	9.2
Workers	0
	Total: 85 out of 100

Source: Adapted from Authenticitys (2019)

By having successfully passed the B Corp Certification process Authenticitys was able to reinforce its social identity and show transparency. While B Corp is one of the tools that allows for differentiation, in itself a certification does not make a social entrepreneurship venture unique. Such uniqueness is only found through the innovative social business model.

CHAPTER CASE 5.2

Reviving and celebrating local culture: a case study of the Caiman Ecological Refuge

(Source: The Long Run; Ecological Refuge Caiman (https://caiman.com.br/); Instagram (@refugioecologicocaiman)

Synopsis

The present case study illustrates how the **Caiman Ecological Refuge**, Brazil revived and celebrated cattle ranching culture as a key element for conserving the Pantanal Wetlands and for sustaining successful ecotourism and ranching businesses. To achieve this, Caiman Ecological Refuge used tourism as a tool to build up the Pantaneiros' self-esteem and pride in their culture and has hosted and promoted cultural festivities and traditional practices that were reinstated by working closely with the Pantaneiros. In order to bring about a cultural change, it has also been necessary to address other social challenges, such as lack of education and healthcare and prevalence of violence. Reviving the Pantanal culture through tourism has resulted in the conservation of both cultural and natural heritage, since Pantaneiros have become more aware of the value of their biodiversity and their traditions, as they realise the interest that these awaken in tourists. This has helped in addressing the challenges that Caiman faces in conserving the Pantanal's integrity, such as increased agriculture activity and countering the lack of interest from young generations to become cowboys or stay in the region, and the loss of extensive cattle ranching.

About Caiman Ecological Refuge

Caiman Ecological Refuge is located on a 53,000 hectare ranch that integrates cattle ranching, ecotourism and conservation in the Pantanal Wetlands in the State of Mato Grosso do Sul, Brazil (Figure 5.3).

Figure 5.3 Baiazinha aerial view.
 (Photo Credit: Caiman Ecological Refuge).

It was established by Roberto Klabin in 1985, in order to preserve the Pantanal – the world's largest wetland plain, designated as a UNESCO World Natural Heritage and World Biosphere Reserve – while maintaining a successful cattle business and respecting and celebrating local culture.

Nearly 150 people live at the Caiman ranch, which holds 16,000 heads of cattle that coexist in the area with wildlife and which is a destination for ecotourism, comprising four lodges (Sede, Baiazinha, Cordilheira and Casa RK). Ecotourism and the cattle operation are underpinned by a strong conservation programme that has focused on the establishment of a 5600-hectare private reserve of natural heritage ('Dona Aracy') and the support of three major conservation projects: (1) the Hyacinth Macaw Project, which focusses on the survival of the world's largest macaw; (2) the Onçafari Project that is contributing to the conservation of jaguars and (3) the Blue-Fronted Parrot Project that is researching and recovering that species.

Challenges

The Pantanal cultural heritage derives from the blend of the Portuguese, Indigenous and Paraguayan people. Cattle ranching, which has coexisted with the natural environment for over 250 years, has been a main influence for the local culture, permeating the way people behave, dress, live and eat, influencing folklore and customs.

However, fifty years ago the culture of cattle ranching and the Pantaneiros (cowboys) was poorly valued and living conditions were precarious. People were very poor and hunted game for food. A culture of aggression and violence dominated the region, where people resorted to weapons to solve conflicts and there was limited access to education and healthcare. Furthermore, the commemoration of cultural events and traditional practices was limited. A small 'club' celebrated some festivities, such as days of Catholic saints, but the gatherings focused on eating and dancing without exalting the value of traditions and customs, nor the unique biodiversity of the Pantanal.

The lack of cultural identity and low quality of life resulted in little interest from young people in becoming cowboys and remaining in the area, reducing the labour force for cattle ranching and fostering a loss of the Pantaneiros' cultural values. This also resulted in a low level of empowerment of local people in conserving the Pantanal and resisting the pressure to replace extensive cattle ranching with intensive modern schemes or agricultural production in areas encroaching the Pantanal, as well as a lack of environmental awareness and little opposition to hunting or trading wildlife, putting the Pantanal at a crossroads Figure 5.4.

116 SOCIAL ENTREPRENEURSHIP AND IMPACT ASSESSMENT

Figure 5.4 Cowboys.
(Photo Credit: © Rafael de Andrade).

Solutions

Roberto has made extensive efforts to revive the Pantaneiros' cultural identity as a means to protect the Pantanal's integrity and to ensure the sustainability of cattle ranching. He strongly believes that the Pantanal can only be maintained in its natural state if extensive cattle ranching continues to be the major economic driver of the region, along with other complementary sustainable activities such as ecotourism, which respect and tap the potential of Pantanal as a first-class wildlife viewing destination.

Hence, in order to revive and celebrate culture in the Pantanal, Roberto has revived traditional practices and folklore in a participatory way; has used ecotourism to recognise and demonstrate the value of the Pantanal's culture and has promoted and created awareness of the Pantaneiro culture.

REVIVING FOLKLORE AND PRESERVING TRADITIONS

Pantanal customs and traditions are a central element of Caiman Ecological Refuge's philosophy and operations. In order to recover cultural elements such as traditional festivities, folklore, food, music and clothes, Roberto hired a local ranch manager who helped him better understand the culture and engage with the cowboys at Caiman. This way, they asked the Pantaneiros how and what should be done to properly organise traditional festivities. For example, to recover and host the Lasso Festival they asked the cowboys what would be the best place to set an arena for lasso competitions, how many people and who they should invite, which ranches around the Pantanal could be involved, what kind of music they should play, what are the most important traditional dishes of the Pantaneiros, what kind of music they would hear, what clothes they would wear, etc. (Figure 5.5).

Figure 5.5 Pantaneiro festival.
(Photo Credit: © Rafael de Andrade).

Following this, Caiman Ecological Refuge organised, hosted, promoted and financially supported the Caiman Lasso Festival, and has continued to do so for over twenty-four years. During the festival, Caiman carries out its own lasso competition and brings together local food and barbecues, live typical music from traditional bands and typical dances such as the square dance. Over the last twenty years the event has evolved from the Pantaneiros competing with each other to a demonstration of skill on the horse and lasso, where the whole community can join and enter, including children. Today, the Lasso Festival is a real celebration of Pantanal culture by the whole community (farm workers, neighbours and the surrounding community). Handicrafts are exhibited, explained and sold by surrounding communities, including Indigenous people, and traditional folk groups are represented, showcasing their music and talent. Caiman guests now have more possibilities than before to interact with the Pantanal and its culture. In line with this evolution, Caiman changed the name of the Festival to 'Traditional Pantaneiro Festival'.

Other important community events that Caiman has financially supported and promoted are the Christmas Party, Catholic masses and the Birthday Party, which is held monthly. The first two are key to maintain the local religion, while the Birthday Parties provide a space to interact, stimulate culture and improve relationships among the cowboys and their families.

In addition to reviving traditional festivities within the Ranch, Caiman has supported participation in other cultural events that transcend the ranch's borders. For example, every month lasso festivals happen across the state, hence, Caiman has financed lasso competition fees and has provided food and transportation for the horses and the families of the cowboys. The ranch also makes a few donations of cattle to be used in competitions in other towns. This way Caiman promotes culture in the whole region and encourages the development and demonstration of the skills of its own cowboys.

Caiman has also aimed to maintain traditional practices as part of its day-to-day activities. In order to do so, they invested in building Stables, the Cowboys Shad and the Social Club, which serve as a space for leisure activities and for cowboys to gather around with their families. In this area, cowboys can produce tools and clothes such as leather belts, saddle blankets, reins, chaps and lassos, using traditional methods.

IMPROVING QUALITY OF LIFE OF THE PANTANEIROS

Improving the quality of life of the Pantaneiros and offering good working conditions were important to motivate traditional families to stay on the ranch and maintain their lifestyle, as well as to improve education, relationships and positive values across the community. Hence, Caiman provided the cowboys with free housing, dentists, first-aid training and schools for their children and has regularly invited health professionals to raise awareness about health-related aspects as well as good nutrition and has provided them with meat and milk from the ranch and a good restaurant. Environmental education, conservation classes and outdoor activities are also carried out regularly.

RECOGNISING THE VALUE OF THE PANTANAL'S CULTURE AND ENVIRONMENT THROUGH ECOTOURISM

As part of the strategy to preserve and revive the local culture at the Pantanal, Caiman identified the need for both cowboys and outsiders to recognise the value of the Pantanal's culture. Caiman has used ecotourism as a main tool in valuing the Pantaneiros' culture because it gives the cowboys the opportunity to showcase the culture, instilling pride in their skills and techniques.

Caiman offers tourist experiences specially designed to appreciate and learn about the Pantaneiros' traditions and lifestyles. For example, during a 'cowboy day' or a 'cattle drive with typical lunch' tour, guests can learn about handling cattle and saddling horses, interact with cowboys, practice the lasso and herding whip and become part of Tereré, a traditional mate tea-drinking ritual of the cowboys. Guests visit the Cowboys' Corral where they are shown daily activities of a cattle ranch such as herding, branding, vaccinating and castrating or visit the Mangueiro, where the cowboys gather the cattle. Tourists are also taken to the Cowboys Shad where former cowboys, now guides, provide a Pantanal Cultural Workshop and where guests can admire the traditional equipment that cowboys produce themselves. Similarly, guests can try traditional foods like meat on a wooden skewer while listening to the cowboys tell the Pantanal's tales or join the Quebra-Torto breakfast, a very nutritious meal cowboys make before leaving in the morning to work with the cattle, and learn about its fascinating history (Figure 5.6).

Figure 5.6 Cordilheira outdoor space.
(Photo Credit: Caiman Ecological Refuge).

Furthermore, ecotourism has stimulated local artisans to produce traditional handcrafts, which are sold at the lodge, helping maintain cultural artefacts and promoting economic development.

Caiman has also used ecotourism to help cowboys recognise the value of the biodiversity of the Pantanal, bringing a positive cultural change towards environmental conservation. With the development of wildlife viewing as part of the ecotourism experience at the Caiman Refuge, cowboys became key in finding and reporting key wildlife sightings (e.g., giant ant-eater, jaguar, etc.) to the bilingual tour guides. As a result, cowboys, who used to be indifferent to biodiversity, became aware of the importance of the Pantanal's wildlife and realised the significant role they played in sustaining the ranch and ecotourism. Similarly, cowboys began to realise that ecotourism opened new job opportunities for them and their families, which could only be sustained if wildlife was preserved (Figure 5.7).

Figure 5.7 A jaguar.
(Photo Credit: Caiman Ecological Refuge).

CREATING AWARENESS AND PROMOTING THE PANTANEIROS' CULTURE

Besides using tourism to create awareness and share the lifestyle and traditions of the Pantaneiros, the Caiman Ecological Refuge has promoted the Pantaneiro lifestyle and culture locally, nationally and internationally through different media and strategies. This has been important because it helps create awareness among Brazilians and foreigners about the value of the Pantanal and the ways in which tourism and cattle ranching have helped maintain the natural environment and culture.

Caiman has developed a website, blog and social networking. It created an institutional film, folders and other promotional materials that help promote the traditions, and a photo book of the Lasso Festival to raise awareness about the importance of the local culture, which is available to all guests at the Caiman Lodge. Similarly, it has appeared in local newspapers, magazines and TV programs.

Furthermore, Roberto has developed networks and collaborations with numerous neighbouring ranches and key stakeholders in order to protect the Pantanal's culture and biodiversity. For example, he:

- Established an NGO called S.O.S. Pantanal, which has helped him gain a reputation as a respected conservationist that has allowed him to invite different actors to participate in Pantanal's cultural and environmental conservation.
- Invited politicians to the Lasso Festival to reinforce the conservation of the Pantanal and its culture.
- Promoted cultural revival and environmental conservation in other ranches in the Pantanal.

Positive impacts

- The Pantaneiros' culture was revived and now remains as an integral part of the operation and management of the Caiman Ecological Refuge.
- The Lasso Festival has become the most important event of the year at the Caiman Ecological Refuge. State and municipal politicians, media, ranchers, entrepreneurs, guests and the local society in general are invited to the Festival and interact with the culture and the cowboys, attracting more than 800 people annually.
- Ecotourism has changed the way cowboys perceive themselves and their culture, as they realised that people are interested in them and in their traditions, helping them recognise the value of their own culture.
- Caiman's cowboys have increased their self-esteem and pride in their culture by showcasing to tourists their abilities and customs, as well as through participating in traditional competitions and parties, where Caiman's cowboys have earned themselves a reputation of being among the best within the wider area. On average, Caiman has supported one or two teams (five cowboys on each team) and their families to attend four competitions per year.
- Increased awareness and appreciation of the Pantaneiros' traditions by tourists.
- Engaged with neighbouring landowners and government in the wider Pantanal area and Mato Grosso do Sul region, which has strengthened efforts to conserve the Pantanal. In 2016, Roberto managed to get the two governors of the states where the Pantanal is located, to discuss the region's conservation and consider passing an environmental law concerning the Pantanal's protection.
- Achieved a balance between environmental conservation, the preservation of the Pantanal's culture and respect for the traditional activities of the community.

- Ecotourism has increased the cowboys' awareness of the importance of the Pantanal's conservation.
- Improved quality of life due to better healthcare and education.
- Hunting ceased as cowboys had assured and free access to meat from the ranch to feed their families.

Downsides

The cowboys' numbers may decrease as they get more involved in tourism, which could result in a change of culture. However, Caiman is actively promoting the maintenance of the cowboys' culture and tries to maintain a balance between ranching and tourism.

Lessons learned

- Listen to the people in the local community. Trying to revive cultural traditions should be a participatory process, where the local actors lead and define the characteristics of their own traditional events and activities.
- Offer guests a 'real' cultural experience. Do not create a 'fake' experience or a show for ecotourism purposes only.
- Having a strong culture and sense of belonging to the Pantanal has a major positive impact on environmental conservation by the local community, contributing to maintaining the Pantanal as the most preserved biome in Brazil.
- Approaching traditional customs as a 'living entity' rather than as something 'dead' from the past positively influences the success of the business.
- Integrating cultural aspects into guest experiences as a core element of Caiman's tourism product and hosting traditional festivities such as the Annual Caiman Lasso Festival have revived culture and have built self-esteem among cowboys.
- Attracting government officials from other states to the Lasso Festival effectively promotes and helps preserve the Pantanal culture within Brazil, and raises awareness of the need to conserve the region and protect it against intensive agriculture.
- Media activities and publications about the festival and other activities have been a very useful tool to promote and share the Pantanal culture in a national and international context.

- The extensive knowledge and experience in cattle ranching among Caiman's community members is essential not only for the operation of a successful ecotourism business, but also for the management of the Pantanal environment and habitats.

Improving the quality of life in the ranch was a key element to enhancing positive cultural values. Tourism and cattle ranching should focus on equity and distributing profits throughout all members of the community, in order to provide opportunities for real prosperity in the region, which helps retain local people and cultural traditions.

EXERCISES

Group discussion

Take some time to review chapter case 5.1 and visit the company's website (https://authenticitys.com/en/) as well as the B Corp website (https://bcorporation.net/)

1. Can you find other tourism or hospitality businesses certified B Corp?
2. Are there other certification systems you are aware of in the field of sustainability in tourism or hospitality? In which ways are they similar or different to B Corp certification? (e.g., set of criteria, focus of certification, marketing potential, etc.)
3. Authenticitys developed 'The Ultimate Responsible Travel Guide'. What are the tips provided by Authenticitys? Will that change the way you travel in the future?

Group research & discussion

Take some time to review chapter case 5.2 and visit the company's website (https://caiman.com.br/en/)

1. Can you describe in your own words the challenges faced and the solutions provided by the Caiman Ecological Refuge?
2. What are the positive impacts and downsides associated with establishing the Caiman Ecological Refuge?
3. What is a World Heritage Site and a World Biosphere Reserve?
4. After reading the 'Lessons Learned', would you have further recommendations?

> **Individual research**
>
> Write an essay about the social impact assessment (SIA) and social return on investment (SROI) using the tourism and hospitality sectors to illustrate your analysis. Keep in mind some of the following points:
>
> 1. Clearly defining SIA and SROI
> 2. Presenting industry examples
> 3. Providing recommendations to tourism and hospitality social businesses

Notes

1. Invited chapter co-author: Claudia Langer, University of Balearic Islands, Spain.
2. Greenwashing is generally associated to the fact that a company claims their products and services as more environmentally sound as they really are. Such behaviour is also denominated deceptive manipulation (Siano, Vollero, Conte, & Amabile, 2017) and refers to purely symbolic practises as opposed to substantive practises, such as green supplier championing (Blome, Foerstl, & Schleper, 2017).

References

Alegre, I., & Berbegal-Mirabent, J. (2016). Social innovation success factors: hospitality and tourism social enterprises. *International Journal of Contemporary Hospitality Management, 28*(6), 1155–1176. https://doi.org/10.1108/IJCHM-05-2014-0231

Alkier, R., Milojica, V., & Roblek, V. (2017). Challenges of the social innovation in tourism. *ToSEE, 4*(2004), 1–13. https://doi.org/10.20867/tosee.04.24

Altinay, L., Sigala, M., & Waligo, V. (2016). Social value creation through tourism enterprise. *Tourism Management, 54*, 404–417. https://doi.org/10.1016/j.tourman.2015.12.011

Aquino, R. S., Lück, M., & Schänzel, H. A. (2018). A conceptual framework of tourism social entrepreneurship for sustainable community development. *Journal of Hospitality and Tourism Management, 37*(September), 23–32. https://doi.org/https://doi.org/10.1016/j.jhtm.2018.09.001

Authenticitys. (2019). *2018 Social Impact Report.* https://www.authenticitys.com/en/impact/

B Lab. (n.d.). *Our History B Corporation.* https://www.bcorporation.net/what-are-b-corps/the-non-profit-behind-b-corps/our-history

Blome, C., Foerstl, K., & Schleper, M. C. (2016). Green supplier championing and greenwashing: An empirical study on leadership and incentives. *Academy of Management Proceedings, 1*, 16–47. https://doi.org/10.5465/ambpp.2016.16147abstract

Borzaga, C., & Bodini, R. (2014). What to make of social innovation? Towards a framework for policy development. *Social Policy and Society, 13*(03), 411–421. https://doi.org/10.1017/S1474746414000116

Bosma, N., Schott, T., Terjesen, S., & Kew, P. (2015). *Global Entrepreneurship Monitor – Special Topic Report Social Entrepreneurship.* https://www.gemconsortium.org/file/open?fileId=49542

Boston Consulting Group. (2019). *Social Impact Careers at BCG.* https://www.bcg.com/careers/working-at-bcg/social-impact.aspx

Bremser, W. G. (2014). A growing interest in sustainability. *The CPA Journal, 84*(3), 15–17.

Brown, L. B. (2009). *Plan 4.0: Mobilizing to Save Civilization.* New York NY: Norton.

Cahan, S. F., Chen, C., Chen, L., & Nguyen, N. H. (2015). Corporate social responsibility and media coverage. *Journal of Banking and Finance, 59,* 409–422. https://doi.org/10.1016/j.jbankfin.2015.07.004

Carter-James, A., & Dowling, R. (2017). Guludo beach lodge and the Nema Foundation, Mozambique. In P. Sheldon & D. Roberto (Eds.), *Social Entrepreneurship and Tourism: Philosophy and Practices* (pp. 221–236). Cham Switzerland: Springer.

Daye, M., & Gill, K. (2017). Social enterprise evaluation: Implications for tourism development. In P. Sheldon & D. Roberto (Eds.), *Social Entrepreneurship and Tourism: Philosophy and Practices* (pp. 173–194). Cham Switzerland: Springer.

Dichter, S., Adams, T., & Ebrahim, A. (2016). *The Power of Lean Data.* https://ssir.org/articles/entry/the_power_of_lean_data

Ebrahim, A., & Rangan, V. K. (2014). What impact? A framework for measuring the scale and scope of social performance. *California Management Review, 56*(3), 118–141. https://doi.org/10.1525/cmr.2014.56.3.118

European Commission. (2011). *Social Business Initiative – Creating a favourable climate for social enterprises, key stakeholders in the social economy and innovation* {SEC(2011) 1278 final}. https://doi.org/10.1080/01402390.2011.569130

Florman, M., Klingler-Vidra, R., & Facada, J. (2016). *A Critical Evaluation of Social Impact Assessment Methodologies and a Call to Measure Economic and Social Impact Holistically Through the External Rate of Return Platform.* Working Paper (1602). LSE Enterprise, London.

Franzidis, A. (2018). An examination of a social tourism business in Granada, Nicaragua. *Tourism Review, 74*(6), 1179–1190. https://doi.org/10.1108/TR-04-2017-0076

Global Social Venture Competition. (n.d.). *GSVC Social Impact Guidelines,* 1–6.

Global Social Venture Competition. (2018). *Global Partner Network – GSVC.* http://gsvc.org/about/global-community/

Grieco, C., Michelini, L., & Iasevoli, G. (2015). Measuring value creation in social enterprises: A cluster analysis of social impact assessment models. *Nonprofit and Voluntary Sector Quarterly, 44*(6), 1173–1193. https://doi.org/10.1177/0899764014555986

Honeyman, R. (2014). *The B Corp Handbook* (1st ed.). Oakland CA: Berrett-Koehler Publishers, Inc.

Karakas, F., Manisaligil, A., & Sarigollu, E. (2015). Management learning at the speed of life: Designing reflective, creative, and collaborative spaces for millennials. *The International Journal of Management Education, 13*(3), 237–248. https://doi.org/10.1016/J.IJME.2015.07.001

Kline, C., Boluk, K., & Shah, N. (2017). Exploring social entrepreneurship in food tourism. In P. Sheldon & D. Roberto (Eds.), *Social Entrepreneurship and Tourism: Philosophy and Practices* (pp. 135–154). Cham Switzerland: Springer.

Knowles, B. (2014). *Cyber-sustainability: Towards a Sustainable Digital Future.* Lancaster University, Faculty of Science and Technology, UK. http://eprints.lancs.ac.uk/id/eprint/68468

Long, D., Clark, C., Rosenzweig, W., & Olsen, S. (2004). Double bottom line project report: Assessing social impact in double bottom line ventures. *Business,* 1–70. https://doi.org/10.1016/j.rser.2014.08.006

Maas, K. (2008). *Social impact measurement: Towards a guideline for managers.* EMAN-EU 2008 Conference: Sustainability and Corporate Responsibility Accounting – Measuring and Managing Business Benefits, 75–79. https://core.ac.uk/download/pdf/12354878.pdf

Maas, K., & Grieco, C. (2017). Distinguishing game changers from boastful charlatans: Which social enterprises measure their impact? *Journal of Social Entrepreneurship, 8*(1). https://doi.org/10.1080/19420676.2017.1304435

Mair, J., & Marti, I. (2006). Social entrepreneurship research: A source of explanation, prediction, and delight. *Journal of World Business, 41*(1), 36–44. https://doi.org/10.1016/j.jwb.2005.09.002

Majer, H., Altenburger, R., Bachner, C., & Steckenbauer, G. C. (2015). Nachhaltige Innovationen. https://doi.org/10.1007/978-3-662-49952-8_2

McLoughlin, J., Kaminski, J., Sodagar, B., Khan, S., Harris, R., Arnaudo, G., & Mc Brearty, S. (2009). A strategic approach to social impact measurement of social enterprises. *Social Enterprise Journal, 5*(2), 154–178. https://doi.org/10.1108/17508610910981734

Millar, R., & Hall, K. (2013). Social return on investment (SROI) and performance measurement. *Public Management Review, 15*(6), 923–941. https://doi.org/10.1080/14719037.2012.698857

Moody, M., Littlepage, L., & Marron, J. (2013). Valuing SROI: Social return on investment techniques and organizational implementation in the Netherlands and United States. *Johnson Center at Grand Valley State University; Lilly Family School of Philanthropy at Indiana University Research and Publications, 6*. https://scholarworks.gvsu.edu/jcppubs/6

Murray, J. H. (2012). Choose your own master: Social enterprise, certifications, and benefit corporation statutes. *American University Business Law Review, 2*. http://heinonline.org/HOL/Page?handle=hein.journals/aubulrw2&id=11&div=&collection=

Nicholls, J., Lawlor, E., Neitzer, E., & Goodspeed, T. (2009). A guide to Social Return on Investment. Development, *Social Enterprise Journal, 3*(1), 55. https://doi.org/10.1108/17508610780000720

OECD. (2009). Transforming innovation to address social challenges. https://www.oecd.org/sti/inno/44076387.pdf

Rachel, G. B. (2012). The quadruple bottom line and nonprofit housing organizations in the United States. *Housing Studies, 27*(4), 438–456. doi: 10.1080/02673037.2012.677016

Siano, A., Vollero, A., Conte, F., & Amabile, S. (2017). "More than words": Expanding the taxonomy of greenwashing after the Volkswagen scandal. *Journal of Business Research, 71*, 27–37. https://doi.org/10.1016/J.JBUSRES.2016.11.002

Sloan, P., Legrand, W., & Simons-Kaufmann, C. (2014). A survey of social entrepreneurial community-based hospitality and tourism initiatives in developing economies: A new business approach for industry. *Worldwide Hospitality and Tourism Themes, 6*(1), 51–61. https://doi.org/10.1108/WHATT-11-2013-0045

Social Value. (2013). Supplementary Guidance on Using SROI.

Sood, S., Tulchin, D., Yi, S., Li, H., Parakh, R., Jhanwar, R., & Xu, D. (2014). *Quadruple Bottom Line*. http://upspringassociates.com/wp-content/uploads/2014/09/TipSheet13QBL.pdf

Stenvall, A., Laven, D., & Gelbman, A. (2017). The influence of social entrepreneurship in tourism on an Arab Village in Israel. In P. Sheldon & D. Roberto (Eds.), *Social Entrepreneurship and Tourism: Philosophy and Practices* (pp. 279–293). Cham Switzerland: Springer.

The Economist. (2009). *Triple bottom line*. https://www.economist.com/node/14301663

The Rockefeller Foundation. (2003). *Social impact assessment – A discussion among grantmakers*. https://doi.org/10.3152/147154603781766400

United Nations Public Administration Network – Centre for Good Governance. (2006). *A Comprehensive Guide for Social Impact Assessment*. http://www.rlarrdc.org.in/images/Guide%20to%20SIA.pdf

von der Weppen, J., & Cochrane, J. (2012). Social enterprises in tourism: an exploratory study of operational models and success factors. *Journal of Sustainable Tourism, 20*(3), 497–511. https://doi.org/10.1080/09669582.2012.663377

Weinreb, S. (2018). *Mission Driven Business? Here's Why To Become A B Corp, According To Four Certified Companies.* https://www.forbes.com/sites/saraweinreb/2018/04/30/mission-driven-business-here-are-six-reasons-to-consider-b-corp-certification/#54d959197def

World Health Organisation – Regional Office for Europe. (2017). Social return on investment. http://www.euro.who.int/__data/assets/pdf_file/0009/347976/20170828-h0930-SROI-report-final-web.pdf?ua=1

Zahringer, L. (2014). *The Quadruple Bottom Line: Adding purpose to the mix.* https://www.seechangemagazine.com/?p=772

Chapter 6

Hospitality social entrepreneurship: the nexus of hospitality, sustainable development and entrepreneurship

This chapter explores the linkages between sustainability innovation and entrepreneurship. Following a brief review of entrepreneurship and social entrepreneurship concepts, the chapter explores the attributes of social entrepreneurs. It also investigates the ways in which hospitality has become a major activity in society and an increasingly important sector in terms of economic and social development. In particular, the chapter discusses tourism, luxury, sustainability and the role of social entrepreneurs in guaranteeing a cohesion between these concepts.

The chapter concludes with two case studies: (1) Soneva, where environmental and social involvement meets luxury and (2) Sustainability Master Plans: a roadmap to developing sustainable destinations. A set of additional exercises is provided at the end, based on individual or group research and discussions.

Introduction

The authors of *The Limits to Growth: The 30-Year Update* argue that in enacting sustainability "no one will get credit, but everyone can contribute" (Meadows, Randers, &

Meadows, 2004, p. 209). This is a call to action for the hospitality industry; a sector particularly fertile for activating sustainable development and entrepreneurship.

The inclusion of sustainable development in the hotel industry calls for making a number of decisions, not only to improve typical business performance, but also to build a good relationship with the social, economic, and environmental context in which it operates. Since – given its reach – the damages caused by the hotel industry have an impact on the environment and human and labor rights, as well as on economic aspects, the hotel and tourism industry needs to develop a joint approach to a social and environmental economy, based on a new business model and on creating value-added activities.

Social entrepreneurship stands as the liaison for achieving this integration, and although social entrepreneurship is an emerging academic research field, the phenomenon itself is not new. While previous chapters have looked into defining the term 'social entrepreneurship', emphasis was given to the term 'entrepreneurship' since 'social' only modifies the entrepreneurial spirit (as discussed in Chapter 2). If the concept of 'entrepreneur' does not have a clear meaning, no change can be brought about when modifying it with social will. Specifically, for such purposes we should identify innovative projects driven by entrepreneurs to address social needs. However, the goal of social entrepreneurship is to go beyond traditional philanthropy and cooperate through social responsibility (see Chapter 5). Social entrepreneurs have always lived in our communities, even if they have not always been called that. Moreover, many institutions that are taken for granted today were originally developed by social entrepreneurs. The origins of entrepreneurship can be traced back to different sources. On one hand, social entrepreneurship is related to generating revenue through non-profit entrepreneurship. On the other, it is seen as a wider concept that defines it as a process that looks to identify, address and solve social issues (Desa, 2007). Social entrepreneurs look for the most effective method to fulfil their social missions (see Chapter 5). We need a much more strategic and innovative approach to drive social and economic value creation beyond its limits to generate transformative benefits for society (Austin, Stevenson, & Wei-Skillern, 2006). This is a requirement for the social entrepreneurship spirit.

Entrepreneurship and sustainability

In Chapter 1, sustainability is discussed in great length. For the purpose of this chapter, we will review sustainability linked with entrepreneurship. According to Seidman, "Sustainability is much more than our relationship with the environment. It is about our relationship with us, with our communities and with our institutions" (2007, p. 58). This relates to Nahapiet and Ghoshal's (1998) definition of value creation, which – according to the authors – is evidenced in those organizations focused on offering physical facilities and encouraging the development of strong relationships among different community players, while investing their own resources to attain such goal. As explained by Ana Teresa Muro (2005) in the book titled Textos en Sustentabilidad Empresarial – Integrando las Consideraciones Sociales, Ambientales y Económicas en el corto y largo plazo (Articles on Corporate Sustainability – Integrating the Social, Environmental and Economic Considerations in the Short and Long Term) (Gardetti, 2005), Wheeler, Colbert and Freeman (2003) assert that a company can embrace different levels of commitment to value creation through corporate culture. Moreover, they argue that an organization is sustainable when it recognizes the interdependences and synergies between the firm, its stakeholders, value-based labor networks and the social bonds that are developed within a society. Such an organization seeks to maximize the creation of value simultaneously in economic, social and ecological terms. Along this line, Grayson and Hodges (2004) refer, with the same term, to companies that provide the alignment of business values, purpose and strategy with the social and economic needs of customers and consumers, while embedding responsible and ethical business policies and practices throughout the company. These guidelines may be implemented to define the concept of social entrepreneurship proposed by Toke Bjerregaard and Jakob Lauring, based on a definition by Mair and Martí (2006), according to which social entrepreneurship can be understood as a process involving the innovative use and combination of resources to pursue opportunities to catalyze social change and/or address social needs.

Entrepreneurship: the nexus of sustainability and innovation

Many sustainability-improving innovations (which tend to require some level of technological radicalness) are carried out by smaller firms, reflecting the theoretically and empirically well-established negative association between firm size and the level of technological radicalness of an innovation (Harms et al., 2010; Markides & Geroski, 2005; Schaltegger & Wagner, 2008; Schumpeter, 1934). This implies a significance of entrepreneurship in the nexus of sustainability and innovation. Therefore, addressing the entrepreneurship, innovation and sustainability nexus from the point of view of small and medium-sized firms is an important contribution. Concerning innovations that are not suitable for the mass market but that can survive in a niche one – these frequently go together with providing supply for a peer group initially, especially in the case of startups (Wagner, 2012).

Moreover, when reviewing the existing literature in social entrepreneurship, we find that defining what social entrepreneurship is, and what its conceptual boundaries are, is not an easy task (Cho, 2006; Johnson, 2000; Mair, Robinson, & Hockerts, 2006). According to Johnson (2000), this is in part because the concept is inherently complex and in part because the literature in the area is so new that little consensus has emerged on the topic. Nevertheless, a few definitions have emerged. Schuyler (1998) describes social entrepreneurs as individuals who have a vision for social change and who have the financial resources to support their ideas. Thompson, Alvy and Lees (2000) describe social entrepreneurs as people who realize where there is an opportunity to satisfy some unmet need that the state welfare system will not or cannot meet, and who gather together the necessary resources (generally people – often volunteers – money and premises) and use these to make a difference.

The entrepreneur and entrepreneurship

Based on the above – and in order to delve into the concept of social entrepreneurship to discuss and establish the nexus of hospitality, sustainable development and entrepreneurship – the meaning of entrepreneurship will now be reviewed. As noted by Mona Anita Olsen K. and Mykletun R. J. (2012), Sewell and Pool (2010, p. 6) define entrepreneurship as "the desire, motivation and skills necessary to start and manage a successful business" And, later, they point out that, in line with Kobia and Sikalieh, "A clear cut and controversy-free definition is nowhere within reach. Entrepreneurship is also often confused with innovation – to many these two words are very similar, but to others there is a huge difference between the two" (Kobia & Sikalieh, 2010, p. 120). An entrepreneur can be defined more clearly as a leader. As stated by Brian Smith at the Business Leader Seminar organized by the Sustainable Enterprise Academy (2002, 2003): "Leaders know what it is [that is] important to them". In addition, to achieve a profound social change the role of personal values is very important: Many authors such as Young and Tilley (2006), Tilley and Young (2009), Choi and Grey (2008), Hall and Vredenburg (2003) and Dixon and Clifford (2007) have documented the relationship between sustainability and personal values on one hand, and, on the other, how idealistic values regarding environmental and social goals can be translated into valuable economic assets (Dixon & Clifford, 2007). Such leaders show transformational leadership behavior (Gardetti, 2016), inspiring and guiding the fundamental transformation that sustainability requires (Egri & Herman, 2000). And, to that end, leaders creatively and continually manage that tension between their vision of the future and current reality, creating hierarchies of meaning and purpose (Gardetti, 2016; Sustainable Enterprise Academy, 2003, 2004). Moreover, a widely accepted foundational objective of entrepreneurship education is to encourage students to create their own business and develop the skills and competencies needed to be successful in their own ventures (Harkema & Schout, 2008). As for value creation, the same authors believe that it consists in leveraging available resources to create something of value (Olsen & Mykletun, 2012).

Entrepretality

'Entrepretality' is a term created by Olsen and Mykletun (2012) to describe the objective of entrepreneurship education in the hospitality industry. 'Entrepretality' is the process of using available resources to create value by enhancing the service-value proposition for a customer, client or other being. The term and its focus on the value of a service output starkly contrasts with the most widely recognized view of entrepreneurship in hospitality academia. As Brizek and Khan (2008) note, in hospitality academia entrepreneurship is related to those who create start-ups and new ventures. However, this understanding in the academia is limiting because it solely focuses on new venture creation and neglects looking at the basis of hospitality education – creating a service-value proposition for a customer. Entrepretality will become more important in an increasingly competitive, shifting and global economy. Intensifying global competition, corporate downsizing and de-layering and rapid technological progress have heightened the need for organizations to become more entrepreneurial to survive and prosper (Li, Tse, & Zhao, 2009). It will be necessary for university programs to be flexible enough to adjust to the changing needs of the global economy. To support resilience in the hotel industry, let me take Jen Morgan's words when she asserted, "To leapfrog ahead, we need pioneering and brave people, communities and organizations who are willing and able to challenge that status quo and to experiment for change" (2011, p. 153).

Social entrepreneurship versus commercial entrepreneurship

Companies, regardless of the sector they belong to, their dimension or their geographical location, are increasingly asked to provide innovative solutions to manage complex social problems, from community development to social exclusion and poverty reduction (Margolis & Walsh, 2003). Social entrepreneurship has been increasingly catalyzing the interest of academics, companies, and the business debate for about a decade. The concept of social entrepreneurship has been widely reported in the mass media and is seen as an emerging discipline within many business schools. According to Austin et al. (2006), social entrepreneurship is an innovative, social value-creating activity that can occur within or across the nonprofit, business and public sectors. The first key element to stress here is innovation. Entrepreneurship is a creative process that pursues an opportunity to produce something new. Replicating an existing organization, activity or process is an important managerial activity, but unless it brings an important new dimension or element, it is not very entrepreneurial. The second key element is social-value creation. This is the fundamental dimension that differentiates social entrepreneurship from commercial types (Austin et al., 2006). Generating social value is the explicit, central driving purpose and force of social entrepreneurship. The third key dimension is the *loci*, or hub, since social entrepreneurship transcends sectors and organizational forms. It can occur in all sectors and in their collaborative interactions. For social entrepreneurs, value is found in the form of large-scale transformational benefits that affect either sectors or society at large. In terms of personal characteristics, social entrepreneurs may be described as visionary change makers who implement innovative ways of addressing pressing social problems (Grenier, 2007). Social entrepreneurship signals an imperative to drive social change and it is that potential payoff, with its lasting, transformational benefit to society, that sets the field and its practitioners apart. Social entrepreneurship, as a practice and a field for scholarly investigation, provides a unique opportunity to challenge, question and rethink concepts and assumptions from different fields of management and business research. Social entrepreneurship is seen as differing from other forms of entrepreneurship in the relatively higher priority given to promoting social value and development versus capturing economic value. While there are many possible definitions that have been set forth in the early literature, the foremost definitions share the fundamental virtue of creating a broad umbrella for this study on social entrepreneurship (Dzisi & Otsyina, 2014). Academic research can play a major role in understanding the limitations and challenges faced by entrepreneurs, corporate directors, politically responsible people, investors and consumers, in order to move towards sustainability (Wüstenhagen, Sharma, Starik, & Wuebker, 2008). Social entrepreneurship, an emerging discipline within many business schools, is defined as an innovative, social value-creating activity that can occur within or across the nonprofit, business, and public sectors (Austin et al., 2006, as cited in Dzisi & Otsyina, 2014). A relatively new concept easily confused with corporate social responsibility (CSR) by many, it is the conscious integration of social, cultural and environmental programs into entrepreneurial ones. According to Moufakkir and Burns (2012), social entrepreneurship is an agent of change, a global phenomenon that plays a significant role in the socio-cultural evolution. According to Muñoz (2009), it is a dynamic process undertaken by individual entrepreneurs who are proactive, risk taking and mission oriented, and who decide to replicate a socially-driven venture in a new location in order to catalyze societal and policy reform through entrepreneurial methodologies anchored in innovation and an adaptive spirit (Muñoz, 2009). Moreover, this author conceives social entrepreneurs as persons with the ability to make a favorable impact within business and socioeconomic environments. Again, it has been observed that while the inherent benefit provided by socially directed activities has not changed over the years, the modalities of implementation have evolved. Additionally, there is a need to anchor entrepreneurial thinking and venture sustainability in socioeconomic activities. Thompson et al. (2000) identified the relevance of vision formulation, leadership ability and consideration of the long-term impact of the venture. Mort, Weerawardena and Carnegie (2003) pointed out the need for value creation alongside efficiencies in management and decision-making, while Overholt, Dahle and Canabou (2004) alluded to the integration of entrepreneurial thinking and action, concretization of goals and aspirations and venture continuity. Social entrepreneurship is growing rapidly and attracting increased attention. As a result of its increasing popularity, all sorts of activities are now being called social entrepreneurship (Martin & Osberg, 2007). Wyndham in 2006 developed its core values and saw CSR as not just a program, but as a way of living that embodies the individual's vision and values (Bohdanowicz & Zientra, 2008). Also at the Scandic and Rezidor Groups, membership of the executive team has been expanded to include vice presidents who are responsible for sustainable business and community development (Ergul & Johnson, 2011).

A review on entrepreneurship & social entrepreneurship

This section provides a summary of the main strands of thinking around entrepreneurship. A detailed discussion can be found in Chapter 2. Dees and Hass (1998) pointed out that the word entrepreneurship is a mixed blessing. On the positive side, it connotes a special, innate ability to sense and act on opportunity, combining out-of-the-box thinking with a unique brand of determination to create or bring about something new to the world. Joseph Schumpeter, a renowned economist, described entrepreneurs as the innovators who drive the "creative-destructive" process of capitalism (Schumpeter, 1961). According to him, the function of entrepreneurs is to reform or revolutionize the pattern of production. Entrepreneurs can do this by exploiting an invention or, more generally, an untried technological possibility for producing a new commodity or an old one in a new way, by opening up a new source of materials supply or a new outlet for products through reorganizing an industry (Schumpeter, 1961). Schumpeter's entrepreneurs are the change agents in an economy. By serving new markets or creating new ways of doing things, they move the economy forward.

Moreover, Wennekers and Thurik (1999) were emphatic that truly Schumpeterian social entrepreneurs will significantly reform or revolutionize their industries. Dees (2001) acknowledges that social entrepreneurs are the reformers and revolutionaries described by Schumpeter, but with a social mission. In other words, they make fundamental changes in the way things are done in the social sector and, because their visions are bold, they attack the underlying causes of problems rather than simply treating the symptoms. Dees and Hass (1998) also added that social entrepreneurs may act locally, yet their actions have the potential to stimulate global improvements in a variety of areas – education, healthcare, economic development, the environment, arts, etc.

Social entrepreneurship involves the recognition, evaluation and the exploitation of opportunities (Austin et al., 2006) and demonstrates "risk-tolerance, innovativeness and pro-activeness"; similar to conventional entrepreneurship, but does so in the social area (Peredo & McLean, 2006, p. 59) Specifically, the fundamental premise of social entrepreneurship is to use business knowledge and entrepreneurial principles to solve critical dilemmas facing a society regarding economic, social and environmental problems (Germak & Singh, 2010). Therefore, such entrepreneurs are more concerned with satisfying the social needs of communities (Newbert, 2003; Thompson, 2002) rather than commercial needs (Roberts & Woods, 2005). French economist Jean-Baptiste Say described an entrepreneur as one who shifts economic resources out of an area of lower productivity and yield and into an area of higher productivity and greater yield (Wennekers & Thurik, 1999). Entrepreneurs create value. Dees and Hass (1998) concur that many of the entrepreneurs that Say and Schumpeter have in mind serve their function by starting new profit-seeking business ventures, but starting a business is not the essence of entrepreneurship. Though other economists may have used the term with various nuances, the Say-Schumpeter tradition that identifies entrepreneurs as the catalysts and innovators behind economic progress has served as the foundation for the contemporary use of this concept (Dees & Hass, 1998).

Engaging in a process of continuous innovation, adaptation and learning, entrepreneurs are innovative. They break new ground, develop new models and pioneer new approaches. Innovation can take many forms. It does not require inventing something wholly new; it can simply involve applying an existing idea in a new way or to a new situation. Dees and Hass (1998) explained further that entrepreneurs need not be inventors. They simply need to be creative in applying what others have invented. Their innovations may appear in how they structure their core programs or in how they assemble resources and fund their work. On the funding side, social entrepreneurs look for innovative ways to assure that their ventures will have access to resources as long as they are creating social value (Dees, 2001). This willingness to innovate is part of the modus operandi of entrepreneurs. It is not just a one-time burst of creativity. It is a continuous process of exploring and learning.

One of the most frequently cited definitions of social entrepreneurship comes from Dees (2001). Mair et al. (2006) noted that this definition combines an emphasis on discipline and accountability with notions of value creation taken from Say, aspects of innovation and change agents from Schumpeter, the pursuit of opportunity from Drucker and resourcefulness from Stevenson. In brief, this definition can be stated as follows: Social entrepreneurs play the role of change agents in the social sector by

> adopting a mission to create and sustain social value (not just private value), Recognizing and relentlessly pursuing new opportunities to serve that mission, Engaging in a process of continuous innovation, adaptation and learning. Acting boldly without being limited by resources currently in hand, and Exhibiting heightened accountability to the constituencies served and for the outcomes created.
>
> (Dees, 2001, p. 4)

Although social sector leaders will exemplify these characteristics in different ways and to different degrees, the closer a person gets to satisfying all these conditions, the more they fit the model of a social entrepreneur (Ergul & Johnson, 2011). Those who are more innovative in their work and who create more significant social improvements will naturally be seen as more entrepreneurial.

Differentiating attributes of social entrepreneurs

The characteristics and motivations of social entrepreneurs was discussed in detail in Chapter 4. Following here is a discussion and summary of some differentiating attributes of social entrepreneurs.

Adopting a mission to create and sustain social value: According to Dees and Hass (1998) this attribute is the core of what distinguishes social entrepreneurs from business entrepreneurs even from socially responsible businesses. For a social entrepreneur, the *social* mission is fundamental. This is a mission of social improvement that cannot be reduced to creating private benefits (financial returns or consumption advantages) for individuals.

Recognizing and relentlessly pursuing new opportunities to serve that mission: Dees (2001) further explained that where others see problems, entrepreneurs see opportunity. Social entrepreneurs are not simply driven by the perception of a social need or by their compassion, rather they have a vision of how to achieve improvement and they are determined to make their vision work. They are persistent and improve, while taking into consideration the risk of failure. Entrepreneurs tend to have a high tolerance for ambiguity and learn how to manage risks for themselves and others. They treat the failure of a project as a learning experience, not a personal tragedy (Dees & Hass, 1998).

Acting boldly without being limited by resources currently in hand: Social entrepreneurs do not let their own limited resources keep them from pursuing their visions. They are skilled at doing more with less and at attracting resources from others. They use scarce resources efficiently and leverage their limited resources by drawing in partners and collaborating with others. They explore all resource options, from pure philanthropy to the commercial methods of the business sector. They are not bound by sector norms or traditions. They develop resource strategies that are likely to support and reinforce their social missions. They take calculated risks and manage the downsides, so as to reduce the harm that will result from failure. They understand the risk tolerances of their stakeholders and use this to spread the risk to those who are better prepared to accept it.

Exhibiting heightened accountability to the constituencies served and for the outcomes created: Because market discipline does not automatically weed out inefficient or ineffective social ventures, social entrepreneurs take steps to assure they are creating value. This means that they seek a sound understanding of the constituencies they are serving.

Some of the key characteristics of business entrepreneurs as outlined in the literature are attitudes, motivations, capabilities, skills, perspectives, behaviors and origins (Dees & Hass, 1998). It would be logical to do the same for social entrepreneurs and some incipient efforts along this line can be found in the literature. Mair et al. (2006) observed that social entrepreneurs are one species in the genus 'entrepreneur'. They are entrepreneurs with a social mission. However, because of this mission, they face some distinctive challenges and all definitions ought to reflect this. For social entrepreneurs, the social mission is explicit and central. This obviously affects how they perceive and assess opportunities. Mission-related impact becomes the central criterion, not wealth creation.

Distinguishing between social entrepreneurs and business entrepreneurs, Dees and Hass (1998) argued that wealth is just a means to an end for social entrepreneurs; whereas with business entrepreneurs, wealth creation is a way of measuring value creation. This is because the latter are subject to market discipline, which determines, in large part, whether they are creating value. If they do not shift resources to more economically productive uses, they tend to be driven out of business. Markets are not perfect, but over the long haul, social entrepreneurs work reasonably well as a test of private value creation, specifically the creation of value for customers who are willing and able to pay (Dees and Hass). An entrepreneur's ability to attract resources (financial capital, academic capital, social capital, etc.[1]) in a competitive marketplace is a reasonably good indication that the venture represents a more productive use of these resources than the alternatives it is competing against. The logic is simple. According to Johnson (2000), social entrepreneurs who can pay the most for resources are typically the ones who can put those resources to higher valued uses, as determined in the marketplace.

The magnitude of the environmental and social challenges that our planet is facing calls for a dramatic shift towards new solutions (Wüstenhagen et al., 2008).

Against this background, and in line with the definition given by Gasse (2007 as cited in Spence, Boubaker Gherib, & Biwolé, 2008, p. 51): "Entrepreneurship is the action of mobilizing resources to launch projects and create firms whose products and services meet the needs of society". From this definition, we may infer that the attitude of an entrepreneur should be that of a leader and a visionary who anticipates certain situations or contexts in order to create different realities. An entrepreneur's vision can be defined as an "image projected in the future of the place we want our product to have in the market, as well as the image of the type of organization we need to achieve these goals" (Filion, 1997, in Spence et al., 2008, p. 56). As explained by Spence et al. (2008), an opportunity is therefore considered as a future situation that is both desirable and feasible. Verstraete and Fayolle talk about "opportunity recognition" and "business creation", implying that entrepreneurship theory applies only to for-profit organizations, hence leaving aside social entrepreneurs (Filion et al., 2001; Verstraete & Fayolle, 2005). Moreover, entrepreneurs can be considered a source of wealth for the firm and society in general, based on their ability to create value (Spence et al., 2008). An entrepreneur's attitude towards failure is a key factor of entrepreneurial orientation. The owner/manager's propensity to develop new opportunities, innovate and act proactively and their attitude towards risk is usually a key factor in firms' success (Churchill & Muzyka, 1994; Covin & Slevin, 1989; Julien & Marchesnay, 1996; Knight, 1997; Miller & Friesen, 1982; Quariel & Auberger, 2005; Spense et al., 2008; Stevenson & Jarillo, 1990). In their role as leaders, entrepreneurs need to have a proactive attitude based on their values, in order to improve both society and the environment, build a project based on ethics and collaboratively interact with the rest of the community, with respect and care.

More than economic players

This worldview that conceives entrepreneurs not only as economic players, but also as social and environmental players, helps us define sustainable entrepreneurship. Therefore, the first definition given by Schaltegger and Wagner is as follows:

> Sustainable entrepreneurship is characterized by some fundamental aspects of entrepreneurial activities which are less orientated towards management systems or technical procedures, but rather focus more on the personal initiative and skills of the entrepreneurial person or team to realize market success with environmental or societal innovations.
> (Schaltegger & Wagner, 2012, p. 31)

However, as this definition fails to include the entrepreneur's action towards his or her own organization, these authors give a wider definition of the term: "Sustainable entrepreneurship can thus be described as an innovative, market-orientated and personality-driven form of value creation by environmentally or socially beneficial innovations and products exceeding the start-up phase of a company" (Schaltegger & Wagner, 2012, p. 32). This definition takes into account intrapreneurs, who substantially change and shape the environmental and business growth development of the company (Jorna, 2006; Schaltegger & Wagner, 2012).

Sustainability innovations

The decision of a company to get involved in sustainability innovation activities can be triggered by a number of factors, which can, for instance, relate to changes in regulation; initiatives of important stakeholders, such as NGOs, or changes in the management team of a firm (Schaltegger & Wagner, 2012). "Sustainability innovations are in many cases, radical innovations" (Schaltegger & Wagner, 2012, p. 40). Sustainability innovation is, by definition, characterized by high social benefits; therefore, if social benefits cannot be appropriated and the private benefit is low, this would be particularly detrimental to society (Schaltegger & Wagner, 2012).

Entrepreneurship and sustainable development

It is still very difficult to evaluate the sustainable entrepreneurship approach in terms of its contribution to sustainable development. Additional research and experiments are required to determine the specific role of entrepreneurs in sustainable development (Hall, Daneke, & Lenox, 2010). On one hand, entrepreneurship can help create sustainable development in low-income economies for many reasons. By working out a feasible business model that includes all the costs and possible revenues, an enterprise can be organized in such a way that long-lasting positive impact can be achieved more readily than in the colonial or development-aid approach, without using human and natural resources faster than they can be replenished. On the other hand, addressing societal harms and constraints does not necessarily raise costs, because the (new) enterprises can innovate by using new technologies, service systems and management approaches and, as a result, achieve better productivity and expansion of their markets.

Entrepreneurship can create independence and reappraise self-esteem, in a way countering the negative results of development aid. Entrepreneurship facilitates a fast learning process. Individual entrepreneurs quickly adapt their strategies and learn quickly, because the market results of their efforts provide direct feedback in terms of profits or losses. The possibility for new entrepreneurs to even make financial profits provides the entrepreneur with another drive to start an entrepreneurial initiative and decreases the dependence on donors from high-income economies. This lack of financial dependence on high-income economies contributes to the self-esteem and financial stability of low-income economies.

Based on the above, the adoption of an entrepreneurial approach yields a holistic approach, by combining different aspects that are usually undervalued in development aid initiatives. For example, marketing, financial models, stakeholder analyses, etc. Even though these aspects may sound very commercially and financially driven, they also contribute to the success of initiatives aiming at mainly social and ecological value creation. Entrepreneurship creates equality in communication among different stakeholders.

Moreover, an entrepreneurial approach is sustainable in time because it makes individuals in low-income economies responsible for their own situation and helps them improve their daily lives by granting them the opportunity to start a business. It is also more sustainable from the perspective of a high-income economy: Rather than merely being a donor and having to face more and more resistance against development aid, the actors in the high-income economy now become investors. Besides, high-income economies are familiar with entrepreneurship.

Finally, the approach stimulates the entrepreneurs' learning because their income will serve as feedback mechanism on their way of working. Social and ecological sustainability can be stimulated by the investors. Entrepreneurship creates a basis for dialogue in which the initiative for development is gradually taken over by actors in the low-income economy. The technical innovation introduced also requires social innovation. Moreover, in developing economies, entrepreneurship implies that, since there is no business context to trust as a common base of resources in terms of knowledge, materials and people, its ability to innovate and be resilient to challenges and unexpected circumstances (i.e., its ability to create value) becomes more necessary in these contexts.

In order to integrate the concepts of sustainable development, social entrepreneurship and sustainability, one can refer to the text written by Gulen Hashmi (2017),[2] who developed the concept of value creation based on the SLOW model, which is described in the following case.

BOX CASE 6.1

The SLOW model – sustainable luxury for overall well-being

The SLOW model focuses on sustainability strategies and practices in luxury goods/services companies based on a value-creation model that takes into consideration both shareholder value and social value.

The SLOW (Sustainable Luxury for Overall Wellbeing) value-creation model is a theoretical contribution about the sustainable management of luxury within a value-creation context, focused on the different types of sustainability engagement in the luxury industry that leads to shareholder value and social value. In the pursuit of the sustainable management of luxury, the industry needs to start with sustainability challenges and creating value through social and environmental excellence, while managing the business in a way that delivers shareholder value.

This SLOW value-creation model builds on the True Business Sustainability Typology (Dyllick & Muff, 2015), which is based on concerns (inputs), organizational perspective (processes) and the type of value created (outputs) as the typical elements of a business process.

The SLOW value-creation model further expands the True Business Sustainability Typology on one of the three elements of the business process model: type of value created. The model redefines sustainable management of luxury with regard to both shareholder value (on one axis) and social value (on another). The vertical axis is built on the luxury company's need to create shareholder value while the horizontal axis is built on the luxury company's need to create social value for overall wellbeing. Taking into consideration the nature and the current sustainability practices of the luxury sector, the four plots of the SLOW model distinguish between 'self-indulgent luxury', 'refined luxury', 'thoughtful luxury' and SLOW, which represent the different types of sustainability engagement relevant to the luxury industry.

Value creation goes beyond shareholders and considers other stakeholders who are also indirectly involved in the business itself. This stakeholder perspective is built on the premise that the interests of many non-shareholders are also viewed as 'ends', rather than the 'means'. Value is largely created by clean traceability, reaching beyond tangible beauty. Luxury brands with this type of sustainability engagement use traceability as a starting point for creating value along their supply chain. For these luxury brands, sustainable luxury means clear traceability, which can be defined as a journey to the past to understand where a product comes from, its components, raw materials and their extraction (Gardetti & Girón, 2014).

The SLOW value-creation model, in this sense, aims to provide luxury industry professionals and academia with a tool to understand and differentiate between the various types of sustainability engagement that lead to varying degrees of shareholder value and social value. Due to their high profile and high potential to make a relatively higher positive impact as compared to other industries, luxury brands have a bigger responsibility for solving sustainability challenges and prioritizing social value over shareholder value.

The SLOW value-creation model is a theoretical contribution that sets the scene for further empirical research in the sustainable management of luxury. Although the SLOW model was elaborated with reference to assessments of some of the top, most valuable luxury brands' sustainability engagements, the adoptability of SLOW still needs to be applied to other luxury brands in the industry. SLOW offers important insights for luxury brand managers and sustainability experts who aspire to resolve today's social challenges with business acumen. Last but not least, the SLOW value-creation model can be considered an important contribution to transcending the social entrepreneurship mindset in these times when there's growing need for awareness of, "It's not how big companies grow, but how they grow big" in order to improve today's current economic paradigm.

Hospitality, tourism and luxury

The hospitality industry should recognize and take responsibility for mistakes and failures. The excessive use of resources is particularly concerning for resorts that rely on nature to provide guests with memorable experiences (Shivdasani, 2017).

A number of countries including China, Mexico and some island nations have explicitly chosen to pursue luxury tourism as a development strategy (Brenner & Aguilar, 2002; Scheyvens, 2007; Wang & Wall, 2007).

Arguments for such policies include:

- A belief that luxury tourism is the best match for the interests of the fastest growing tourism markets;
- An expectation that this will attract higher-spending tourists, which will support greater economic benefits for the destination economy (Gulette, 2007);
- A desire to promote a more positive destination (Wang & Wall, 2007).

The rise of the concept of sustainable luxury as a response to growing demand for luxury tourism equates to increasing concerns about global sustainability (Moscardo, 2017). The definition of luxury consumption given by Tynan, McKechnie and Chhuon suggests that luxury consumption should be defined as goods and services "that are high quality, expensive and non-essential products and services that appear to be rare, exclusive, prestigious and authentic and offer high levels of symbolic and emotional/hedonic values through customer experiences" (Tynan, Mckechnie, & Chhuon, 2010, p. 158).

According to Gianna Moscardo (2017), luxury tourism can be defined as tourism products and services that are promoted as and perceived by tourists to be associated with characteristics included in the definition of luxury, with the exception of a high price. This is because price is a little more complicated in the case of luxury tourism. Tourists can experience travel products and services that would be luxuries in their home countries for considerably less money when they travel to destinations where lower wages and standards of living allow for the provision of luxury at a cheaper price.

Wiedmann, Hennigs and Siebels (2009) classified luxury consumption motivations into five groups: (1) price/costs; (2) functional values, including usability, uniqueness and quality; (3) social values, including conspicuous consumption; (4) status-seeking and prestige, individual or personal values such as hedonism or self-indulgence and materialism and (5) self-identity as a person of taste or as a connoisseur. Luxury is seen by De Banier "as having seven culturally specific common characteristic elements which are exceptional quality; hedonism (beauty and pleasure); price (expensive); rarity (which is not scarcity); selective distribution and associated personalized services; exclusive character (prestige, privilege) and creativity (art and avant garde)" (De Banier et al., 2012, in Poelina & Nordensvard, 2017, p. 152).

The discussions of growth in luxury consumption and the emerging middle class in BRIC (Brazil, Russia, India and China) nations also highlight the importance of travel to these consumers, with growth in demand for both luxury travel options and shopping for luxury goods as a key travel activity (Park & Reisinger, 2009). As the use of luxury as a tourism development tool and demand for luxury tourism grows, research investigating luxury tourism consumption has begun to emerge. Luxury tourism is associated with exclusivity, privileged access, intensive and extensive service, privacy, spacious personal facilities, quality in facility appearance, furnishings and service attributes such as food and dining options, comfort and uniqueness (Ahn & Pearce, 2013; Mohsin & Lockyer, 2010).

Moscardo (2017) suggests that luxury tourism is likely to have significant negative impacts both on the visited destination and more broadly through the global nature of the tourism distribution system. There is considerable discussion of tourism and sustainability and pressure from consumers, NGOs and governments to adopt sustainable practices. The outcome is pressure on tourism businesses to adopt sustainability initiatives and actions. Moreover, there is a trend towards limiting the size of tours and resorts, requiring self-sufficiency in energy and water usage, more effective and green waste management systems and the use of sustainable building products and methods. As a result, there is now considerable overlap in many locations between ecotourism and luxury tourism.

Also according to Moscardo (2017), many authors (Ahn & Pearce, 2013; Weinstein, 2010) argue that it is possible to redesign and alter key aspects of luxury to limit negative impacts. Further, it is argued that luxury consumers are increasingly aware of and concerned about sustainability issues and so are actively seeking more responsible luxury options (Bendell & Kleanthous, 2007). Related to this claim is the argument that luxury consumption is shifting from social to individual motives, with a greater emphasis on unique experiences (Yeoman & McMahon-Beattle, 2006). These arguments together are suggest that luxury tourists may be prepared to accept changes in key characteristics of the luxury tourism experience if they are linked to less negative impacts and they may accept less in the way of comfort, indulgence and tangible facilities in exchange for more engaging experiences (Moscardo & Benckendorff, 2010).

Hospitality, tourism and sustainability

Tourism can be seen as contributing to sustainability only if it is developed and managed in such a way as to address issues related to the environment, society and the economy. Since natural capital cannot be replaced with other forms of capital, it must be maintained and enhanced (Lawn, 2012).

Therefore, to combine so many factors like sustainability and social entrepreneurship with an industry – in this case, the hotel industry, which has a great impact on different aspects and, in turn, is closely related to other industries – may seem complicated, especially if we add the luxury component. However, while these concepts have been recently developed in the academic field, there are more and more examples about entrepreneurs who choose the path of sustainable tourism for their business.

As soon as we start analyzing each concept, we realize that they are closely related: Each has a double aspect, since every decision we make has an impact both on the context and on ourselves. Entrepreneurs are aware of this and use it to their advantage, implementing short-term actions to generate long-term improvements.

A social entrepreneur who manages to put these elements together based on his principles is a transformational leader of reality with every action taken, step by step. A leader generates wealth in the economic sense of the term, but – above all – on a social (cultural), personal (spiritual and intellectual) and environmental (care) level.

Opportunities to make small positive changes are plenty in the hospitality industry. Those changes may not negatively impact either the profitability or guests' perception of products and services, yet they can generate considerable good for both the environment and society. In fact, sometimes those changes can enhance guests' experiences. Additionally, bold steps can fundamentally redress the balance between business and society, and shift back to the original purpose of the corporation as a service to society.

CHAPTER CASE 6.1

Case study: Soneva – when environmental and social involvement meets luxury

> Luxury goes hand in hand with sustainability. A sensible starting point is that luxury can be considered as placing an importance on durability in line with the concept of fewer but better.
>
> (Hashmi, 2017, p. 23)

Soneva Fushi was opened in 1995 by Eva and Sonu Shivdasani as a vision of crafted villas, paying attention to every detail, that would cater to a niche market of travelers looking for an alternative to conventional resorts. Not only is this luxury resort located on a remote island in the northern Baa Atoll region of the Maldives, it lacks the extravagance most people equate with luxury, including a 'no news, no shoes' policy, encouraging guests to enjoy the natural environment through activities that have a low impact on the environment and surrounding communities.

"Soneva Fushi resort is part of group of hotels distinguished by their adherence to and promotion of the concept of 'intelligent Luxury'. This phrase refers to the combination of sustainable, local, organic wellness, learning, fun experiences.[3] This attempt to integrate sustainability and luxury is often cited as a leading example of successful Sustainable Luxury tourism" (Moscardo, 2017, p. 175).

Soneva Fushi addresses social and environmental concerns in each decision-making process and regularly monitors key sustainability indicators to identify areas for improvement and necessary action plans. Steps towards maintaining a sustainable resort include its low impact design, a ban on all bottled water imports, experimentation with deep seawater cooling and installation of solar panels. In addition, the resort is actively involved with community development projects that support surrounding communities and improve the long-term sustainability of the Maldives as a place to live and as a tourism destination. The success of Soneva Fushi is testament to the success of the 'intelligent luxury' concept without compromising economic viability or guest experience.

> Johan Rockström of the Stockholm Resilience Centre illustrates earth's challenges brilliantly in his Planetary Boundaries framework. The idea is simple: our finite world has limits, or a budget, to speak in business terms. Nine boundaries have been identified, four of which are over budget, including climate change, biodiversity loss and the nitrogen and phosphorus cycle. The Planetary Boundaries concept highlights that we are in trouble; however, it also shows that if we act fast, it is possible to reverse the dire state we are in. The 1987 Montreal Protocol managed to reverse ozone depletion that was transgressed. However, to duplicate the success, we have to act fast.

> The breakthroughs of the Paris Agreement on climate change and the launch of the UN Sustainable Development Goals are beacons of hope for current and future generations, and they remind us that there can only be environmental progress with social equity.

> There are two main areas to focus on within the hospitality industry: climate change and nitrogen/phosphorus cycle. This means switching to renewable energy and food that does not require excessive use of fertilizers.
>
> (Shivdasani, 2017, pp. 36–37)

The price of renewable energy is rapidly decreasing and is becoming competitive with fossil fuel. The main challenge is the relatively high price for energy storage.

> We have invested the funds through the Soneva Foundation in carbon mitigation projects. Also we have a strong focus on moving over to renewable energy. Soneva Fushi has installed 7kWp solar PV that covers our electricity needs during the day through a power purchase agreement, which has reduced our energy bill by 25% without need for heavy investments.
>
> (Shivdasani, 2017, p. 37)

> A significant group of customers mentioned observation of sustainable practices; however, the study revealed a gap between the WCED (1987) definition and the notion of sustainability by ordinary tourists. First of all, very few people used the term 'sustainability,' most used terms 'eco-,' 'environmental,' 'green' and 'nature'. Customers understood sustainability primarily as care about the natural environment. What appealed to the guests most was appearance of the villas, which were blended with the natural environment and lush vegetation. Other remarks included two main points- recycling and growing own produce.
>
> (Robbins & Gaczorek, 2015, p. 179)

Resorts and hotels are often central to a community, so the aim of Soneva's team is to raise awareness and change people's behavior. For instance, in 2008 they took the decision to stop offering branded bottled water, instead each resort serves water filtered, mineralized, alkalized and bottled on site in reusable glass bottles. The initiative not only eliminates plastic waste but also cuts out unnecessary transportation miles – as well as carbon emissions and fuel use – and is more cost effective. They have used the additional revenue to give around 750,000 people access to safe water around the world. Every action taken by Soneva is guided by the belief that companies must become solutions to the environment where they develop their business, instead of having a negative impact.

Soneva's approach is focused on low volume, high quality and wealthy clientele. This was a conscious decision.

> What attracted us to the Maldives was its natural beauty and we knew that to preserve that, one needed to limit the number of people coming. I strongly believe that combining luxury and sustainability is the right business model and that when done right is the most successful business model. However, I had no idea that our intensely personal vision of a locally crafted villa and environmentally responsible lifestyle would form the basis of a successful collection of world-class resorts.
>
> (Shivdasani, 2016, p. 140)

'Intelligent luxury' is Soneva's vehicle for delivering this inspiration to their guests. Luxury is defined as something that is a rarity, and in today's society, that is peace, time and space. Luxury is about sand between the toes and dinner under the canopy of a billion stars. Luxury is about reconnecting with oneself and the natural environment. In addition, they strongly believe that sometimes the more sustainable option is actually the more luxurious one.

The focus on sustainability and luxury also translates into repeat business. At Soneva Fushi, the percentage of return guests exceeds 50%, which surpasses hotel industry averages. The values of a company matter to those who consume its products.

Corporations have grown increasingly independent. In many cases, the emphasis has moved away from the creation of public good towards the creation of wealth for shareholders, and, as such, the contract between firms and society has broken down. Today, corporations measure success through profit, share price and dividends. However, it is possible to measure everything except that which makes life worthwhile. It seems that corporations are no longer mandated by society to do good, and yet they still enjoy the benefits that limited liability brings.

Shivdasani strongly believes that all companies, hotel businesses included, must have a purpose beyond profit. They must play a greater role in the world beyond just enriching their shareholders. It is about changing the approach to business success. In his opinion, the profitability purpose can coexist in harmony with social and environmental goals.

SOCIAL ENTREPRENEURSHIP IN HOSPITALITY

CHAPTER CASE 6.2

Physical master plans: a roadmap to developing sustainable destinations

(Source: The Long Run; HM Design (www.h-m-design.com))

Synopsis

This case study explores how **HM Design** creates physical master plans as a roadmap to successfully developing high-end sustainable tourism destinations. HM Design (https://h-m-design.com/ecotourism-planning-2) utilizes relevant information on physical, metaphysical and cultural elements of the site to deeply understand the context, opportunities and limitations of each destination. In addition, they identify participatory planning processes with different stakeholders, using local knowledge wisely and prioritizing respect for animals, plants, local people and the spirit of the place as key elements for site planning and developing tourism destinations that truly respect and integrate with the natural and local context.

About HM Design

HM Design (www.h-m-design.com) is a specialized eco-planning and eco-design firm established in 1990 by Hitesh Mehta. It is a multi-international award-winner and has built projects and consulted in over sixty-four countries. Its goal is to create unique low-impact projects that balance the economic, environmental, social and spiritual aspects of each site.

Challenges

Site planning for sustainable high-end tourism faces challenging dichotomies as it needs to ensure that:

- Luxury and excellent service is provided according to the expectations of traditional high-end guests, while also being economically, socially, environmentally and spiritually sustainable;
- It creates a guest experience that is refined and exclusive, yet humble and natural;
- The design is beautiful and maximizes benefits for tourists, while minimizing environmental impacts and construction costs;
- It identifies the optimum locations for ecotourism facilities and interpretive experiences, where guests can enjoy the best of nature without jeopardizing the essence and socio-environmental balance of the place;
- It allows diversification of tourism products and accommodation to cater to the different tastes of varied ecotourists.

Solutions implemented

- HM Design puts in place a participatory planning process, where different stakeholders such as the community, the clients and tourists are taken into account. Although the specific process for each destination could vary, in a general sense these are the steps that the company follows:

    1. Compilation of base documentation
    2. Office-based review and analysis of base documentation
    3. On-site presentation on research and site analysis to clients
    4. Site reconnaissance and ground-truthing
    5. On-site metaphysical (nature connection) workshops
    6. Stakeholder planning workshop and charette
    7. Progress presentation to clients and approval of site/master plan.
    8. Office-based finalization of site analysis (includes metaphysical analysis)
    9. Refinement of approved site/master plan and further research
    10. Client and stakeholder review and final revision of plans
    11. Final submission

- A key element in the process for HM Design is collecting reliable information not only regarding physical aspects of the place, but also the metaphysical and socio-cultural ones.

PHYSICAL UNDERSTANDING

HM Design collects base data about the characteristics and attributes of the place, in order to be able to create a 'Suitability Analysis' that presents a realistic development and conservation plan, and proposes a design that minimizes costs while also being in harmony with the place. Some of the visual information that HM Design generates and layers together to build a Composite Analysis include:

- Elevation analysis: it is important to determine areas that will have good views and cool breezes.

- Slope analysis: it is important to understand which areas are sensitive to development in terms of erosion and cutting and filling to create building platforms and other impacts that could alter topography and hydrology. For example, in some regions and sites, developing infrastructure on slopes above 30% can result in excessive grading, which could cause erosion, instability and slope failure. Furthermore, it could result in higher construction costs due to civil engineering and grading.

- Slope aspect analysis: this shows the direction that each slope of the site faces. It is important for solar access, cooling breezes and views. It is also important for the energy of the place, which in some countries – such as India, where the majority of the population is Hindu and practices Vaastu Shastra – the connection between energy and directional alignments is a key aspect of the culture and architectural and site landscape integration with nature.

- Hydrology: this can be used to determine the direction and concentration of water flow. In sustainable design, constructions should not be developed on ridges or areas of water flow, especially where flows meet and where water could be captured. Similarly, vegetation should be preserved or replanted in areas where water flows to prevent erosion and improve water quality.

- Vegetation analysis: this allows an identification of areas with dense vegetation or primary forest, as well as the habitats where native, endemic or threatened species exist, in order to avoid developing those areas and in this way protecting the most pristine and vulnerable systems in the destination. Additionally, vegetation analysis is also important for sustainable design as it provides useful information to manage solar access (Figure 6.1).

METAPHYSICAL UNDERSTANDING

- HM Design consults with nature and learns from its elements in order be able to include all natural aspects and be in tune with the spirit of

150 SOCIAL ENTREPRENEURSHIP IN HOSPITALITY

Figure 6.1 Hydrology analysis of the Peninsula Sanctuary – a luxury sustainable tourism resort in Nicaragua. (Photo Credit: HM Design).

the place, so as to understand the destination in a truly holistic and sustainable way.

- HM Design studies the 'chi' or the sacred energy of each site. For example, in the Crosswaters Ecolodge and Spa in South China, HM Design brought in a Feng Shui master with twenty years of experience to help them to understand the 'chi' of the mountain and river site. (https://h-m-design.com/eco-architecture-crosswaters-ecolodge).

- The company conducts metaphysical workshops with the Master Plan team and ecopsychology is applied to reintegrate the intelligence of the natural world with people's perceptual awareness and thought processes. For example, HM Design brought in a professional ecopsychologist on three projects (Ario Eco-Ranch, Kwanari Ecolodge and Chaa Creek Reserve) to conduct deep-ecology nature (ocean, forest, river and cosmology) connection workshops to help the consultants and clients immerse themselves into the landscape (Figure 6.2).

Figure 6.2 An ecopsychologist conducting a 'Forest Connection' workshop with the client, consultants and indigenous stakeholders (Mayans) for the Master Plan for Chaa Creek Reserve, Belize. (Photo Credit: Hitesh Mehta).

- The participants of the workshops employ the 'Six Senses Technique', in which each person uses each of the five basic human senses to discover and experience the site. For example, when employing the sense of sight, only the eyes remain open and the rest of the senses are blocked off in order to create focus and increase sensitivity, while reflecting the observations that arise through each respective sensorial experience (Figure 6.3). These exercises provide greater

152 SOCIAL ENTREPRENEURSHIP IN HOSPITALITY

awareness of the site and show the diversity of experiences that the ecosystem could offer. (International Ecolodge Guidelines, 2002)

Figure 6.3 A metaphysical workshop participant conducting a 'sound' sensorial site immersion.
(Photo Credit: Hitesh Mehta).

- HM Design then asks all workshop participants to use their 'sixth sense', referring to immersing themselves into the site and communicating with the voice of nature. Participants are asked to choose an element of nature (e.g., the river, ocean, rock, butterfly, bird, soil, etc.) and transcend their bodies and minds to embody or become the element, to listen to it and then write down on a piece of paper the element's perspective on the proposed development.

- Participants write about their ecosystem experiences and then discuss their feelings and insights with others in a group to learn about the others' experiences.

- HM Design then collates all these metaphysical thoughts and places them on the wall above the drawing board as one of the guiding principles for the Master/Site Plan.

SOCIO-CULTURAL UNDERSTANDING

- For HM Design, a sustainable master plan or architectural design must also be aligned with a deep knowledge of the culture and history of local people.

- Preliminary research on the culture of the place is carried out and local people, such as rangers, village chiefs, medicine men, shamans, etc., are involved in the on-site visits, utilizing their deep knowledge and understanding of the place as well (Figure 6.4). For example, in

SOCIAL ENTREPRENEURSHIP IN HOSPITALITY 153

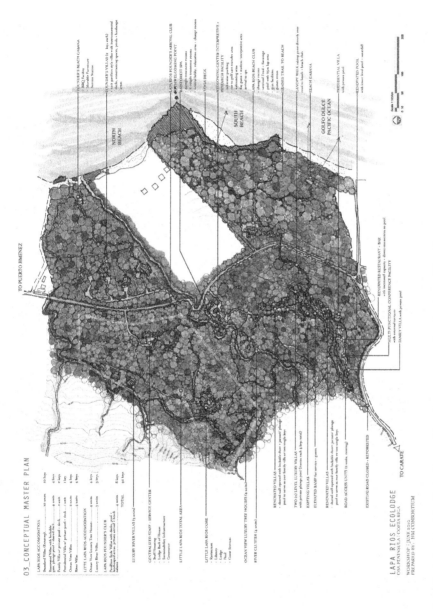

Figure 6.4 Sustainable biodiversity and tourism master plan for Lapa Rios Reserve. (Photo Credit: HM Design).

the Lapa Rios Ecolodge – a Long Run GER Member – research was carried on the history of the Osa Peninsula's cultural and natural landscapes (https://h-m-design.com/lapa-rios-sustainable-master-plan).

- HM Design draws inspiration from the way local people live and make use of the materials around them. For example, for the design of Plataran Menjangan Lodge and Spa, typical Balinese villages were meticulously studied, taking into account not only spatial distribution but also the social dynamics within Balinese people.

Lessons learned

- Integrated, multi-disciplinary and participatory approaches that incorporate local knowledge when planning and designing are necessary for sustainable tourism development.
- Sustainable Master Plans and architectural designs should be a response to the local context, which includes all three elements – physical, metaphysical and cultural – and it should not be imposed. Plans should be aligned harmoniously with nature and culture.
- Rich and reliable sources of data are needed in order to understand how environmental and cultural systems can influence overall design and vice versa. Secondary data plays an important role, but it is crucial to validate information on-site and involve different stakeholders in data collection.
- A detailed site analysis helps identify the opportunities and constraints for tourism development, enabling the maximization of development opportunities and the market potential of various products while minimizing disturbances to the environment.
- Sustainable physical master planning should look at the big picture, but at the same time focus on small details like site plans, in order to ensure that it is treating the site in a holistic way and as a whole system that takes into account the small interconnections between nature, society, culture, energy and the guests' experiences (Figure 6.5).
- Location is crucial to the success of any high-end sustainable tourism destination, both due to the experience offered and environmental protection in the long term.
- The design of the tourism products should be aligned both with people and nature. For example, a resident naturalist can teach astronomy, about the cosmos, indigenous plants, mammals, etc. or guests could also be involved with local artists and folkloric groups.

SOCIAL ENTREPRENEURSHIP IN HOSPITALITY 155

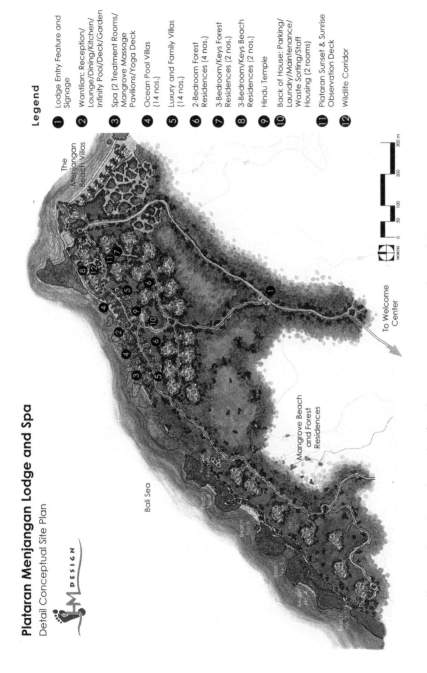

Figure 6.5 An illustrated conceptual site plan for Plataran Menjangan Lodge and Spa. (Photo Credit: HM Design).

- Metaphysical workshops take the understanding of a place to a higher level, allowing a deeper connection with nature. Journaling the process is very important as is setting aside time for the group engaging, as the former captures information in a deeper and more creative way, while the latter enhances trust, respect and sharing among team members.

EXERCISES

Group discussion

As mentioned before, "Integrated, multi-disciplinary and participatory approaches that incorporate local knowledge when planning and designing are necessary for sustainable tourism development".

1. After reading chapter case study 6.1, do you believe Soneva is a case of sustainable tourism development? Why?

2. If the road to sustainability is visualized as a path or a journey, how can Soneva continue expanding it sustainable horizons?

Group research & discussion

Take some time to review chapter case 6.2 and visit the company's website (HM Design, www.h-m-design.com).

1. How does an entrepreneur manage the different aspects of starting a business and being a changemaker?

2. In your opinion, is it necessary first to recognize and analyze a problem that needs to be solved, or can transformational leaders generate business in a responsible, ethical way without studying the different problems that the community or environment presents? Why?

3. Which characteristics would you highlight from transformational leaders?

4. How does HM Design build up sustainable plans? Where, and on which aspects, do they focus?

5. Which of the steps that they take into consideration as part of their action plan do you consider the most important? State at least three reasons why you think this way.

> **Individual research**
>
> Write an essay about the role of leadership in changing hospitality towards more sustainability. Keep in mind some of the following points:
>
> 1. What is the role and impact of social entrepreneurs in hospitality versus larger hotel chains' CSR programs in driving change?
> 2. How did you derive your conclusions?
> 3. Can you support your essay with industry examples?

Notes

1. In his book *Distinction: A Social Critique of the Judgement of Taste*, Pierre Bourdieu (1979) explained the different types of capital – economic resources being the economic capital, knowledge being the academic capital, and the ability to create bonds being part of the social capital. However, cultural capital is given by the context and the construction based on the above elements.
2. Text summarised and adapted for this chapter from Hashmi, G. *Redefining the Essence of Sustainable Luxury Management: The Slow Value Creation Model* in Gardetti, M.A (2017), *Sustainable Management of Luxury*. Springer Nature Singapore. Singapore. 3–28.
3. http://www.soneva.com/slow-life.

References

Ahn, Y. H., & Pearce, A. R. (2013). Green luxury: A case study of two green hotels. *Journal of Green Building* 8(1), 90–119. College Publishing, USA

Austin, J. E., Stevenson, H., & Wei-Skillern, J. (2006). Social entrepreneurship and commercial entrepreneurship: Same, different, or both? *Entrepreneurship Theory and Practice*, 30(1), 1–22. SAGE Journals, UK

Bendell, J., & Kleanthous, A. (2007). *Deeper Luxury*. WWF-UK, UK

Bjerregaard, T., & Lauring, J. (2012). The social sustainability of entrepreneurship. An ethnographic study of entrepreneurial balancing of plural logics. In M. Wagner (Ed.), *Entrepreneurship, Innovation and Sustainability* (pp. 170–187). Greenleaf Publishing, UK.

Bohdanowicz, P., & Zientara, P. (2008). Hotel companies contribution to improving the quality of life of local communities and the wellbeing of their employees. *Tourism and Hospitality Research*, 9(2), 147–158. SAGE Journals, UK

Brenner, L., & Aguilar, A. G. (2002). Luxury Tourism and regional economic development in Mexico. *The Professional Geographer*, 54(4), 500–520. Taylor & Francis Group, UK

Brizek, M., & Khan, M. (2008). Understanding corporate entrepreneurship theory: A literature review for culinary/food service academic practitioners. *Journal of Culinary Science & Technology*, 6(4), 221–255. Taylor & Francis Group, UK

Cho, A. H. (2006). Politics, values and social entrepreneurship: a critical appraisal. In J. Mair J. Robinson, & K. Hockerts (Eds.), *Social Entrepreneurship* (pp. 34–56). Palgrave Macmillan.

Choi, D. Y., & Grey, E. R. (2008). The venture development processes of "sustainability" entrepreneurs. *Management Research, 30*(3), 377–395.

Churchill, N. C., & Muzyka, D. F. (1994). *Entrepreneurial management: A converging theory for large and small enterprises.* Working paper 94/64/ENT/SM, INSEAD, European Institute of Business Administration, Paris.

Covin, G. J., & Slevin, D. P. (1989). Strategic management of small firms in hostile and benign environments. *Strategic Management Journal, 10*, 75–87.

Dees, J. G., & Hass, M. P. (1998). *The meaning of "Social Entrepreneurship".* The Kauffman Center for Entrepreneurial Leadersship, USA

Dees, G. (2001). *The Meaning of Social Entrepreneurship.* http://www.fuqua.duke.edu/centers/case/documents/dees_SE.pdf#search=%22social%20entrepreneurship%22.

Desa, G. (2007). Social entrepreneurship: Snapshots of a research field in emergence. *International Social Entrepreneurship Research Conference (ISECR)* (3rd ed.)

Dixon, S. E. A., & Clifford, A. (2007). Ecopreneurship: A new approach to managing the triple bottom line. *Journal of Organizational Change Management, 20*(3), 326–345. Emerald Insight, UK

Dyllick, T., & Muff, K. (2015, March). Clarifying the meaning of sustainable business: Introducing a typology from business-as-usual to true business sustainability. *Organization & Environment, 29*(2), 156–174. SAGE Journals, UK

Dzisi, S., & Otsyina, F. A. (2014). Exploring Social Entrepreneurship in the Hospitality Industry. *International Journal of Innovative Research & Development, 3*(6), 233–241.IJSR, India

Egri, C. P., & Herman, S. (2000). Leadership in North American environmental sector: Values, leadership styles and contexts of environmental leaders and their organizations. *Academy of Management Journal, 43*(4), 523–553. AOM, USA

Ergul, M., & Johnson, C. (2011). Social entrepreneurship in the hospitality and tourism industry: an exploratory approach. *The Consortium Journal of Hospitality and Tourism, 16*(2), 40–46. Journal Guide, USA

Ersoy, A. (2014). The role of cultural intelligence in cross-cultural leadership effectiveness: A qualitative study in the hospitality industry. *Journal of Yaşar University, 9*(35), 6099–6260. Yaşar University, Turkey

Filion, L. J. (1997) Le champ de l'entrepreneurial: historique, evolution, tendances. *Revenue Internationale PME, 10*(2), 129–72.

Filion, L. J. (2001). *Realiser son project déntreprise.* Les Éditions Transcontinentale, Canada

Gardetti, M. A. (2005) Desarrollo sustentable, sustentabilidad y sustentabilidad corporativa. In Gardetti (Ed.) *Textos en Sustentabilidad Empresarial Integrando las Consideraciones Sociales, Ambientales y Económicas en el corto y largo plazo.* p. 37–77LA-Bell, Buenos Aires

Gardetti, M. A. (2014). Stories from the social pioneers in the sustainable luxury sector: a conceptual vision. In M. A. Gardetti & M. E. Girón (Eds.), *Sustainable luxury and Social Entrepreneurship* (pp. 23–34). London: Routledge.

Gardetti, M. A. (2016) Transformational Leaders. In M. A. Gardetti & M. E. Girón (Eds.), *Sustainable Luxury and Social Entrepreneurship. More Stories from the Pioneers* (pp. 25–32). London: Routledge.

Gasse, Y. (2007). Creation et gestion de lénterprise. In L. J. Filion (Ed.), *Management des PME, de la creation a la croissance.* FPPI, Canada

Germak, A. J., & Singh, K. K. (2010). Social entrepreneurship: Changing the way social workers do business. *Administration in Social Work, 34*(1), 79–95. Taylor & Francis, UK

Grayson, D., & Hodges, A. (2004). *Corporate Social Opportunity! 7 Steps to Make Corporate Social Responsibility Work for Your Business*. Greenleaf Publishing, UK.

Grenier, P. (2007). Vision and values: what they mean for social entrepreneurs. *International Social Entrepreneurship Conference Research (ISECR)* (3rd ed.), Copenhagen.

Gullete, G. S. (2007). Migration and tourism development in Huatulco, Oaxaca. *Current Anthropology, 48*(4), 603–611. The University of Chicago Press Journal, USA

Hall, J., & Vredenburg, H. (2003). The challenge of innovating for sustainable development. *MIT Sloan Management Review, 45*(1), 61–68. MIT, USA

Hall, J. K., Daneke, G. A., & Lenox, M. J. (2010). Sustainable development and entrepreneurship: Past contributions and future directions. *Journal of business venturing, 25*, 439–448. Elsevier, The Netherlands

Harkema, S., & Schout, H. (2008). Incorporating student-centred learning in innovation and entrepreneurship education. *European Journal of Education, 43*(4), 513–526. Wiley, UK

Hashmi, G. (2017) Redefining the essence of sustainable luxury management: The slow value creation model. In Gardetti, M. A (Ed.), *Sustainable Management of Luxury* (pp. 3–28). Springer Nature, UK.

Johnson, S. (2000). Literature review on social entrepreneurship. *Canadian Centre for Social Entrepreneurship*, University of Alberta School of Business, Canada

Jorna, R. (2006). *Sustainable Innovation. The Organizational, Human and Knowledge Dimension*. Greenleaf Publishing, UK.

Julien, P.A., & Marchesnay, M. (1996). *L'entrepreneuriat*. Economica colection. Gestion poche.

Knight, G. A. (1997). Cross cultural reliability and validity of a scale of measure firm entrepreneurial orientation. *Journal of Business Venturing, 12*, 213–225. Elsevier, The Netherlands

Kobia, M., & Sikalieh, D. (2010). Towards a search for the meaning of entrepreneurship. *Journal of European Industrial Training, 34*(2), 110–127. Emerald Insight, UK

Lawn, P. (2012). The economics of sustainable development. In G. Moscardo, G. Lamberton, G. Wells, W. Fallon, P. Lawn, A. Rowe, J. Humphrey, R. Wiesner, R. Pettitt, B. Clifton, D. Renouf, & W. Kershaw (Eds.), *Sustainability in Australian Business* (pp. 99–132). Wiley & Sons.

Li, L., Tse, E., & Zhao, J. (2009). An empirical study of corporate entrepreneurship in hospitality companies. *International Journal of Hospitality & Tourism Administration, 10*(3), 213–231. Taylor & Francis, UK

Mair, J., & Marti, I. (2006). Social entrepreneurship research: A source of explanation, prediction, and delight. *Journal of World Business, 41*(1), 36–44. Elsevier, Tne Netherlands

Mair, J., Robinson, J., & Hockerts, K. (2006). *Social Entrepreneurship*. Palgrave Macmillan, UK

Margolis, J. D., & Walsh, J. P. (2003). Misery loves companies: Rethinking social initiatives by business. *Administrative Science Quarterly, 48*, 268–305. SAGE Journals, UK

Markides, C., & Gerosky, P. (2005). *Fast Second. How Smart Companies Bypass Radical Innovation to Enter and Dominate New Markets*. Jossey-Bass USA

Martin, R. L., & Osberg, S. (2007). *Social Entrepreneurship: The Case for Definition*. Stanford Social Innovation Review, USA.

Meadows, D., Randers, J., & Meadows, D. (2004). *Limits to Growth: The 30-Year Update*. Chelsea Green Publishing, UK.

Mohsin, A., & Lockyer, T. (2010). Customer Perceptions of service quality in luxury hotels in New Delhi, India: An exploratory study. *International Journal of Contemporary Hospitality Management, 22*(2), 160–173. Taylor & Francis, UK

Morgan, J. (2011). Leading by nature. In J. Marshall, G. Coleman, & P. Reason (Eds.), *Leadership for Sustainability: An Action Research Approach* (pp. 148–153). Greenleaf Publishing, UK

Mort, G. S., Weerawardena, J., & Carnegie, K. (2003, February). Social entrepreneurship: Towards conceptualization. *International Journal of Nonprofit and Voluntary Sector Marketing, 8*(1), 76–88. Wiley, UK

Moscardo, G. (2017). Sustainable luxury in hotels and resorts: Is it possible? In M. A. Gardetti (Ed.), *Sustainable Management of Luxury*. Springer Nature, UK.

Moscardo, G., & Benckendorff, P. (2010). Sustainable Luxury: Oxymoron or comfortable bedfellows. In *Proceedings of the 2010 International Tourism Conference on Global Sustainable Tourism*.p. 709–728 Mbombela: Nelspruit South Africa.

Moufakkir, O., & Burns, P. M. (2012). Introduction. In O. Mouffakir & P. Burns (Eds.), *Controversies in Tourism*. CABI Publishing, UK

Munoz, M. J. (2009). Social entrepreneurship in China: Trends and strategic implications. *Buletinul, 61*(2), 1–12.

Muro, A. T. (2005). Responsabilidad social y corporativa y acción social: diferencias y relación con la estrategia de negocios y la cultura operativa. In Gardetti (Ed.) *Textos en Sustentabilidad Empresarial Integrando las Consideraciones Sociales, Ambientales y Económicas en el corto y largo plazo*. p. 109–128 LA-Bell, Buenos Aires

Nahapiet, J., & Ghoshal, S. (1998). Social capital, intellectual capital, and the organizational advantage. *The Academy of Management Review, 23*(2), 242–266. AOM, USA

Newbert, S. L. (2003). Realizing the spirit and impact of Adam Smith's capitalism through entrepreneurship. *Journal of Business Ethics, 46*, 251–161. Springer, UK

Olsen, M. A., & Mykletun, R. J. (2012). *Entrepretality: Entrepreneurship Education in the Hospitality Industry*. http://scholarship.sha.cornell.edu/articles/35

Overholt, A., Dahle, C., & Canabou, C., (2004). Social capitalists. *Fast Company, 78*, 45–57.

Park, K. S., & Reisinger, Y. (2009). Cultural differences in shopping for luxury goods: Western Asian and Hispanic tourists. *Journal of Travel Tourism Marketing, 26*(8), 762–777. Taylor & Francis, UK

Peredo, A. M., & McLean, M. (2006). Social entrepreneurship: A critical review of the concept. *Journal of World Business, 41*(1), 56–65. Elsevier, The Netherlands

Poelina, A., & Nordensvard, J. (2018). Sustainable luxury tourism, indigenous communities and governance. In M. A. Gardetti and S. S. Muthu (Eds.), *Sustainable Luxury, Entrepreneurship and Innovation, Environmental Footprints and Eco-design of Products and Processes* (pp. 147–166). Springer, UK

Quariel, F., & Auberger, M. N. (2005). Management responsible et PME: une relecture du concept de "responsabilité sociétale de l'enterprise". *Revue des Sciences de Gestion: Direction et Gestion, 40*(211/212), 111–126. Revue des Sciences de Gestion, France

Robbins, D., & Gaczorek J. (2015). Luxury and sustainability in tourism accommodation—an exploration of how to reconcile apparently incompatible objectives using a case study approach. In: Proceedings of the BESTEN Think Tank XV *The Environment-People Nexus in Sustainable Tourism: Finding the Balance* (pp. 166–186). Kruger National Park, South Africa.

Roberts, D., & Woods, C. (2005). Changing the world on a shoestring: The concept of social entrepreneurship. *University of Auckland Business Review*, 45–51. University of Auckland, Australia.

Schaltegger, S., & Wagner, M. (2008). Types of sustainable entrepreneurship and conditions for sustainability innovation: From the administration of a technical challenge to the management of an entrepreneurial opportunity. In R. Wüstenhagen, J.

Hamschmidt, S. Sharma, & M. Starik (Eds.), *Sustainable Innovation and Entrepreneurship. New Perspectives in Research on Corporate Sustainability series* (pp. 27–48). Edward Elgar Publishing, UK.

Scheyvens, R. (2007). Poor cousins no more: valuing the development potential of domestic and diaspora tourism. *Progress in Development Studies, 7*(4), 307–325. SAGE Journals, UK

Schuyler, G. (1998). Social entrepreneurship: Profit as a means, not an end. *CELCEE: Kauffman Centre for Entrepreneurial Leadership Clearing House on Entrepreneurial Education, 98*(7). P. 1–4

Seidman, D. (2007). *How We Do Anything Means Everything*. John Wiley & Sons.

Sewell, P., & Pool, L. (2010). Moving from conceptual ambiguity to operational clarity: employability, enterprise and entrepreneurship in higher education. *Education & Training, 52*(1), 89–94. Emerald Insight, UK.

Shivdasani, S. (2016) Soneva Thailand. In M. A. Gardetti & M. E. Girón (Eds.), *Sustainable Luxury and Social Entrepreneurship. More Stories from the Pioneers* (pp. 139–159) Greenleaf Publishing, UK.

Shumpeter, J. A. (1961). *The Theory of Economic Development*. Harvard University Press, USA.

Soneva. (2018). http://www.soneva.com/slow-life.

Spence, M., Boubaker Gherib, J. B., & Biwolé (2008). V. O. A framework of SMEs' strategic involvement in sustainable development. In R. Wüstenhagen, J. Hamschmidt, J., S. Sharma, & M. Starik (Eds.), *Sustainable Innovation and Entrepreneurship* (pp. 49–70) Edward Elgar Pubblishing, UK.

Stevenson, H. H., & Jarillo, J. C. (1990). A paradigm of entrepreneurship: Entrepreneurial management. *Strategic Management Journal, 11*, 11–28. Wiley, UK

Sustainable Enterprise Academy. (2002). *Business Leader Seminar's Report*. York University, Canada.

Sustainable Enterprise Academy. (2003). *Business Leader Seminar's Report*. York University, Canada.

Thompson, J. (2002). The world of the social entrepreneur. *The International Journal of Public Sector Management, 15*(5), 412–431. Emerald Insight, UK

Thompson, J., Alvy, G., & Lees, A. (2000). Social entrepreneurship—a new look at the people and the potential. *Management Decision, 38*(5), 328. Emerald Insight, UK

Tilley, F., & Young, W. (2009). Sustainability entrepreneurs: Could they be the true wealth generators of the future? *Greener Management International, 55*, 79–92. Greenleaf Publishing, UK

Tynan, C., Mckechnie, S., & Chhuon, C. (2010). Co-create value for luxury brands. *Journal of Business Research, 63*(11), 1156–1163. Elsevier, The Netherlands

Verstraete, T., & Fayolle, A. (2005). Paradigmes et entrepreneuriat, *Revue de l'entreprenuriat, 4*(5), 33–52. l'Académie de l'Entrepreneuriat et de l'Innovation, France

Wagner, M. (2012) Entrepreneurship, innovation and sustainability. An introduction and overview. In M. Wagner (Ed.), *Entrepreneurship, Innovation and Sustainability*. Greenleaf Publishing, UK.

Wang, Y., & Wall, G. (2007). Administrative arrangements and displacement compensation in top downtourism planning—a case from Hainan Province, China, *Tourism Management, 28*(1), 70–82. Elsevier, The Netherlands

Weinstein, J. (2010). Green luxury no oxymoron. *Hotels, 44*(2), 30.

Wennekers, S., & Thurik, R. (1999). Linking entrepreneurship and economic growth. *Small Business Economics, 13*, 27–55.

Wheeler, D., Colbert, B., & Freeman, R. E. (2003). Focusing on value: Reconciling corporate social responsibility, sustainability and a stakeholder approach in a network world. *Journal of General Management, 28*(3), 1–28. SAGE Insights, UK

Wiedmann, K.-P., Hennigs, N., & Siebels, A. (2009). Value-based segmentation of luxury consumption behavior. *Psychology & Marketing, 26*(7). 625–651. Wiley, UK

World Travel & Tourism Council. (2016). Goals and targets. In *Environmental, social, & governance reporting in travel & tourism* (pp. 11–14). World Travel & Tourism Council.

Wüstenhagen, R., Sharma, S., Starik, M., & Wuebker, R. (2008). Sustainability, innovation and entrepreneurship: Introduction to the volume. In R. Wüstenhagen, J. Hamschmidt, S. Sharma, & M. Starik (Eds.), *Sustainable Innovation and Entrepreneurship* (pp. 1–23). Edward Elgar Publishing, UK.

Yeoman, I., & McMahon-Beattle, U. (2006) Luxury markets and premium pricing. *Journal of Revenue & Pricing Management, 4*(4), 319–328. Palgrave McMillan, UK

Young, W., & Tilley, F. (2006). Can business move beyond efficiency? The shift toward effectiveness and equity in the corporate sustainability debate. *Business Strategy and the Environment, 16*(6), 402–415. Wiley, UK

Chapter 7

Hospitality and tourism as natural agents of social change

This chapter examines trends and changes in the hospitality and tourism markets in relation to social entrepreneurship. It opens with a discussion on the role of hospitality and tourism in developing tourism destinations. The chapter also discusses the role and responsibilities of larger corporate players in achieving change even if this sector is not usually considered within the social entrepreneur realm.

The chapter concludes with an evaluation of the enhanced role of hospitality in tackling global societal and environmental problems. A set of additional exercises is provided at the end of the chapter, which are based on individual or group research and discussions.

The chapter closes with two case studies: (1) Thinking Outside of the Box for Community and Business Sustainability: A Case Study of Nomad Lodges and (2) "Le Marche in Valigia" ("Le Marche in a suitcase"): a community-based, experiential tourism venture.

Introduction

Peter Drucker, author and management consultant, once wrote that "to survive and succeed, every organization will have to turn itself into a change agent" (2001, p. 19). The world is faced with many enormous challenges, not least of which is climate change, along with increasing polarity of incomes and inequality (Sheldon & Danielle, 2017). Change agents are desperately needed.

Social entrepreneurship and the development of tourism markets

For many years, it has been claimed that tourism may provide some alternatives to the need for extractive and environmentally destructive industries and, with the correct tools, provide meaningful, well-paid jobs and social and environmental value through such methods as pro-poor tourism and community-based tourism (Scaglione, Marx, & Johnson, 2010).

The exponential growth and economic impact of hospitality and tourism is well documented with an increase from 25 million international tourists in 1950 to over 1.42 billion by 2018 (UNWTO, 2018; World Bank, 2020). If domestic tourism is included in this, the figures are even more manifest, with domestic tourism being estimated in the region of 8 billion tourists annually (Sheldon & Danielle, 2017). However, the 2020 COVID-19 pandemic has put a halt to this continuous growth, bringing the total international arrivals for the year back to 2012 levels, at around a billion arrivals (at the time of book completion in May 2020) (UNWTO, 2020). Most experts argue for a strong industry resilience.

On the supply side, there has been both a consolidation and a concentration in the number of hospitality chains as can be seen in Table 7.1. A similar consolidation and concentration has taken place in the airline industry as well.

As may be noted, Marriott today has almost double the number of rooms of the top operator in 2000 (Cendant) and almost five times the number of rooms of the top operator in 1975, Holiday Inn (Johnson, 2002a).

There has also been considerable disruption in the industry through the so-called 'sharing economy', with room sharing platforms of the Airbnb type rising in competitiveness in the traditional hotel sector and at the same time causing significant problems to many cities. The effects of such platforms have been felt especially in Europe, where the opportunity for opening up previous privately-owned rooms to tourists has been increasingly viewed as a negative force by city officials due to over-tourism and gentrification.

These are complex problems and include wider, non-tourism issues, as outlined by Koens, Postas, and Papp (2016).

Historical development of social entrepreneurship in hospitality and tourism and definition of a tourism social enterprise

Although the name of Thomas Cook was at one point synonymous with travel, a less widely known fact is that he was a social entrepreneur who believed strongly in the power of travel "for the …advancement of Human Progress" (Turner and Ash as quoted in Higgins-Desboiles [2006, p. 1193]) The first "father of modern mass tourism" started his tour operator and travel agency business with short train

Table 7.1 Comparison of leading hotel companies, 1975–2018, by number of rooms.

Rank	1975 Company	Rooms	2000 Company	Rooms	2018 Company	Rooms
1	Holiday Inn	274,969	Cendant Corp	548,641	Marriott Int'l	1,254,805
2	Sheraton corp.	109,999	Bass Hotels & resorts	496,005	Hilton Worldwide	870,982
3	Ramada Inns. Inc.	94,621	Marriott Int'l	404,792	InterContinental Hotel Group	799,923
4	Hilton Hotel Corp.	61,621	Accor	389,437	Wyndham Hotel Group	792,331
5	Trust House Forte	60,705	Choice Hotels Int'l	349,392	Choice Hotel Int'l	554,798
6	Howard Johnson	59,800	Hilton Hotel Corp.	314,628	Best Western Hotels & Resorts	294,851
7	Balkantourist	51,800	Starwood Hotels	215,207	Hyatt Hotel Corp	191,575
8	Days Inn Inc.	37,983	Carlson (Radisson/SAS)	119,710	Radisson Hotel Group	179,367
9	Quality Inns Int'l	32,954	Hyatt	87,969	G6 Hospitality	125,529
10	Travel Lodge Int'l	31,492	Sol Melia	82,733	Magnusson Hotels	101,306

Source: Johnson (2002a) and Statistica (2020).

journeys within England that developed later into international tours to India, Egypt and the Middle East. Cook was quick to see the potential of the development of a travel market due to increasing prosperity, urbanisation and leisure time.

Although the success of Cook's early excursions is well documented, the fact that he had an extensive social agenda underpinning his work is often under-reported. He believed that "excursionism", as he called it, could act as an agent of democratisation (ibid).

Often hospitality and tourism are regarded as one 'industry' but some earlier writers have disputed this label: A respected tourism researcher opined that tourism is "a social/economic phenomenon that acts both as an engine of economic progress and a social force" (Krippendorf, 1994, quoted in Freya-Desboiles, 2006, p. 1204). He viewed tourism as more than an industry, rather as a sector. We may, in fact call tourism an 'industry of industries', like the automotive sector.

Definition of a social tourism enterprise

Historically, hotel companies often developed internationally by building high-end hotels in primary destinations. This too-often resulted in "an island of prosperity in a sea of poverty" (Johnson, 2002a). Over the course of the past three decades, hospitality companies have focused more on working with local communities and changing that perception. The aspirational need for equity in the industry may be seen as long ago as the 1980s with the Manila Declaration (Freya-Desboiles, 2006), which claimed that the "ultimate aim is the improvement of the quality of life and the creation of better living conditions for all peoples" (WTO, 1980, p. 1).

Sheldon and Danielle (2017) articulated a definition of a social tourism enterprise:

> A process that uses tourism to create innovative solutions to immediate social, environmental and economic problems in destinations by mobilizing the ideas, capacities, resources and social agreements from within or outside the destination, required for its sustainable social transformation.
>
> (p. 7)

This may be considered an excellent definition as it deals with the aspect of the longevity/sustainability of the impact, with the main goal being improving the destination's environmental, social and economic factors.

Suitability of hospitality and tourism for social entrepreneurship

Although there have been increasingly negative images of tourism ills in both the popular media and academic press, tourism may still be regarded as a major factor in social value-creation (Sigala, 2016) and tourism entrepreneurship can lead to social change (de Lange & Dodds, 2017). Indeed, tourism can act as a social force that serves human development through a wider vision of its role in global community; moreover, social enterprises in tourism may empower local communities, support sustainable regional development and improve the social capital and quality of communities by promoting a sustainable lifestyle and food provision, even in developed economies. "However[,] social enterprises are particularly important in the context of developing economies that government institutions do not sufficiently do enough to support entrepreneurial activity in the tourism sector" (Altinay, Sigala, & Waligo, 2016, p. 405). Lombardi (2017) stresses the opportunities and impact of the role of employment in hospitality, travel and tourism. These industries often offer entry-level jobs to youth in developing countries. He quotes that by 2022, travel and tourism will employ 328 million people and will create 73 million new jobs. Many hospitality and tourism corporations are especially seeking to develop brands throughout Asia and Africa, thereby providing young persons with the opportunity of employment and careers. Companies that incorporate youth development into their business models through investments in pre-employment training and on-the-job professional development help attract to and retain young people in the industry. In a model that is symbiotic, by offering young people employment that has an upward trajectory, hospitality and tourism companies are fulfilling their labour needs for the future. This is one of the main reasons that corporations such as Marriott and Hilton stress youth training programs, apprenticeships and internships.

On a macro scale, de Lange and Dodds (2017) view social enterprises (used synonymously with social entrepreneurship) as playing an important role in sustainable tourism in the following ways:

1. Through the development of new, innovative enterprises – this grows the sector by giving more options to tourists;
2. This, in turn, may increase competitive pressures on existing firms;
3. Social tourism enterprises may also serve to create a base for other, more profitable activities in the community (for example in the Turkish olive oil enterprise case study presented in Chapter 3, local employment was provided not just in making high-quality olive oil, but also in pottery, making and food and beverage provision within the village's economy).
4. Tourism social enterprises may help in the expedition and enactment of environmental and social regulations by offering special expertise, goods and services that existing companies may struggle to meet. "New start-ups may accelerate the sustainability of the industry while supporting new government regulations" (p. 1984).
5. Tourism social enterprises may promote local economic development and thereby attract attention from international companies. These forces result in the existing tourism industry becoming more sustainable.

Sigala (2016) gives specific examples of how Tourism Social Enterprises work in different sectors of the industry including:

- Social festivals (responsible social identity construction)
- Heritage sites (responsible re-enactment of history)
- Restaurants (social way of food production & provision)
- Accommodation (supporting community development and equal entrepreneurial activities
- Social sports tourism (fostering lifestyle values and wellbeing)
- Souvenirs/community involvement (to enable community development) – enterprises may be seen as ideal vehicles for social change (location, investment, facilities).

The concept of social entrepreneurship (SE) has been reinforced by leaders in the industry actively spearheading SE philosophies and projects. One such example is Jonathan Tisch, the CEO of a major hotel corporation (Loews Hotels). Tisch has written two books on the subject of community service and civic SE – *The power of we-succeeding through partnerships* (2004) and *Citizen you: How social entrepreneurs are changing the world* (2011). In many ways, it may be seen that hospitality and tourism organisations offer an excellent fit for SE and that it can play a role in increasing sustainable tourism (de Lange & Dodds, 2017).

Importantly, social tourism can be key in developing countries that may be constrained by a lack of governmental entrepreneurial support and extremely limited resources (Sigala, 2016). Looking at the related field of social innovation, Kohler and Chesbrough (2019) have been researching the role of platforms in crowdsourcing for a unique model of tourism social enterprise.

Their example provides a framework for creating crowdsourcing platforms for social innovation. The example of travel2change.org, which refined their four prototype social programs in tourism, is a very effective model. Important steps in the process are to: define the value unit (this could be ideas, products, services or designs); identify the platform actors (these could include tour operators, travel agents and local community leaders); inspire creation (an example could be cleaning a beach or trail, etc.) and combine the mechanisms that drive users and finally to ensure curation (guarantee both the quality and quantity of the value unit). The mechanism may be social, algorithmic or editorial to make sure that the platform finds the 'sweet spot' between the different stakeholders.

Major hospitality corporations often display signs of SE that take the form of linkages with the environment and/or with the local community in which the property is located. This may be seen in efforts to reduce environmental impact through sustainability initiatives, including reduction of single use plastics, reducing food waste, and energy management systems.

There have been a number of academic evaluations of international hotel chains' initiatives related to sustainability including Scandic hotels, Fairmont hotels and resorts (Johnson, 2002b) and the Fair Hotels scheme. Ergul and Johnson (2011) found that half their hotel manager respondents applied principles of sustainability to confront negative attention received by the industry. This leads to a discussion of the role of social 'intrapreneurs' who are concerned with creating social and sustainable value within already existing organisations.

Corporate hospitality: displaying signs of social entrepreneurship

As stated previously, many initiatives have been tied in with environmental protection and sustainability (often as cost-saving measures on the part of the hotel corporations). Increasingly, however, there are also efforts to partner with local communities.

Several leading hospitality companies are paying attention to sustainability and the triple bottom line approach (TBL). Three major hospitality corporations that stress social and environmental considerations (Marriott, Hilton and Accor) align their company goals with the UN Sustainable Development Goals (SDGs) and the 2025 Sustainability and Social Impact Goals.

Overall all three major chains have names for their schemes that serve to anchor them in the mind of employees and customers: "Nurture our planet" (Marriott), "Travel with purpose" (Hilton) and "Acting every day for Positive Hospitality" (Accor).

There are several major themes common to the groups; Marriott stresses the need to do more and Accor stresses that the need is urgent.

The different areas of interest may be divided into community involvement (including emergency aid relief after disasters), reduction of environmental impact through sustainable hotel operations and employment opportunities (especially related to diversity, youth, women and refugees).

Accor

Accor may be considered one of the forerunners of combining environmental factors with other elements. The company was the first major hotel chain to advance environmental action dating back over twenty-five years, when it became the first major hospitality corporation to establish an environmental department (1994).

Just over a decade later, in 2005, they produced online tools to manage energy and water consumption, which evolved into a product named 'Gaia' by 2016. Gaia now enables hotels to carry out self-assessments, shares information and aligns with objectives. In 2011 Accor started Planet 21, with a four-tier ranking system that was repurposed with new objectives from 2016 to 2020. The company now has "Planet 21 in Action", which involves employees, customers, buildings, food, communities and business partners.

Marriott

Marriott also stresses its commitment to the environment and the community through a number of themes, including "Nurture our world" and "Serve our world" along with "Empowering through opportunity", and by sustaining responsible operations.

The first two emphasise making communities better places to live, work and visit, in terms of community engagement, volunteering, and doing good. The "Empowering through opportunity" theme stresses Marriott's role in addressing unemployment and underemployment, especially for some of society's most affected groups, including youth, women, people with disabilities, veterans and refugees. Responsible operations for hospitality enterprises are fostered through integrating sustainability into the value chain, thereby attempting to mitigate some of the effects of climate change. Many of the goals tie in with the Millennium Development Goals (MDG).

For example, there is a goal of:

> By 2025, invest at least $5M to increase and deepen programs and partnerships that develop hospitality skills and opportunity among youth, diverse populations, women, people with disabilities, veterans and refugees. This ties back to MDG numbers 4, 5, 8, 10, 16, 17.

Hilton

Hilton's scheme is known as "Travel with purpose", which is the company's Corporate Social Responsibility strategy. The company states that they will double their investment in social impact and reduce their environmental footprint by 50% by 2030. It will be interesting to see if they meet these objectives. Comparable to Accor's digital sustainability tracking system, Gaia, Hilton has developed 'Lightstay' for over 5600 of their hotels. Hilton also has a number of specific goals that align with the SDGs and Millennium Development Goals. As with Marriott, Hilton stresses the role that the company can play in employment through such schemes as apprenticeships, internships, education and training, etc.

Some selected goals from the company website may be seen in Table 7.2.

Table 7.2 Goals and progress of Hilton

Goal + Progress	Notes
Adopt a global standard for responsible travel and tourism, complementing our existing environmental certifications	Our entire portfolio of more than 5,600 hotels is certified to ISO 9001 (Quality Management), ISO 14001 (Environmental Management) and ISO 50001 (Energy Management), the largest ISO certified building portfolio in the world. Hilton is currently evaluating opportunities to adopt a global standard for responsibility
Embed human rights due diligence across our global operations	We embedded human rights due diligence in our Enterprise Risk Management System and new country development review. We have rolled out anti-trafficking training to all of our hotels, including franchise properties, with 68% of General Managers having completed the training module to date.
Reduce Scope 1 and 2 carbon intensity by 61% (GHG emissions/m^2—2008 baseline). Progress: 34% Reduction	In 2018, Hilton became the first major hotel brand to set science-based carbon targets aligned with climate science and the Paris Climate Agreement. Since 2008, we have achieved a 34% reduction in Scope 1 and 2 carbon emissions. All Hilton properties are required to use LightStay to set energy reduction targets in line with our 2030 goals. Hotels are also required to identify a continuous improvement project that will help drive energy conservation, and LightStay measures each hotel's performance and progress. In 2018, Hilton also became the first major hotel brand to join The Climate Group's EP100 initiative by committing to improve our energy productivity in line with our 2030 carbon targets.
Zero soap to landfill by recycling all used guest soap bars where available. Progress: 4,350+ Hotels recyle soaps	More than 4,350 of our 5,600+ properties worldwide recycle soap. We launched a new brand standard in 2018 requiring all Hilton Garden Inn and Hampton by Hilton properties in the United States, Canada, Dominican Republic and Puerto Rico to recycle soap bars and amenity bottles through our soap recycling partner, Clean the World. We also expanded soap recycling to all properties in India in partnership with Sundara.

(Continued)

(Continued)

Goal + Progress	Notes
Reduce food waste sent to landfill by 50% in our managed operations (2017 baseline)	Through our partnership with the World Wildlife Fund, we established our food waste baseline and launched a new food waste reduction program in the Americas. We will expand this food waste program globally and collaborate with our Team Members to adapt it locally.
Double our investment in programs that contribute to sustainable solutions and economic opportunity for all (e.g. women, veterans, persons with disabilities, etc.—2017 baseline	In 2018, Hilton announced an initial investment of $1 million to drive sustainable travel and tourism in Africa. We also joined the Tent Partnership for Refugees, pledging to impact 16,000 refugees by 2030 by providing hospitality skills training, in-kind donations and volunteer hours to refugee organizations, and offering employment opportunities. We partner with Project SEARCH, a training and education program for individuals with developmental disabilities, and have graduated 355 students from the program since 2013, employing 107 of them and maintaining a turnover rate of 19% over a five-year period. See our Inclusive Growth fact sheet for more information
Train employees at Hilton managed hotels on relevant environmental and social issues and engage guests in supporting responsible travel in destination hot spots	In 2018, we continued to evaluate and evolve our trainings to empower our Team Members to be responsible social and environmental stewards. Through on-property pilots, we are also working to identify natural opportunities to engage our guests around sustainable travel. We require or encourage the following trainings for Team Members, and will continue to expand upon this framework for the future: Preventing Human Trafficking (mandatory for all General Managers), Responsible Sourcing (mandatory for all Supply Management), Sustainable Seafood (mandatory for Supply Management and Food & Beverage Leaders of managed properties) and LightStay[a] (mandatory for all General Managers and Chief Engineers).

Source: Hilton Environmental Impact, available at: https://cr.hilton.com/environment.

a LightStay is Hilton's corporate responsibility measurement platform that measures hotels' environmental and social impact.

Altinay et al. (2015) make the point that although there are many studies on hospitality and tourism that underscore creativity, innovation and entrepreneurship in the industries, the social element has been neglected. They give an example of a case study of Guludo Beach Lodge (GBL), a tourist/visitor accommodation facility in Mozambique on the south-eastern coast of Africa. The lodge operates alongside and invests in the Nema Foundation that is its associated charity (which receives 5% of the lodge's revenues, but also fundraises inde pendently, e.g., through donations from guests). The Foundation seeks to identify and tackle the root causes of poverty and environmental devastation in specific communities. "The aim of both organisations is to bring benefits to the local area at a minimum environmental, developmental and operational cost" (GBL/NEMA founder). The combination of its economic and social goals, including a clear commitment to the social purpose, renders this organisation a social enterprise.

Criticisms of traditional hospitality and tourism development

There is a more than a little irony in the fact that many of the ills of the industry are due to the travel agencies and packaged tours that followed on from Cook's work.

Tourism was initially regarded as a cleaner and greener alternative to the smokestack and extractive industries seen to be polluting and destructive to the environment.

More recently, the total effects of tourism on physical, social and cultural environments has become more obvious and green tourism, ecotourism and conscious tourism have been the subjects of both tourism promotion and academic research.

Criticisms of the 'traditional' development of hospitality and tourism include the fact that much of the financing in the industries are often from home markets, with resultant major leakages to the local economy (it has been estimated, for example, that in all-inclusive resorts, 95% of every tourist dollar is actually spent outside of the local economies, providing little economic benefit to the local community (Sheldon & Danielle, 2017)). In addition, although hospitality enterprises are often major employers, the industry has suffered from a reputation of long and unsociable hours, low pay, above-average instances of harassment in the workplace and stressful and irregular work conditions.

Hospitality and tourism enterprises were able to amass profits due to the benefits of low labour costs and not paying their fair share in terms of environmental pollution and over-usage of natural resources. In many, if not most, destinations modern tourism has been synonymous with price-based strategies, resulting in undifferentiated mass tourism markets (Sheldon & Danielle, 2017), with the only thing changing being the major generating country (from western Europe in the 1970s to Japan in the 1980s to China in the 1990s).

These criticisms of tourism development are taken even further by Hall (2017), who maintains that travel and tourism have been subject of 'green washing' to a large extent.

174 HOSPITALITY, TOURISM AND SOCIAL CHANGE

Hall argues that the concept of 'green growth' and the promotion of tourism and the 'green economy' has perhaps developed part of the orthodoxy of sustainable tourism. He, therefore, concludes that efficiency and market-based approaches are only a small component of what is required in reducing tourism's environmental impacts and instead posits the need for degrowth and a sufficiency-based approach.

Conclusion

There is an urgent need to change from the demand side model because it is outstripping the planet's ability to replace and renew natural and cultural resources. Examples of over-tourism in both environmental and human terms are well documented, including many of the major cities in Europe (Barcelona, Venice and Amsterdam) and worldwide (e.g., Big Sur, California; Mount Everest and elsewhere). The 2020 pandemic has put a stop to much of international tourism, however, it is expected that those destinations will continue to attract a large number of tourists once the situation returns to normal. But 'normal' needs to be reassessed when it comes to tourism development.

Whilst accepting the data that underpins these examples, an alternative view to the cynical exploitation of green washing may be seen. Indeed, there is

> pressure on tourism and hospitality companies to be more responsible socially and environmentally is growing rapidly. Members of both the boomer and millennial generations - the two primary sources of consumer spending power - are increasingly aware of the impact of their travels to host communities.
> (Sheldon & Danielle, 2017, p. 8)

CHAPTER CASE 7.1

Thinking outside of the box for community and business sustainability: a case study of Nomad Lodges

(Source: The Long Run; Nomad Lodges, www.nomadlodges.com)

Synopsis

This case study illustrates how working closely with the community, stakeholders and outsiders can foster innovation to develop sustainable tourism projects that truly respect the ways of life of local communities. By keeping an open mind and using a participatory approach and two-way communication, **Nomad Lodges** (Colombia) has designed a different business model that fully integrates with the customs of the Indigenous people that live adjacent to the area where the planned ecolodge is being built (Figure 7.1).

Figure 7.1 Field working with the communities.
(Photo Credit: © Nomad Lodges).

About Nomad Lodges: Amazon project

Nomad Lodges is an ambitious ecotourism project that envisions the development of a network of luxury ecolodges in South America, built in harmony with the environment. Nomad Lodges Amazonas is the first of these; the planning phase started in June 2014 and it is expected to open in December 2021. Nomad Lodges is located in 500,000 hectares in the Colombian Amazon, bordering Brazil and Peru, within the biodiverse territory of 'Aticoya', an association between the Tikuna, Yagua and Cocama Indigenous communities.

The goal of Nomad Lodges is to design a sustainable project that respects and integrates profoundly with the particular ways of life of the Indigenous communities they are surrounded by, while offering high-quality services that meets guests' expectations.

Challenges

Conventional, and often standardised, 'Western' operating norms, which are implemented to deliver high-quality service, do not fit in with the Indigenous peoples' concept of life, work and time. For the Tikuna, Yagua and Cocama communities, life is about reaching a balance with the environment, and therefore, daily activities are adapted to the rhythm of nature, rather than a 'nine to five' schedule. Fishing, growing crops and working can be influenced by the rain or the moon cycle. Similarly, social activities have a determinant role in the community life. 'Mingas', for example, are a collective activity where all the families reunite to discuss or work on a specific issue and can be summoned with only one or two days' notice. Since participating in Mingas is a priority for community members, work may be postponed to attend or organise these gatherings.

As a result, the major challenge for Nomad Lodges was to find a way to manage the high level of uncertainty and unreliability as well as the availability of mainly unskilled labour within the communities, in order to offer consistent and high-quality service, without changing the dynamics of the communities' way of life and rhythm (Figure 7.2).

Figure 7.2 Monitoring natural and cultural places with local communities. (Photo Credit: © Nomad Lodges).

Solutions implemented

Nomad Lodges adopted the following three approaches as key elements in developing a sustainable project that respects local communities:

HOSPITALITY, TOURISM AND SOCIAL CHANGE 177

PARTICIPATORY PLANNING AND TWO-WAY COMMUNICATION WITH THE COMMUNITY FROM THE START

- Before starting the project, Nomad Lodges took extensive time to get an in-depth understanding of the Indigenous communities' way of life. For forty-five months they sat down with the communities and listened carefully in order to learn and understand their social structures, daily lives and knowledge of the cosmos as a whole.

- The next step was to explain to the communities what the Nomad Lodges concept was all about, along with the benefits it could bring to them and the role that they could play in the success of the project. It was an open two-way communication, as Nomad Lodges equally learnt about people's concerns and interests, while the communities learnt about the project and increasingly identified with it.

- Then, Nomad Lodges discussed with the communities specific issues including the operation of the lodge, conservation of the area and the importance of sustainability in general. It required plenty of time and excellent communication to explain environmentally friendly practices, which were new concepts to the communities, but necessary to ensure sustainability. For example, recycling or adequately disposing waste that did not come from nature, instead of throwing them in the forest as locals would normally do with fruits and vegetables waste.

- Open and informal communication between Nomad Lodges and the communities has been continuous during the four years of planning and development of the project, which has been key to engaging with the community and making them part of the whole process.

CREATING TRAINING AS A SOCIAL ACTIVITY FOR THE COMMUNITY

- Nomad Lodges worked together with the National Learning Service (SENA) to start a tourism and hospitality training programme for the three surrounding communities, which included trainings on customer service, cooking classes, food hygiene, waste management and English, amongst others.

- Trainings are carried out in a similar way to a Minga, a collective activity where everybody in the community works together. It was important to design trainings as a Minga, as this enabled Nomad Lodges involve all members of the community in the project, which provided an equal opportunity for all, not just a few families, to benefit from it. This, in turn, avoids jealousy and conflicts amongst the members of the communities and their families. In addition, trainings carried out in form of Mingas facilitated the communities' acceptance of the project since it did not require a change in their habits nor did it impose a new way of working, further enhancing the integration of the project with local traditions.

- To organise trainings, Nomad Lodges always have to speak first to the Curaca (Chief) to be able to gather the community and register everyone who is interested in a particular training. Once fifty to sixty people have registered, Nomad Lodges coordinates with a teacher from the SENA to organise the training.

- To support the training, all three – Tikuna, Yagua and Cocama – communities are in charge of food and setting up the classrooms, contributing in some way to the organisation of the sessions. For example, one community would bring vegetables, another fish and another would cook.

- On average, each training lasts for one week. Apart from learning new skills, it also represents an opportunity to spend more time as one community, as well to exchange knowledge between the different peoples.

- Nomad Lodges closely monitors the attendance of the training, as it is key for them that people show continued interest and commitment by attending every class and completing the trainings. Only those community members who are genuinely interested and have confirmed that interest during the trainings will be hired, as they are likely to be more reliable (Figure 7.3).

Figure 7.3 Cultural activity with the younger generation.
(Photo Credit: © Nomad Lodges).

COLLABORATING WITH OUTSIDERS TO CREATE A NEW OPERATING MODEL

- Nomad Lodges worked in collaboration with young and motivated students from the Ecole Hôtelière de Lausanne (Switzerland) for eight weeks in order to find an innovative business model that allowed Nomad Lodges Amazonas to achieve international quality and service standards, while respecting the harmony of Indigenous activities and traditions with nature.

- Nomad Lodges decided to work with students because, unlike CEOs or general managers, their ideas are not influenced by previous experiences. Not ignoring that feedback from experts is valuable and can be used as a point of reference, for Nomad Lodges it was important to have a fresh and relatively unbiased point of view since they wanted to develop a completely new concept.

- The 'outside of box' model developed is based on a flexible organisation with a high level of rotation among staff and management. Since Indigenous people are not used to long-term jobs, but rather work on a 'mission', Nomad Lodges will assign a person to a specific job for one or two days, after which they will rotate to another person who has the same capacities and acquired the same skills through the training scheme. Similarly, if one community summons a Minga with short notice, Nomad Lodges can quickly replace staff with people from any of the other two communities.

- To ensure the success of the model, extensive training and motivation were identified as key elements to ensure that sufficient qualified staff will be available for rotation without jeopardising the quality of the service Nomad Lodges wants to provide.

- The model also envisions a 'puzzle-like' structure for managerial positions. Nomad Lodges aims to retain a general manager for one year, but is preparing for shorter periods of time as well. After the first three to four months, a person will be assigned to assist the general manager in every managerial aspect. In case the general manager was to leave, the assistant should have acquired sufficient knowledge of the operation in order to replace him or her or to train a new one.

- In addition, for managerial positions, Nomad Lodges will seek out outstanding young hospitality professionals from abroad, who are motivated, open minded, capable of understanding and adapting to a continuously changing environment and are happy to live in remote areas. Motivation and a desire for a unique experience are the key elements that Nomad Lodges will seek in its future managers. These same values and motivations will be essential for the general manager and chef, although they will need to have more years of experience. Local people will have the opportunity to land managerial positions if they wish to do so in the long term.

- Nomad Lodges will continue its collaboration with the Ecole Hôtelière de Lausanne (Switzerland) by incorporating students aged between twenty-two and twenty-four years, as trainees into the lodge for a period of three to six months, and graduates, who are on average over twenty-four years, will be considered for managerial positions.

Positive impacts

- Preserves local traditions and cultures by respecting their ways of living and habits.
- Increases employment and revenues for local communities, helping them become economically independent. The high rotation and equal opportunities to participate in the project results in more jobs and equal benefits for all members. [Highlight: 340–360 people trained to date.]
- Empowers communities to defend and protect their land from external pressures to extract natural resources in unsustainable ways, by reducing dependence on subsidies and, hence, becoming less prone to manipulation. Also, increasing awareness amongst the communities of the value of the natural and cultural heritage for the tourism business, empowering communities to conserve their territories and traditions for the next generation.
- Increased awareness of illegal activities on the land owned by the communities.
- Increased motivation amongst local teenagers to stay in the region.
- Foster good relations between different Indigenous communities, which can increase collaboration and governance over the territory.
- High engagement and strong relationships with local communities increases the probability of business success and sustainability in the long term.

Downsides

- Developing an innovative and sustainable project has been a long process, which required more time and money investments compared to other conventional projects.

Lessons learned

- Innovative ways of doing business must be designed to respect and align with local customs and traditions, instead of imposing conventional or standardised ways of operating. Communities' wellbeing is the priority.
- Interdisciplinary work is crucial for innovation. Asking, listening and co-creating with all stakeholders (e.g., local communities, public institutions and tourists) as well as with people that are not necessarily part of the project (e.g., students and professionals from other industries) is highly advisable to achieve innovative and efficient solutions that can support businesses reaching new and unexpected heights.
- Community engagement is essential to meet social and business sustainability goals. It is key to be open minded to ideas and suggestions, and address concerns of the communities from the beginning of any project and throughout its development, in order to continuously adapt, innovate and improve, thereby creating a mutually beneficial business.
    - High community engagement can be achieved by:
    - Having adequate communication and consultation;
    - Putting in place participatory planning mechanisms that are accessible to the local communities and within the local context;
    - Educating not only the community to develop the skills needed for the business, but also project developers, who should learn from local knowledge and lifestyle;
    - Involving all members of the communities in decision making and developing activities;
    - Collaborating with each other;
- As a backbone of all of the above, respecting the communities in every way.
- Building strong relationships and strong communication channels with the local communities requires openness, transparency and respect for their ancestral knowledge, customs and opinions.
- Mechanisms of communication must be selected and implemented according to the context of local communities.
- Networking across the members of The Long Run inspires and helps building solutions. However, every member should also reflect on the

182 HOSPITALITY, TOURISM AND SOCIAL CHANGE

4Cs (Conservation, Community, Commerce and Culture) with people from outside of the tourism network. This will allow them to use and bring in new knowledge to continuously develop the business and find new creative solutions (Figure 7.4).

Figure 7.4 Organising field working with local authorities. (Photo Credit: © Nomad Lodges).

Being a pioneer in the implementation of a new concept or business model requires a lot of work, time and effort. It is a learning process where mistakes are made and many difficulties are faced along the way. However, those experiences are a fundamental part of building up new knowledge that supports better planning and implementation of the project, and that will facilitate the development of future similar projects. Nomad Lodges started exploring alternative ways of functioning after trying to work futilely in a conventional way with lawyers, engineers, architects and politicians who didn't understand the project.

CHAPTER CASE 7.2

"Le Marche in Valigia" (Le Marche in a Suitcase)

With acknowledgements to Teresa Benetti for background research and information

Context

Le Marche in a Suitcase (LMIS) https://www.turismarche.it/en/projects/le-marche-in-valigia/ is a project created by Roberto Ferretti and the Agritur-Aso Association, which is an European Union-awarded project

Le Marche (the Marches) is a region in north-central Italy that is bordered by its more well-known tourist relatives of Emilignia-Romagna to the north, Abruzzo to the south and Umbria and Tuscany to the west. It is fairly common to say that it is not well known outside of Italy. Twenty years ago, it was said that "some people predict that the Marches will follow the tourist-filled tracks of Tuscany and Umbria" (Automobile Association, 2000, p. 164). The promise of increased tourism has, to a large extent, been unfulfilled, however. Yet the region has a beautiful coastline, exquisite medieval villages and towns, beautiful countryside and genuine, welcoming hospitality. It is home to one of the landmark villages studied in the famous 'Mediterranean diet'. Whilst the region does not have a signature product such as Parma ham or Chianti, the local food and wine is of excellent quality. The region is renowned for high-quality artisanal producers, who make handmade shoes, purses, hats and bags for such designer labels as Gucci and Dolce and Gabbana. As a sign that perhaps the tourist forecast quoted previously from the Automobile Association may begin to bear fruit, Le Marche was ranked number 2 in the Lonely Planet's list of must-see places in 2020.

The region was hit by a series of earthquakes in October 2016 and, four years later, is still struggling to recover.

In an innovative attempt to increase tourism to the region, local entrepreneurs and tourist professionals decided to take matters into their own hands by forming an Association ("Agritur-Aso") in 2009, that included local bed and breakfast owners, vineyards, olive oil farms and other tourist facilities and farms.

Local author, food expert and botanist, Roberto Ferretti was installed as the president and the project "Le Marche in Valigia" ("Le Marche in a Suitcase") was created, with the aim of promoting tourist, agricultural and social development in the region.

The idea of the project stemmed from the request from many satisfied tourists who spent their holidays in the Le Marche region, staying at the Association's facilities, to promote the beauty of the region to their friends back home. Many voluntarily agreed to help and the project started the promotional journey first in Italy, then in Europe and eventually in many other countries all over the world. The idea was therefore formed of bringing the Marche region, "in a suitcase" to showcase the rich cultural, musical and gastronomic heritage of the region.

Mission

The mission of LMIS is to encourage people around the world to become familiar with the Le Marche region through 'relationship tourism'. The philosophy behind the project is sustainable tourism based on the development of relationships, experiences and intercultural exchanges. In this context, the exchange of products and hospitality is not merely seen as a commercial transaction, but involves the establishment of personal relationships, ultimately creating a rewarding and positive experience for all who are involved.

This project was made possible with the contribution of local farmers, wine makers, olive oil producers, local food and beverage suppliers, who entered into the project and whose products are used and on display during those events. Their collaboration was encouraged by their trust with the Agritur-Aso association and, when possible, stakeholders are included in the delegation during some events.

Involvement in the project and contributions:

The composition of the delegation of LMIS varies, however, it invariably includes the initial person who has contacts with the location where the event is organised, in Italy or abroad. There will be a delegation from Le Marche who present a series of events and dinners. The dinners will include information on local food and culture, some audience participation in making some of the dishes from scratch, and the service of a set menu composed of local food from the region. During the course of the meal, there may be an olive oil tasting and an Italian opera singer will sing famous pieces to the audience. It makes for a unique, authentic and magical evening.

The initiative is self-funded by those who organise the events and there is no public funding.

Some events are financed by personal contributions to supplement the contributions of all participants. In order to organise these events, a strong motivation is required to play a role as a 'voluntary ambassador' of the region, based on the love for the territory and a desire to learn and meet people from other cultures, not based only on economic return.

The project has been active for ten years and the achievements can be summarised by some observational data (personal estimates by Roberto Ferretti).

There have been organised events in fifty-seven locations in fifteen countries (Slovakia, Belgium, France, Poland, UK, Malta, Germany, Slovenia, Croatia, Denmark, Italy, Japan, Australia, USA and Sweden) and four continents. Over 8000 participants have attended the events, each of which typically lasts around three hours. Between 10 and 50% of the participants in each event have visited Le Marche in the following years and have stayed in one of the accommodations listed during the events.

These tourists often brought their partners or family along, or came in small (seven to sixteen participants) or large groups (up to forty to fifty people). When a group decided to visit the region after participating in one of the events, they benefitted from promotional initiatives to facilitate their trip. A popular incentive offered by Agritur-Aso was to offer each member of the group fixed-price accommodation in several locations, as individual bed and breakfast or country houses did not have the capacity to accommodate the whole group. This is called 'albergo diffuso', or 'diffused hotel', wherein the hotel is not one building with all of the rooms, but rather several properties offering the same price and similar facilities.

Around 98% of the tourists who have visited the region through this project are first-time visitors, even though many of them have visited Italy several times. One example is that after the event in Malta, a progressively increasing number of groups of tourists, comprising parties of up to fifty people, have visited each year since 2016: In the first year one group visited, in the second year two groups and in the third year three groups of fifty people visited the region, staying in the local facilities for four to seven days. In 2019, two small groups of seven and fifteen people came from Sweden. Also, in 2019, two groups of seven and fifteen people arrived from France. After a LMIS event in Japan in March 2018, forty people arrived from there, mostly as couples or in small groups of friends.

Future orientation of the project

The goals for the future include introducing LMIS to more countries, increasing the number of stakeholders and empowering the initiative between all the small enterprises and tour operators, especially those that normally would not be able to afford expensive advertising and marketing campaigns due to size (SMEs). In addition, the plan is to include institutions such as the Comuni and Regione (local councils/municipalities and regional administration) with the hope that the LMIS format could be included in their programs for tourism promotion. It is hoped that the project will be recognised for creating a specific tourist cluster base focused on interpersonal relationships and different experiences, which is the opposite of classic mass tourism. In order for this to continue, continued support from local institutions is very important.

APPLICABILITY OF THE PROJECT IN OTHER REGIONS

The principles of LMIS project, with the philosophy of sustainable tourism, human relations and the culture of gifts, are largely shared and endorsed by people all over the world who love to travel.

The creators of the project hypothesise that replicating the project in other regions would not only be feasible but also be beneficial for the advancement of the region to those who will recognise it. The practical realisation of the project in different regions should necessarily involve training and empowerment of the tourism entrepreneurs both from the private and public sectors. Higher education institutions could play a fundamental role in this process through education and in collaboration with trade associations and experts involved in the tourism sector. The local University of Macerata, especially Professor Alessio Cavicci, has been a major player in promoting studies into the importance of local food and beverage products for the regional economy, through the involvement of Ph.D. and other graduate students in local place branding projects. This has resulted in the region and the LMIS receiving recognition and an award from the European Union for experiential tourism in the category of sustainable tourism awards for 'Culinary, heritage, food and gastronomy tourism'.

EXERCISES

Group research & discussion

Take some time to review chapter case 7.1 and visit the company's website (www.nomadlodges.com).

1. Discuss the concept of 'change agent'; to what extent can the hospitality industry be a 'change agent'? Explain.
2. What were some of the challenges faced by Nomad Lodges? What were the solutions implemented?
3. How important is the concept of stakeholder relationship in SE?

4. Looking at the overall lessons learned from the Nomad Lodges case study, what can large hotel corporations learn from social entrepreneurs and in particular, concepts such as Nomad Lodges?

Group discussion

Take some time to review chapter case 7.2 and visit the project's website (https://www.turismarche.it/en/projects/le-marche-in-valigia/).

1. To what extent is this project replicable in other regions or countries?
2. Similar to the case on Nomad Lodges, what is the importance of stakeholder relationship in the overall success of the project?
3. What are your recommendations in regards to the expansion of the project?

Individual research

Write an essay about the concept of 'change agent'. Keep in mind some of the following points:

1. How do you define 'change agent'? What are the main criteria you consider essential in describing the concept?
2. Provide examples of change agent in the hospitality industry. How did you make your choice?
3. Are change agents necessary in our society? And if so, why?

References

Altinay, L., Sigala, M., & Waligo, V. (2016). Social value creation through tourism enterprise. *Tourism Management*, 54, 404–417

de Lange, D., & Dodds, R. (2017). Increasing sustainable tourism through social entrepreneurship. *International Journal of Contemporary Hospitality Management*, 29(7), 1977–2002.

Drucker, P. (2001). The next society: A survey of the near future. *The Economist*, 356(32/November 3), 3–20.

Ergul, M., & Johnson, C. (2011). Social entrepreneurship in the hospitality and tourism industry: An exploratory approach. *The Consortium Journal of Hospitality and Tourism*, 16,(2), 40–46.

Hall, C. M. (2015). Economic greenwash: On the absurdity of tourism and green growth in Tourism in the Green Economy. In V. R. Maharaj & K. Wilkes (Eds.), *Tourism in the Green Economy* (pp. 361–380).London: Routledge.

Higgins-Desbolies, F. (2006). More than an "industry": The forgotten power of tourism as a social force. *Tourism Management*, 27(6), 1192–1208

Johnson, C. (2002a). *Locational strategies of International Hospitality Corporations in eastern central Europe* [Unpublished Ph.D thesis]. University of Fribourg, Switzerland.

Johnson, C. (2002b). Sustainability and the international hotel industry. In *Travel and Tourism Analyst*. London, UK: Mintel Publications

Koens, K. Postas, A., & Papp, B. (2016). Is Overtourism Overused? Understanding the Impact of Tourism in a City Context. *Sustainability, 10*(12), 4384. https://doi.org/10.3390/su10124384

Kohler, T., & Chesbrough, H. (2019). From collaborative community to competitive market: the quest to build a crowdsourcing platform for social innovation. *R&D Management, 49*(3). https://doi.org/10.1111/radm.12372.

Lombardi, E. (2017). https://www.greenlodgingnews.com/social-enterprise-in-the-hospitality-industry/

Scaglione, M., Marx, S., & Johnson, C. (2010). Tourism and poverty alleviation approaches: A case study comparison. In P. Keller & T. Bieger (Eds.), *Tourism Development after the Crises: Global Imbalances, Poverty Alleviation* (pp. 205–227).Berlin: Schmidt, ISBN 3-503-13002-0. 2011, p. 205–227

Sheldon, P. J., & Danielle, R. (Eds.). (2017). *Social Entrepreneurship and Tourism: Philosophy and Practices*. Cham, Switzerland: Springer Publications.

Sigala, M. (2016). Learning with the market: A market approach and framework for developing social entrepreneurship in tourism and hospitality. *International Journal of Contemporary Hospitality Management, 28*(6), 1245–1286

UNWTO. (2018). *Tourism Highlights*. https://www.e-unwto.org/doi/pdf/10.18111/9789284419876

UNWTO. (2020). *International Tourist Arrivals could fall by 20–30% in 2020*. https://www.unwto.org/news/international-tourism-arrivals-could-fall-in-2020

World Bank. (2020) *International Tourism, Number of Arrivals*. https://data.worldbank.org/indicator/st.int.arvl

WTO. (1980) *Manila declaration on World Tourism*. The World Tourism Conference. https://www.univeur.org/cuebc/downloads/PDF%20carte/65.%20Manila.PDF

Chapter 8

Hospitality environmental entrepreneurship

This chapter starts with a discussion on the ethical issues facing the hospitality industry and expands on the concept of sustainable tourism. It explores the impacts of tourism on climate change and biodiversity collapse, with a focus on identifying opportunities in environmental entrepreneurship, and discusses best practices in that field.

The chapter closes with two case studies that tackle those challenges via their mitigation strategies. These are (1) Estancia Peuma Hue (Argentina) – an environmental and conservation project on luxury sustainable ecotourism and (2) Mashphi Lodge (Ecuador) – a socio-environmental project on biodiversity, education and the local community in the Ecuadorian Amazon. A set of additional exercises is provided at the end of the chapter, which are based on individual or group research and discussions.

Introduction

Who should take a lead in transforming the current system? Nicholas Stern, author of *The Global Deal: Climate Change and The Creation of a New Era of Progress and Prosperity* contends that "individuals, firms and communities should not just wait for governments to sort things out" (2009, p. 124). The hotel industry, being one of the world's largest in terms of geographic expansion, service provision and use of resources, should lead by example. Legrand, Sloan and Chen, suggest that "hotels, motels and all the various forms of accommodation comprise a large sector of the tourism industry and have been shown to have a highly negative influence on the environment". (2017, p. 17).

It can be asserted that over the past few years, most hotel undertakings have made a great effort to find solutions that will help reduce and reverse the major impacts of their business activities on the environment, particularly by taking measures regarding the use of water and their carbon footprints. Whether they are big hotel chains or small undertakings, it is commonplace that these types of measures have tangible benefits in the short term, including real efficiency gains and an improved corporate reputation.

Ethical issues

Another challenge for hotel undertakings is how to conduct business while implementing an ethics policy. Ethical issues arise in four main areas: the supply chain, the local community (in the tourist destination), the workplace and the customers (Legrand et al., 2017). In this area, the highlight is labour exploitation or informal work in the supply chain, exploitation of migrant workers in hotels and restaurants or even human trafficking. Local people at tourist destinations generally perceive that they have little or no share in the economic benefits of the hospitality business in proportion to their effort, while bearing – as mentioned above – a disproportionate burden from the environmental degradation caused by its activities. Moreover, the process to adjust tourist destinations for their commercial operations generally promotes informal employment and low wages, which, in turn, reduces the possibilities of traditional employment, such as fishing and farming and result in increased imports and the subsequent impoverishment of the local economy due to the relevant increased cost of living. As a consequence of the above, many inhabitants move to other places, leaving the new tourist destination deserted.

Codes of ethics

In 1999, the UN World Trade Organization (UNWTO) devised a global code of ethics for tourism, designed to minimise the negative effects of tourism activities on destinations and local communities. This code was officially recognised in 2001 and, a decade later, the UNWTO held the first International Congress of Ethics and Tourism, which offered the first opportunity to test whether or not the hotel industry could implement it. Encouragingly, there is evidence that the industry is assuming a proactive, collective approach to human rights and business ethics, incorporating human rights risk mapping, employee training on responsible business and sustainable local benefits into their operations (Legrand et al., 2017). Major hotel companies have taken significant steps since the beginning of the new millennium to integrate policies on human rights into their stated policies on business conduct and ethics.

Sustainable tourism: definition and practices

Moreover, Frangialli and Toepfer (2005) argue that the tourism sector must take action and assume responsibility for the multitude of sustainability challenges facing the world today. This is why the UNWTO[1] focuses its advisory and technical assistance services on policies, development guidelines, management techniques and measurement instruments that allow national and local governments, as well as the tourism industry, to incorporate sustainability principles into their decision-making processes and day-to-day operations. In 1987, the UNWTO defined sustainable tourism as follows: "Tourism that takes full account of its current and future economic, social and environmental impacts, addresses the needs of visitors, the industry, the environment and host communities" (UNWTO, 1987; UNWTO & UNEP, 2005, p. 12). This is why, the United Nations Environment Programme (UNEP) has initiated a program that aims to integrate environmental sustainability into decision-making in the tourism industry and into consumers' purchasing choices, by disseminating technical know-how and building business networks to catalyse "sustainability" in the tourism sector (Frangialli & Toepfer, 2005).

For example, according to Bruns-Smith, Choy, Chong and Verma (2015), among common green practices are water conserving fixtures and linen-reuse programs. A separate survey of 120,000 hotel customers found that guests are generally willing to participate in sustainability programs, but the presence of green operations still do not override considerations of price and convenience when selecting a hotel. Additionally, the study finds an increased willingness to participate when hotels offer incentives, such as loyalty program points, for participating in environmental programs. Although the link between environmentally sustainable programs and improved customer satisfaction is weak compared to standard drivers like facilities, the room and food and beverage quality, hotels are increasingly expected to maintain sustainability programs as a regular feature of their business. At the same time, the study did find that environmental sustainability programs do not diminish guest satisfaction. Consequently, the decision regarding which programs to implement should rest on cost-benefit analysis and other operating considerations (Bruns-Smith et al., 2015).

In the specific case of the tourism industry, the particular interest in ensuring sustainable operations is worth noting, for the simple reason that its raw materials consist of natural and cultural resources, which should be protected and expanded for their long-term preservation. Along this line, Bruns-Smith argues that

> the link between environmental sustainability and guest satisfaction is modest, to say the least, despite the prevalence of environmentally sustainable programs and the relatively high guest participation in many of those programs. The traditional drivers of satisfaction (room, facilities, and food and beverage quality) still overwhelm the effects of green operations. That said,

green programs do not diminish guest satisfaction, so hotels may consider their cost-benefit analysis, potential for improved employee relations, and reduced risk in addition to "green" satisfaction to determine whether these investments are beneficial. Finally, it seems that many green investments are now considered to be a more or less standard aspect of hotel operation, regardless of cost or satisfaction considerations.

(Bruns-Smith et al., 2015, p. 16)

Tourism spill-over effect

The hotel and tourism industries are significant contributors to environmental degradation and pollution (UNEP, 2013). Many environmental problems result from direct or indirect consequences of individuals' behaviours, including travel behaviour and working behaviour (Spenceley, 2005; UNEP, & UNWTO, 2005). However, in the US, research on environmental behaviour has mostly remained at and around small scales, leading to an unwritten assumption of their 'spill-over' effect into tourism related practices (Thogersen, 1999). In fact, the relation between environmental commitments and behaviour at home and their spill-over effect in tourism context has not received much attention (Barr, Shaw, & Coles, 2011; Higham & Cohen, 2011). Such studies are critical due to the fact that they address conservation ethics in general (De Young, 2000), individuals' values, beliefs and morals (De Groot & Steg, 2008) and, in a wider scope, socio-structural characteristics (Barr, Shaw, Coles, & Prillwitz, 2010). Besides, understanding individuals' pro-environmental behaviour in different settings is crucial in encouraging behaviour change, promoting an environmentally sustainable lifestyle, mitigating adverse environmental consequences in tourism (Barr et al., 2011) and therefore in alleviating environmental pollution. Against this background, to enable better understanding of the existing gap, Bamdad (2019) studied the reasons for not acting pro-environmentally and classified them based on their similarities and dissimilarities. This study revealed that despite being aware of negative consequences of travel behaviour, few guests completely denied the negative impacts of their own vacation behaviour on the environment. Elliott and Devine (1994) believe that denial of negative consequences of a behaviour happens when it causes distress (Elliot & Devine, 1994). However, other participants were aware of the negative consequences, while the majority of participants openly expressed their dissatisfaction and found their contrasting behaviour problematic. Denying or openly admitting the undesirable contrast is an evidence of cognitive dissonance (Festinger, 1985). A possible way to reverse such inconsistency is not only to educate and raise awareness of the negative consequences of bad behaviours on the environment, but also to prove the positive effects that conscious, consistent actions could have on the environment.

Climate change & biodiversity collapse

As the hospitality industry is related to other industries, such as the food, textile, automotive and transport industries, we will analyse their environmental impacts.

According to Legrand et al. (2017), one of the main reasons for the catastrophic losses and degradation of the world's biodiversity is global climate change. According to the European Commission (2011), up to 60% of the world's ecosystems are over-exploited, which results in imminent degradation, since they are used unsustainably. Moreover, the distribution of species is largely determined by climate, as is the distribution of ecosystems and plant vegetation areas. Climate change sometimes shifts these distributions but, for a number of reasons, plants and animals cannot always adjust.

Over-hunting has been another significant cause of the extinction of hundreds of species and the endangering of many more, such as the buffalo in the 19th century and many large African mammals. In Latin America, we can also mention the case of the brown-headed spider monkey –*Ateles fusciceps* – the most endangered primate in Ecuador, whose extinction may lead to an unbalance in its native ecosystem. Most extinctions over the past several hundred years is mainly due to mass consumption and the promotion of food and clothes, which results in big profits for producers, in addition to species and environmental degradation and the subsequent degradation in the bond between humans and between them and other species.

One of the best-known models of commercial exploitation is the whaling industry, where whales are slaughtered for oil and meat. This custom has led to many whale species being brought to the brink of extinction. A century ago, humans could not seriously exploit and threaten whale populations because of rather primitive technology. At that time, a three-year-long whaling trip would kill fewer than a hundred whales. However, in the mid-20th century, more precisely in 1967, about 60,000 were killed yearly, yielding roughly 1.5 million barrels of oil. Not the whaling industry alone, but the fishing industry has also developed exponentially. Larger, faster ships, better nets and other similar improvements have increased the ability of commercial fishermen to catch more fish and put the survival of several species in danger, in addition to polluting their habitats.

Beyond these examples, and however great over-exploitation is, the greatest damage to marine life is as a result of general environmental degradation caused by human activities. We have built societies that operate at the expense of other species. Most sea aquatic life is concentrated in shallow waters close to land, where marine populations that are already exploited by the food industry are also most susceptible to heavy pollution. Moreover, many organisms live in estuaries, the mouths of rivers and streams where fresh and salt waters mix. These areas are threatened because of industrial and human waste in some parts of the world and fertilisers washed off agricultural land that interfere with the delicate natural equilibrium of these environments (Legrand et al., 2017). Therefore, habitat loss and degradation caused by human activity are important causes of flora and fauna extinction. As deforestation proceeds in tropical forests, more loss of biodiversity can be expected. All species have specific food and habitat needs, the more specific these needs and localised the habitat, the greater the vulnerability these species are to loss of habitat through agricultural and livestock enlargement and to roads and cities, and, therefore, the higher the species' possibility of non-survival.

The human population passed the seven billion mark in 2011 and at the start of 2020, the planet is closer to 7.8 billion. Roughly half the world's forests and natural habitats have been transformed, degraded, reduced or destroyed by human activity. For example, tropical forests are important because they are home to at least 50% of the world's biodiversity. Those forests offer great benefits for the development and quality of life, releasing vast quantities of moisture into the atmosphere to fall as rain elsewhere and performing the vital task of absorbing carbon dioxide. The original extent of these forests was fifteen million square kilometres (km^2), which is now about half the original size. Habitat fragmentation is a further discouraging aspect of natural habitat loss that often goes unrecognised. Forests, meadows, bog lands and other habitats that are divided by human development remain generally small and isolated and can only maintain very small animal populations at best. Any species that requires a large home range will not survive in these areas.

Another important aspect regarding human activity is the use of natural resources. Materials removed from the earth are needed to provide humans with food, clothing, housing and transport, in order to develop the expected standard of living in our societies. Some of the materials needed are renewable resources, such as agricultural and forestry products, while others are non-renewable, such as minerals and oil. The demand for non-renewable resources is still strong with important investments in coal-fired power plants and oil fields, despite knowledge and the warning signs. Due to this, world commodity prices maintain their relentless climb higher as vital minerals become depleted. High oil prices are here to stay – although the COVID-19 crisis of 2020 has shown that this may not always be the case as oil prices dropped, temporarily at least – as a result of the overuse and waste of natural resources, which, in turn, has produced several economic crises over the past decades. Janez Potočnik, Chief of the EU Commission for the Environment, stated:

> It is very difficult to imagine [lifting Europe out of recession] without growth, and very difficult to imagine growth without competitiveness, and very difficult to be competitive without resource efficiency. Unless consumers and businesses take action to use resources more efficiently (from energy and water to food and waste, and raw materials such as precious metals), then their increasing scarcity, rising prices and today's wasteful methods of using them will drive up costs yet further and reduce Europe's standard of living." And he added: "We have simply no choice. We have to use what we have more efficiently, or we will fail to compete. Resource efficiency is a real competitiveness issue for European companies.
>
> (Potočnik, 2011)

This stark warning highlights the increasing scarcity and rising prices of some key resources, including energy and water, but also food and raw materials such as metals, ores and minerals. Some essential minerals can be recycled, such as phosphorus, potassium and nitrogen, but the number of people that even the most efficient recycling systems could support may be much lower than today's world population. The bonanza forecast by some economists of cheap bio-fuels is beginning to backfire, since land that was previously used for producing food is now used to produce crops to fuel mobility. The demand for oil-bearing crops is not only reducing the land available to produce food crops in Europe, it is also driving the clearing of rainforests in the East – with Indonesia and Malaysia being the most affected countries in the region – for palm oil plantations. On the demand side, the other reason for the steady food price increases in the early years of the 21st century has been global population growth. On the supply side, the drivers are many, including aquifer depletion, the loss of cropland to non-farm uses, the diversion of irrigation water to cities, the plateauing of crop yields in agriculturally advanced countries and, due to climate change, crop-withering heat waves, melting mountain glaciers, ice sheets and soil erosion. These climate-related trends seem destined to take a far greater toll in the future. An estimated one-third of the world's cropland is losing topsoil faster than new soil is forming through natural processes – and thus is losing its inherent productivity.

In 2002, the United Nations asked 1500 experts to study the social effects of water scarcity in developing countries. One year later, in 2003, teams of executives from the world's largest water, oil and chemical companies tried to forecast the effect of future water scarcity on their own and national economies. Both groups reported back with alarming unanimity and predicted supply, health and economic crises coming sooner rather than later if there was no radical change in the way water is used. Reasons for water shortages can be found in the phenomenal pace at which glaciers are melting. Glaciers that used to gently supply communities in the summer season with a steady water source are now melting so fast as to cause seasonal floods.

Even the present low-level melting is affecting coastal life and coral reefs, which are disappearing. Droughts, too, are becoming more frequent and lasting longer, rains are coming more irregularly and seasonal rains are less defined. However, water stress is caused by poor water management and wasteful irrigation systems. In India, World Bank Group numbers indicate that 175 million people are being fed with grain that is produced by over-pumping, while in China, over-pumping provides food for some 130 million people. Moreover, in the United States, the world's other leading grain producer, the irrigated area is shrinking in key agricultural states such as California and Texas. Due to this waste of water, in the coming years some countries may give up growing certain crops and rearing animals for consumption. When the water needed to grow crops has to be pumped from hundreds of metres below, the true cost of food on supermarket shelves becomes clearer. And this also makes clear that rather than digging deeper, the future will be about recycling water. In fact, wastewater is increasingly being collected from kitchens, gardens and bathrooms, treated and reused all over the world. This technology is used in the manufacturing industry, entertainment and leisure complexes, housing and tourist accommodation facilities. For example, Singapore, a city right on the equator, with seemingly no shortage of fresh water, uses wastewater for all its industries and most of its housing. In fact, cities that do not want to ask their citizens to save water are moving rapidly to desalination – a process conducted in countries with major technological and industrial development, consisting of separating salt from seawater. However, desalination is the most expensive and least sensible option for the time being. Studies suggest that most communities can find additional water more quickly and for less money by improving efficiency and management. The downsides of desalination are the enormous amounts of power needed and the vast quantities of salt that are extracted and must be disposed of. In the next decade, however, the cost is expected to fall as the technology improves, and desalination plants will increasingly be linked to waste heat from factories or solar power stations.

Tourism forms

Today, a large percentage of tourism is based on scheduled trips, all-inclusive packages, low-cost hotels and other trips that follow this pattern. This tourist offer model helps people visit more places at the lowest cost. For example, this kind of visit is very fast, superficial and includes only 'essential' places with the usual work stress. An extreme example could be Caribbean cruise tourist resorts, on which you can travel to a country with no need to know anything about it. Different forms of tourism called 'slow tourism' – which is characterised by environmental and social respect for the territory, while fostering local economic growth – have emerged as an alternative to this way of travelling.

Moreover, traditional tourism is considered a resource-intensive sector, which has a significant environmental impact. In fact, the United Nations has issued several warnings about the huge environmental impact caused by the tourism industry. However, it was in the 1980s and after the Brundtland report (1987) that concepts like 'sustainable tourism' or 'ecotourism' have come up. Since the turn of the millennium, new ways of understanding tourism as 'pro-poor' or 'low-carbon' have continued to emerge. However, 'slow tourism' is deeper and implements forms of tourism that are not trying to move from the current model but to break dramatically with the traditional concept of tourism. It aims for tourists to be part of local life and to connect with the destination, its people and culture. Therefore, the trip's purpose is not to visit a city, but to discover it (Miretpastor, Peiró-Signes, Segarra-Oña, & Mondéjar-Jiménez, 2015).

Sustainable luxury

Most entrepreneurs fall into two categories: decouplers and integrators. Most decouplers started their social business after identifying a need in the market, which was the core motive for the creation of the venture. On the other hand, many integrators first founded their business idea/product out of passion and then created the need for their products in the markets in which they are involved. For the latter, the motive that pushed them to create their social business was the will to do something good for society or the passion for a material. Market opportunity was not what triggered their businesses.

As explained by Gardetti and Justo (2017, p. 349),

> Sustainable luxury is the return to the ancestral essence of luxury, to the thoughtful purchase, to the artisan manufacture, to the beauty of materials in its broadest sense, and to the respect for social and environmental issues. The foundations of sustainable luxury are social entrepreneurship and craftsmanship…Social entrepreneurs are well motivated to break the rules and promote disruptive solutions to the environmental and social issues. They are leaders who transform, inspire, and care deeply about people and the environment (Short et al., 2009). They reappraise native culture and craftsmanship.
> Gardetti and Justo (2017, p. 352)

In the introduction of their book titled *Sustainable Luxury: Managing Social and Environmental Performance in Iconic Brands*, Gardetti and Torres (2014) describe the evolution of the sustainability-luxury relationship between 2003 and 2011 – a relationship that they first noticed in the book *Deluxe – How Luxury Lost its Luster* by Thomas (2007). Some of the aspects of this evolution are as follows:

> The two most important conferences of this sector held in 2009 addressed these issues and focused their discussions on the assessment of these changes in the consumer and the new concept of success for achieving a "sustainable" luxury. One of them, organized by the International Herald Tribune in New Delhi (India) was called 'Sustainable Luxury Conference'. The other, promoted by the Financial Times in Monaco with the attendance of Prince Albert was titled "Business and Luxury Summit - Beyond Green: economics, ethics and enticement
> (Gardetti & Justo, 2017, p. 349)

As to the environmental and social impact, we can mention that most of the social ventures presented have a social impact on a developing community or support causes from which their product is derived. However, the impact those businesses have on their community is very varied. Among the social businesses, entrepreneurs can either focus on the environment, society or environment and society. Yet, even for ventures started out of the passion for nature, such as Estancia Peuma Hue, the business has a positive impact on the society. Thus, no ventures presented in this book are engaged only in sustainable environments and many are active for both society and nature (Gardetti & Justo, 2017).

Below we present two cases of entrepreneurship in the hospitality industry that focus their action not only on environmental preservation and care, but on its improvement as well. One of them, Estancia Peuma Hue, is located in the Argentine Patagonia, while the Mashpi Lodge is located in the Mashpi Cloud Forest in Ecuador. Both are integrated into the natural environment and, in both cases, the key factor is knowledge of the environment and transmission of this, as well as awareness, to tourists, guests and inhabitants. While the hospitality industry still has a long way to go in terms of sustainability and the environment, these types of projects are inspiring, not just because of their achievements and results, but because they stem from the passion, dedication and effort of their founders who, with their previous knowledge and the insights they continue to gain, aim for excellence every day – not only in conducting business, but also in bringing about a positive change in their environment and in society at large.

CHAPTER CASE 8.1

Estancia Peuma Hue: An environmental and conservation project on luxury sustainable ecotourism in Argentina[2]

About Peuma Hue Ecolodge

Peuma Hue is an ecolodge in a valley surrounded by mountains, pristine forest and waterfalls and with two miles of lakeshore; but it is also a place where people instantly relax, connect in different levels to themselves, to nature, to animals, to other guests, to staff, to everything around. It is a luxury ecolodge with healthy and balanced gourmet meals based on our organic garden and homemade products. It is a multi-activity destination where you can horseback ride with a horse whisperer. Golden retrievers can lead you on hikes that will be a delight. You can take a kayak in such a clear lake that you can see the bottom, with its sunken forest and trout swimming around. Besides, you can hike through 500 acres of pristine mountain forest trails with views over lakes, more mountains and valleys that link with the largest hiking network in the country. It is a place where you can practice yoga under the steepest vertical drop of the area with rock needles jutting above or at an intimate Temple to Nature. It is a place where you make friends with people as much as with animals. Our guest book is full of references to how much the connection to our animals, to our staff and to other guests enhanced their experience, through interesting conversations at cocktails while everyone shares their day or life stories in a cosy living room that resembles a home and not a hotel. And yet there is more to it—quite intangible—that has to do with warmth, sharing, thoughtfulness, beauty, peacefulness, joy and also with what is beyond and exceeds us all. For each person it is different and this is something

HOSPITALITY ENVIRONMENTAL ENTREPRENEURSHIP   199

we respect the most. We try to tap into what each one needs. What is important to us is that our guests have a meaningful time here—within their own lifestyle and stage in their lives—and that can make at least a little difference (Figures 8.1 and 8.2).

Figure 8.1 A view of Peuma Hue.
    (Photo Credit: Francisco Bedeschi).

Figure 8.2 Peuma Hue in Winter.
    (Photo Credit: Peuma Hue).

Mitigating impacts

From the beginning, my idea was to work with renewable and clean energy. Technical reasons and lack of means made it impossible when we started, having to bring the power line in from the main road and relying mainly on propane tanks eight times the price of natural gas. *Against all odds in 2017* we decided to start a small hydroelectric project collecting water from a year-round creek and turning it back into the same creek before it reaches our lake. Again, the protection of our forest was key to our concern, so the pipes were brought up by hand, using cables to hall them up a steep slope without cutting any of the beautiful big trees. We made many mistakes. Among them, when we built the houses that were inefficient energy wise. Maintaining the huge property and all the houses, all the hiking and riding trails we opened, the entrance and inner roads, the organic vegetable garden and greenhouse, the lawn, harvesting, our vehicles and boats, salaries, taxes and all the services we provide, all of that raised the costs to extremely high levels for what we can afford. So our next plan—and challenge—is to be more profitable without losing the spirit Peuma Hue has and that makes it so special.

Activities offerings

We offer activities in this amazingly majestic nature; our horse guide is not only a guide, she is the best horse-whisperer and animal communicator I know. We have a hostess who not only introduces Peuma Hue to our guests and organises all the services and activities with detail, but her genuine passion for the place, her smile and love for animals, is contagious. And we offer massages, where our masseur not only blends several techniques but has a way of focusing and 'knowing' your body that results in what most of our guests refer to as their 'best massage' ever. Our gardener has 'eagle eyes' that allowed him to preserve every single little tree of the native forest when cutting the invasive rosehip and manages our garden in a way that only one endeared to the land can do. The thoughtful, caring and professional attitude of our sales person enhances our guests' stay. In addition, we have a dedicated and thoughtful manager who, besides dealing with tons of different aspects with expertise and never losing his temper, achieves the most wonderful spirit in our team, leading and motivating them into a common goal. I could go on and on, referring to the warmth and high quality of each one in our team, where every single person has a special charm and human values that make them unique in what they do. And we have the loving attitude of our animals—among themselves and with guests—some guests referring to them as being in paradise, puzzled by the harmony between those that naturally should be chasing, fighting or threatening each other in some way. So, this is 'luxury' for us; it is the best quality we can offer in what we offer.

Bridging luxury and sustainability

And then there is 'sustainability'. What are we without being balanced with what surrounds us through time? We are in a very special moment in the history of our planet that shows in an overwhelming way and with more clearness than ever before, the devastating effects of the careless doing of humankind. Having been blessed by intelligence and lots of creativity, we disconnected from being in balance among ourselves and with the rest of the planet. We came up with lineal paradigms of everlasting growth, abuse and extraction that are absolutely unsustainable in a finite planet. We at Peuma Hue live in a paradise of beauty, clean waters that are still safe to drink from their sources, pristine forests that host a number of varieties of plant and animal life. I want this to be enjoyed for generations to come, so whatever we wish to offer and open to others needs to be within this understanding. This leads to moderation, to the essence of what is valuable, to thoughtfulness, consciousness and education.

So, based on these principles, we started, step by step, in a land that at that time was far from being looked after. It was depredated and invaded. It took extremely hard work; consuming 100% of my life and that of many others, tons of love and commitment, facing different fears and challenges all these years. We started from scratch; clearing part of the land from the invasive rosehip and allowing the native forest to come back. The trees were kept low due to the harmful effect of local grazing cattle. Slowly and step by step, in our own woodshop, the big logs we bought from sustainable plantations were transformed into our houses, log cabins and furniture. A deep awe and respect for nature drove us to watch for every detail to protect it in all aspects we could, with the means we had at hand. There was so much to learn!! We made so many mistakes!! But we kept going on to fulfil the dream of doing, offering and opening to what we so much love: nature, beauty, the outdoors and activities, animals, a cosy and comfortable place to live, good and healthy food, harmony and to be close to like-minded people. Every step we took surprised us with unexpected hidden beauty. It was amazing to 'rediscover' what was already there but unseen in the thickness of the overgrown brush. And we tried to match this beauty with our best effort in what we built.

Being a social entrepreneur

All I had done as an adult had to do with some kind of service and generating experiences; thus my inability to think in terms of business. My ex-husband was the one who handled that aspect and the early investment plan. The big challenge came when, three years into the project, we divorced and I took full care of Peuma Hue together with my team, including its business side. Peuma Hue is far beyond a business to me and I don't think I ever learned much of that aspect; my mind still keeps thinking in terms of life experiences first. The economic side—it has to be economically self-sustainable, otherwise we cannot go on—has always been the hardest aspect for me. But being at Peuma Hue is a choice of life, and I'm grateful every day I open my eyes to be able to see what I can see from my window, come down the stairs to pat my dogs and cat, watch the smiles of everyone around. There are so many blessings and privileges in this enterprise that they counterbalance by far the hardship and extremely hard work it also involves. It hasn't been a blessing only for me. Most of the people working and visiting feel deeply affected and passionate about the place. So, after everyone foretold I would be broke soon (my own fear as well), somehow we still manage to keep going! I can't take credit for it; there was no shortage of help of all sorts: ideas, suggestions, challenges and learning. As a team we kept on going; our guests, press, loyal travel agents and word of mouth kept referring our guests that help to keep this place alive.

We started the project already knowing it would be opened to tourists—to share it with the world and to be able to economically maintain it—but it would mainly be our home; opened to family, friends and those who appreciate majestic nature in the midst of one of the most stunning National Parks in the world.

So we began by renovating an old, derelict shack which became our temporary home, built our wood shop which transformed logs into our now twelve buildings (five for guests), their furniture and everything we needed. It wasn't easy; it wasn't too well planned either. Tons of hard work and lots of personal commitment in the team we hired made it possible. But together with the son of a friend of mine who was like a foster son to me and who became our general manager for twelve years—an agriculture engineer and a climber himself—we took it on. We did the basic planning of the houses ourselves, taking into account the 360° views. So no matter where you are in the houses, you are always exposed to imposing natural sights. We found an architect that could interpret exactly what we had planned and improved on it, respected the style we wanted; blending logs, wood, stone and massive windows into just beautifully designed houses (Figure 8.3).

Figure 8.3 Peuma Hue's Master Suite.
(Photo Credit: Francisco Bedeschi).

Conclusion

The project kept evolving; looking back it so much exceeds my wildest dreams in so many senses, good and challenging! Neither of us having formal training in either tourism or architecture, this enabled us to focus just on our hearts and on what we liked. Peuma Hue is the expression and the result of everything we care for and value. It is not a one-person enterprise. Every single person hired, working and visiting added and adds to what it has become and is still becoming; drawn by like-minded values of sustainability, concern for nature and a balanced way of life. I feel this place is not only my home; it is where I belong, it is my teacher, it is what structures me. And this happens not only to me, but also to so many of the people visiting, working or joining the team. I can even say that Peuma Hue shapes us as much as we shape Peuma, in a process of constant transformation, on both sides.

CHAPTER CASE 8.2

Mashpi lodge: A socio-environmental project on biodiversity, education and local community in the Ecuadorian Amazon

About Ecuador

Thanks to its privileged geographic location, Ecuador is a favourite destination for nature tourism, or ecotourism, as it is famous all over the world for its multiple ecosystems and unparalleled biodiversity. Moreover, it became well known in many countries after the Ministry of Tourism promoted the image of Ecuador internationally, with special focus on the Galapagos Islands. Nowadays, there is a trend quickly growing in worldwide tourism to visit places with exuberant nature and biodiversity; therefore, nature tourism is one of the main alternatives when choosing a destination, and it must also offer comfort to rest, relax, and perform activities in a natural environment (Moncayo, 2013).

About Mashpi Lodge

Mashpi Lodge is located in the middle of the Andean forest, on the western side of the Ecuadorian Andes Mountains. The area is damp with heavy rains. Thanks to this combination of location and climate, it is one of the most biodiverse ecosystems on the planet, considered a flora and fauna hotspot; hence, it is an ideal place to explore unparalleled and exuberant endemic richness of the kind found in the reserve (Moncayo, 2013).

Due to this, the Mashpi Lodge project has made great efforts to delve into the richness of the area. Using cameras, and after many research studies, it is estimated that there are almost 500 bird species, such as Andean cock-of-the-rock, parrots, toucans, hummingbirds and tangaras. There are also insects, butterflies, monkeys, peccaries, pumas, ocelots and many more animal species. Moreover, the flora includes orchids, mosses, lichens, fungi and ferns, among others.

The importance of the environment

The environmental conditions of the Mashpi area urged the founders to foster its preservation. Therefore, they undertook an ambitious luxury project aimed at preserving and raising awareness of nature, both in theory and in practice, minimising the environmental impact of the activities performed inside the lodge and during its construction. For this purpose, certain strategies were implemented to prevent great environmental damages in the area where Mashpi Lodge is built. Obviously, while any activity performed by human beings has a certain degree of environmental impact, the idea of the project was to preserve the area where the lodge carries out its tourist activities. This is not about implementing a business strategy or isolated environmental actions, but to embrace a philosophy and a holistic and comprehensive approach of seeing the world around us.

Due to the natural richness of the area where Mashpi Lodge operates, the place failed to be positioned as a major tourist destination. Therefore, tourists do not pack in this area – one of the reasons why the lodge has not reached a high tourist inflow, but has had low occupancy rates. In turn, the environmental conditions of Mashpi Lodge have contributed to fostering nature tourism, mainly stressing education about the preservation of natural resources in the area where the hotel carries out business and encouraging environmental responsibility in their tourists and workers, as they commit themselves to taking care of nature in tourist activities (Tamaríz Fadic, 2014).

Actions implemented

The specific actions implemented by Mashpi Lodge include a waste management system, which sorts all the materials that enter the place and sends them to the city of Quito for subsequent recycling. In addition, the lodge has installed a water treatment plant to treat wastewater for subsequent discharge into the forest. Moreover, to prevent water pollution, no dangerous chemicals or pollutants are used in the products offered by the hotel and, in turn, guests are encouraged to use the biodegradable products provided by the lodge. The lodge is currently powered by electric generators, which cause a certain degree of noise pollution in the environment but are protected with isolation chambers to minimise noise. However, there are plans to build a hydroelectric plant for Mashpi Lodge to become self-powered, with no need for any electric generators. Likewise, efforts are made to minimise vehicle traffic inside the reserve with hikes and electric buggies encouraged when the use of transport is required, in order to reduce both noise and CO2 emissions (Durán, 2012).

In connection with species preservation, we can mention the paper prepared by Valeria Sofía Sorgato Casares (2015), which states that Mashpi Lodge, along with the Proyecto Washu Foundation and the Jambelí Refuge, have suggested reintroducing the brown-headed spider monkey – *Ateles fusciceps* – into the Bosque Protector Mashpi for preservation purposes. The reintroduction consists of releasing specimens of a certain species in a place corresponding to their historic habitat; this is considered a conservation strategy for endangered species, such as the brown-headed spider monkey (Fuentes & Alfonso, 2013). Besides, this process needs to communicate and educate the communities adjacent to the reintroduction zone, such as the Mashpi community, for the effective conservation of this primate (Kellert & Reading, 1993). In 2014, the Proyecto Washu Foundation, Mashpi Lodge and the Jambelí Refuge launched the *Ateles fusciceps* reintroduction programme. This project is extremely important for the conservation of this monkey, which is among the top twenty-five most endangered primates in the world and the most endangered species of Ecuador (Peck, Thorn, Mariscal, & Baird, 2011).

It is estimated that there are less than 230 specimens of this species left in the world (Tirira, 2001). The main causes for its endangerment are reduced habitat due to deforestation resulting from poor cattle-raising and agricultural practices, hunting and the trafficking of this species as a pet (Peck et al., 2011). This is supported by studies, which show that 80% of the primary forest of Chocó has disappeared and become agricultural land (Baird, 2007).

Founder's statement

According to its founders – Roque Sevilla, the controlling shareholder and visionary creator of the Mashpi Lodge and Reserve Project among them (Mashpi Lodge, 2018) – *over the course of our operations at Mashpi our main focus and interest have been, to not only be part of the rainforest, but also of the surrounding communities. We provide job opportunities for the people that inhabit the communities that surround our park. We allow and support the growth of these communities in many ways; for example purchasing their crops for our restaurant. We educate and promote the educational process for the families teaching them how to become self-sustainable, recycle, and respect nature by not hunting animals or destroying all the flora and fauna. We invite groups of women, men and children to visit our hotel and all the scientific projects going on in premises so they can understand the impact of their positive and negative behaviours.*

Mashpi Lodge sustains itself thanks to many technological efforts. We collect water from natural springs, process it to be drinkable and then process it again to return it to the rain forest with no impact to the environment. We have many relying projects that allow us to constantly improve the management of waste and teach our team members the benefits of doing so. We bring consumables from the city and make sure that nothing is left behind when used.

The total cost of the project was eight million US Dollars and last year our sales were in the 1.4 M dollars range with a 1.2 M dollars deficit. We expect sales for 2.4 M dollars for the present year with still a deficit of 0.8 M dollars. Our average rate is 561 dollars.

We are proud to announce that we were selected by National Geographic Society as one of the few Unique Lodges of The World, the only one in Ecuador.

Among our sales channels, we can mention Virtuoso, Signature, American Express Fine Hotel and Resorts Program.[3]

Community involvement

Since the tourism industry usually has a huge negative impact on local economies, it is critical to preserve tourist sites in this context, in addition to promoting the social development of those areas where different entities carry out their businesses, thereby encouraging the participation of people from local communities in tourist projects to improve their quality of life. In this regard, Mashpi Lodge included local communities, creating jobs so that people can have a steady source of income, and improving the livelihood of the people surrounding the lodge. Therefore, a large percentage of local adults are employed by Mashpi Lodge, either as guides or in housekeeping and cleaning jobs. Guides learn about the fauna and flora of Bosque Protector Mashpi, which may also have an impact on their children's environmental knowledge and awareness. This is the closest community to the Mashpi Forest, which consists of 98% natural or semi-natural forests, and it is surrounded by the Mashpi River, i.e., locals are in permanent contact with nature (Sorogato Casares, 2015).

Conclusion

As it is a tourist product mainly targeted at an international segment, Mashpi Lodge has luxury premises, top-quality services, excellent cuisine and lavish infrastructure. Thanks to these characteristics, along with the above approach, it has a reputation for exclusivity in the international tourist industry, as it launched a ground-breaking product in the world in the middle of an entirely natural environment (Tamaríz Fadic, 2014).

EXERCISES

Group research & discussion

Tourism in general and the hospitality sector in particular both impact the environment in which they operate.

1. Name some of the impacts of traditional tourism on biodiversity, climate change, diversity, inequalities and local communities. Can you list them in order of importance? How did you derive your ranking?
2. How should an entrepreneur or business leader tackle these issues?
3. Can these issues be isolated and treated separately?

Group research & discussion

Take some time to review chapter cases 8.1 and 8.2. Take some time to visit the respective websites: (http://www.peuma-hue.com/ and https://www.mashpilodge.com/).

1. Estancia Peuma Hue and Mashpi Lodge are different projects, from different entrepreneurs. To what extent does the context affect the enterprise?

2. Which long term and short term initiatives would you highlight for each case? Make a short list of four initiatives you find particularly interesting and explain why.

3. The Peuma Hue case is written from the perspective of the social entrepreneur. What attributes or characteristics would you say the entrepreneur possesses? (You may refer to Chapters 3 and 4 to help answer this question)

Individual research

The tourism industry is one of the largest economic sectors in the world. However, it is vulnerable in many ways (e.g., to pandemics, natural catastrophes, etc.) but also very resilient; many enjoy travelling (and hotels can be used for other purposes than 'rooms for travellers'). Write an essay on the topic of travel and sustainability with the following questions in mind:

1. How will travel change in upcoming years?

2. Do you see a shift towards more responsible travel? Why is this shift so important and urgent?

3. Are large hotel chains in a better position, in regards to taking sustainable actions, compared to smaller social enterprises? Discuss.

4. What are the challenges and opportunities for large hotel chains and for hospitality social entrepreneurs?

Notes

1 The World Tourism Organization (UNWTO) is the United Nations specialised agency responsible for the promotion of responsible, sustainable and accessible tourism. It is the leading international organisation in the field of tourism. It serves as a global forum for tourism policy issues and a practical source of tourism knowledge (World Tourism Organization, 2018a, 2018b).

2 This text was summarised and adapted for this chapter from Hoter, E. *Estancia Peuma Hue, Argentina.* In Gardetti, M.A. and Girón M.E. (2014) *Sustainable Luxury and Social Entrepreneurship. Stories from the Pioneers.* Greenleaf Publishing Limited. Sheffield. 135–149.

3 Information obtained during the process of the 5th Edition of the Award for Sustainability in the Premium and Luxury Sectors, now called "Award for Sustainability in the Universe of Luxury in Latin America".

References

Baird, A. (2007). *RAPID-Development of playback for rapid population assessment of the Critically Endangered brown-headed spider monkey (Ateles fusciceps) in Ecuador*. [MSc Primate Conservation], 14–17.
Bamdad, T. (2019). Pro-environmental attitude-behavior: A spillover or a gap?. In U. Stankov, S. N. Boemi, S. Attia, S. Kostopoulou, & N. Mohareb (Eds.), *Cultural Sustainable Tourism. Advances in Science, Technology & Innovation* (IEREK Interdisciplinary Series for Sustainable Development) (pp. 169–183). UK: Springer.
Barr, S., Gilg, A., & Shaw, G. (2011). Helping people make better choices: Exploring the behaviour change agenda for environmental sustainability. *Applied Geography, 31*(2), 712–720. doi: 10.1016/j.apgeog.2010.12.003
Barr, S., Shaw, G., Coles, T., & Prillwitz, J. (2010). A holiday is a holiday: practicing sustainability, home and away. *Journal of Transport Geography, 18*(3), 474–481. doi: 10.1016/j.jtrangeo.2009.08.007
Bruns-Smith, A., Choy, V., Chong, H., & Verma, R. (2015). Environmental sustainability in the hospitality industry: Best practices, guest participation, and customer satisfaction. *Cornell Hospitality Report, 15*(3), 6–16.
De Groot, J., & Steg, L. (2008). Value orientations to explain beliefs related to environmental significant behavior: How to measure egoistic, altruistic, and biospheric value orientations. *Environment and Behavior, 40*(3), 330–354.
De Young, R. (2000). Expanding and evaluating motives for environmentally responsible behaviour. *Journal of Social Issues, 56*(3), 509–526.
Durán Calisto, A. M. (2012). Mashpi Lodge. *Revista Clave*.
Elliot, A. J., & Devine, P. G. (1994). On the motivational nature of cognitive dissonance: Dissonance as psychological discomfort. *Journal of Personality and Social Psychology, 67*(3), 382–394
Festinger, L. (1985). *A Theory of Cognitive Dissonance*. Palo Alto, CA: Stanford University Press.
Fuentes, N., & Alfonso, F. (2014). *Programa de reintroducción del mono araña de cabeza café (Ateles fusciceps) en el bosque protector Mashpi*, Pichincha, Ecuador, 2–10.
Gardetti, M. A., & Justo, R. (2017). Sustainable luxury fashion: The entrepreneurs' vision. In M. A. Gardetti (Ed.), *Sustainable Management of Luxury, Environmental Footprints and Eco-design of Products and Processes* (pp. 347–360). UK: Springer Nature.
Higham, J. E. S., & Cohen, S. A. (2011). Canary in the coalmine: Norwegian attitudes towards climate change and extreme long-haul air travel to Aotearoa/New Zealand. *Tourism Management, 32*(1), 98–105. doi: 10.1016/j.tourman.2010.04.005.
Hoter, E. (2014). Estancia Peuma Hue, Argentina. In M. A. Gardetti & M. E. Girón, *Sustainable Luxury and Social Entrepreneurship. Stories from the Pioneers* (pp. 135–149). UK: Greenleaf Publishing Limited.
Kellert, S., & Reading, R. P. (1993). Attitudes toward a proposed reintroduction of black-footed ferrets (Mustela nigripes). *Conservation Biology, 7*(3), 569–580.
Legrand, W., Sloan, P., & Chen, J.S. (2017). *Sustainability in the hospitality industry. Principles of sustainable operations* (3rd ed.). London: Routledge.
Mashpi Lodge. (2018). https://www.mashpilodge.com/es/nosotros/

Miretpastor, L., Peiró-Signes, A., Segarra-Oña, M., & Mondéjar-Jiménez, J. (2015). The slow tourism: An indirect way to protect the environment. In H. G. Parsa, N. Narapareddy, S. Jang, M. Segarra-Oña, & R. Chen (Eds.), *Sustainability, Social Responsibility and Innovations in Tourism and Hospitality* (pp. 317–326). USA: Apple Academic Press.

Moncayo, S. (2013). *Mashpi, Reserva de Biodiversidad de Bosque Lluvioso*. Ecuador: Imprenta Mariscal, Ecuador.

Peck, M., Thorn, J., Mariscal, A., & Baird, A. (2011). Focusing conservation efforts for the critically endangered brown-headed spider monkey (Ateles fusciceps) using remote sensing, modeling, and playback survey methods. *International Journal of Primatology, 32*(1), 134–148. https://doi.org/10.1007/s10764-010-9445-z

Potočnik, J. (2011). In *EU warns wasting environmental resources could spark new recession*. https://www.theguardian.com/world/2011/dec/29/eu-environmental-resources-new-recession.

Sorogato Casares, V. S. (2015). *Programa de educación ambiental para la reintroducción del mono araña de cabeza café (Ateles fusciceps) en la comunidad de Mashpi*. Ecuador: Universidad San Francisco de Quito.

Spenceley, A. (2005). Nature-based tourism and environmental sustainability in South Africa. *Journal of Sustainable Tourism, 13*(2), 136–170. https://doi.org/10.1080/09669580508668483

Stern, N. (2009). *The Global Deal: Climate Change and the Creation of a New Ear of Progress and Prosperity*. UK: PublicAffairs.

Tamaríz Fadic, D. J. (2014). *Análisis del Retorno Promocional del Producto Turístico Mashpi Lodge Manejado por la Empresa Turística Metropolitan Touring en el periodo 2012–2013*. Ecuador: Pontificia Universidad Católica del Ecuador.

Thøgersen, J. (1999). Spillover processes in the development of a sustainable consumption pattern. *Journal of Economic Psychology, 20*(1), 53–81.

Tirira, D. (2004). *Estado actual del mono araña de cabeza (Ateles fusciceps Gray, 1866) (Primates: Atelidae) en el Ecuador.* http://www.lyonia.org/downloadPDF.php?pdfID=2.244.1.

UNEP. (2013). Green economy and trade-tourism. *United Nations Environment Programme*. https://www.cbd.int/financial/doc/tourism-greeneconomy.pdf

UNEP & UNWTO. (2005). Making tourism more sustainable. A guide for policy makers. *United Nations Environment Programme and World Tourism Organization*. https://www.e-unwto.org/doi/book/10.18111/9789284408214

UNWTO. (1987). *Sustainable Development of Tourism*. http://sdt.unwto.org/es/content/definicion.

World Bank Group. (2016). *Population, Total*. https://data.worldbank.org/indicator/SP.POP.TOTL

World Tourism Organization. (2018a). *Sustainable Development of Tourism. Definition*. http://sdt.unwto.org/content/about-us-5

World Tourism Organization. (2018b). *UNWTO. Specialized agency of the United Nations*. http://www2.unwto.org/content/who-we-are-0

Chapter 9

Funding and financing hospitality social ventures

This chapter identifies methods to fund and finance social enterprises. In doing so, it reviews traditional and emerging sources of funding and financing and discusses the challenges linked to social enterprise financing.

It also discusses social business incubators and accelerators, supported with prominent examples. A set of additional exercises is provided at the end of the chapter, which are based on individual or group research and discussions.

The chapter closes with the case of Borana Ranch (Kenya) in regards to establishing a financially sustainable conservancy.

Introduction

As an entrepreneur, one must often deal with uncertainties and "there is much that we do not know about the future. But one thing we do know is that business as usual will not continue for much longer" (Brown, 2009, p. 241). This also includes the ways, methods and tools used in funding and financing change agents.

Consequently, this chapter explores the start-up process and identifies methods to fund and finance opportunities. It discusses the challenges linked to scaling-up projects. Literature about funding and financing tourism and hospitality social enterprises is scarce. As in any other business venture, access to capital is crucial to the creation of social enterprises. Several researchers have explored how corporate social responsibility (CSR) in the hospitality industry is deployed, but this tends to be based on social efforts of larger hotel groups. However, proper financing of entrepreneurial projects is essential to provide the necessary impulse. As Lyons and Kickul state, "'Where money and meaning intersect' is becoming the mantra for a new generation of entrepreneurs and investors" (2013, p. 147).

However, a large number of social enterprises "survive only through the largesse of government subsidies, charitable foundations, and a handful of high-net-worth individuals who will make donations or accept lower financial returns on their investments in social projects" (Bugg-Levine, Kogut, & Kulatilaka, 2012, p. 4). Finding and securing funding can look like an obstacle course to a social entrepreneur.

Some researchers argue that social entrepreneurs should make use of alternative and innovative sources of financial support and social value creation (Reis, 1999; Mair & Marti, 2006). Lyons and Kickul argue that "while this deep gulf between profit-maximizing financial investment and "give-it-away" charity is gradually narrowing, social entrepreneurs still find it difficult to monetize the blended value they create" (2013, p. 148). While a detailed list of ways to obtain financing for social enterprises is beyond the scope of this chapter, in part due to the ever-changing programs, tools and support available to entrepreneurs, a review of the key challenges, opportunities and tools is provided.

Challenges in social enterprise financing

For the social entrepreneur, as any other business entrepreneur, finding sources of financing is important to ensure the net positive outcome of the venture. This positive outcome is the blended value creation of social or environmental business endeavors in the communities. Additionally, economically sound enterprises are required for reinvestments in projects or redistribution to communities.

There are multiple challenges associated with challenges in social enterprise financing, as shown in Table 9.1 – Eight Challenges in Social Enterprise Financing

Table 9.1 Eight challenges in social enterprise financing.

Challenge	Description
Beneficiaries/ Recipients of social enterprise's service or product may not pay for it directly	"Social enterprises tend to use transformative and disruptive forces to create impacts that may accrue to a segment of society, or society at large, rather than a discrete set of customers" (Lyons & Kickul, 2013, p. 148)
Funding gap beyond start-up phase	"The demand typically comes from social entrepreneurs who need capital to move beyond the start-up phase of their businesses" (Lyons & Kickul, 2013, p. 149), may these be for-profit or non-profit endeavors

FINANCING HOSPITALITY SOCIAL VENTURES   213

(Continued)

Challenge	Description
Resulting benefits from social enterprise are not solely captured by the enterprise	To seek financing for a social business may be more difficult since the benefits of the business are often linked to the greater good (e.g., benefit to a community) and not the business itself as is often the case in the traditional business market
Varying, different or unpredictable time horizons	"Social enterprises are typically designed to maximize value in the long term, while investors tend to have shorter time horizons." (Lyons & Kickul, 2013, p. 149). In the case of institutional donors (e.g., governmental support), those are often geared toward the start-up process rather than subsequent capital need for growth
Misaligned return expectations	Investors in social enterprise ventures may expect early returns on the investment. However, "given that mission related impact is the goal of a social entrepreneur rather than wealth creation, these return expectations can be misaligned with the income-generation ability of the social enterprise". (Lyons & Kickul, 2013, p. 149).
Using combinations of risk and return	"A conventional business can use its balance sheet and business plan to offer different combinations of risk and return to many different types of investors: equity investors, banks, bond funds, venture capitalists and so on. Not so for many social enterprises". (Bugg-Levine et al., 2012, p. 4)
Sharing of blended value	The public, philanthropic, and private sectors have different goals. Social enterprise financing may be rendered difficult due to the inherent difference in goals. (Lyons & Kickul, 2013).
Showing success	"Social entrepreneurs cannot rely solely on market signals and pricing to indicate to potential investors how successful they have been in achieving mission-related impact" (Lyons & Kickul, 2013, p. 149).

Adapted from Godeke (2006), Godeke and Bauer (2008), Godeke et al. (2009), Bugg-Levine et al. (2012), Lyons and Kickul (2013).

Traditional and emerging financing and funding options for social entrepreneurs

In this chapter the term 'funding' is defined as the money provided to the social entrepreneur by an organization (e.g., charitable donations), the government

214 FINANCING HOSPITALITY SOCIAL VENTURES

(e.g., grants) or an individual (e.g., philanthropy), which is free of interest and without any repayment requirements. The concept of 'financing' is defined as the sum of money provided to the social entrepreneur with an expectation of repayment along with interest fixed within a certain amount of time. Traditional sources of such financing include banks (e.g., in form of loans) or private equity investors (e.g., venture capital for startups). Traditionally, entrepreneurs may seek funding for the start-up phase, with money made available at one point in time, but with equally strong financing to be able to scale and grow the business over time.

Social enterprises are often funded and financed using a combination of three sources: (1) non-market resources such as government subsidies and private donations; (2) market resources such as the sales of products or services and (3) non-monetary resources such as volunteer work (OECD/EU, 2013). But within these broad categories, there is a multitude of possibilities available to social entrepreneurs in regards to funding and financing options, which for many may feel like a jungle of offers. Indeed, "compared to more traditional capital seekers, social entrepreneurs face an ever expanding set of funding options" (Lyons & Kickul, 2013, p. 149). Table 9.2 – Source of Financing and Funding Options for Social Entrepreneurs provides a summary of the sources along with a description of each source.

Table 9.2 Source of financing and funding options for social entrepreneurs.

Sources	Description
Bank loans	This is one of the key traditional financial products used by most mainstream enterprises. Entrepreneurs using bank loans to finance the business incur a debt and are liable to repay the principal amount borrowed along with the interest over a set timeframe. However, "financial institutions generally refuse to lend to social enterprises because they do not meet their established client criteria and are not seen as offering sufficient guarantees" (OECD/EU, 2013, p. 9)
Grants/Subsidies	A grant is offered to fund a specific venture or project with some compliance and reporting requirements but without a financial return expected by the grant-giving organization. These could be government bodies, philanthropic or charitable organizations investing in the social outcome defined by the social enterprise. Public measures are also available in form of "subsidies or tax and social security contribution exemptions for new social enterprises employing (mainly disadvantaged) employees; subsidies for supporting incubators or business innovation centres; and prizes for the winners of competitions of ideas" (European Union, 2020, p. 74).

(Continued)

Sources	Description
Venture philanthropy	Taking roots in the concept of venture capital financing where private equity capital is provided in various rounds of funding (e.g., early stage seed funding, growth funding), venture philanthropy's goal, however, is to support charitable endeavors via finance but also knowledge and expertise. As such, the venture philanthropist is interested in investment that supports the common social good rather than the pursuit of financial profits.
Institutional investment/ investment funds	Examples of institutional investors include pension funds, mutual funds, insurance companies "which manage large portfolios of capital remain a largely untapped source of finance for social enterprises" (OECD/EU, 2013, p.10). For example, the European Union has a series of funding mechanisms in place for social entrepreneurship (see Table 9.3: EU Funding for Social Entrepreneurship)
Individual investment	A common source of funding and financing for social entrepreneurs are individual investors. Those investors can be socially-motivated high-net-worth individuals. In Europe, these individuals would be driving "investments ranging from EUR 100 000 to a few million euro on a long term basis" (OECD/EU, 2013, p. 10). But equally, individual investors can be local, small-scale investors (referred to as 'citizen investors') who, for example, support local initiatives through local groups and circles of investors. In Europe for example, their financing can range from minimal amounts to EUR 10 000. (OECD/EU, 2013, p. 10).
Ethical or social capital markets	Known as the 'capital market with a conscience', ethical or social capital market are "markets in which socially responsible investing occurs." (OECD/EU, 2013, p. 10) with the goal to increase capital pools to finance social enterprises. (Mendell & Nogales, 2009)
Community based investment/ community finance	Similar to Solidarity finance, Community based investment refers to the socially responsible financing of businesses or not-for-profit organizations that have been refused support by traditional financial institutions. Community investors are community development banks, credit unions and microfinance institutions.

(Continued)

(Continued)

Sources	Description
Crowdfunding/ Online platforms	Using crowdfunding, money can be raised from a large number of individuals each contributing a small amount toward the social entrepreneurship venture, typically via internet platforms.
Friends and family	As a sub category of 'individual investment', friends and family may offer a substantial source of financial support in form of donations or loans.
Competitions/ Scholarships	As a sub category of 'grants', innovation centres or governmental programs may provide funding at the early stage of establishing the social enterprise in form of scholarships. Additionally, social entrepreneurs, have access to numerous funding competitions for social entrepreneurs.

Adapted from Godeke (2006), Godeke and Bauer (2008), Godeke et al. (2009), Bugg-Levine et al. (2012), and Lyons and Kickul (2013)

Since access to finance is one of the main obstacles to the growth of social enterprises, Table 9.3 – EU Funding for Social Entrepreneurship provides an overview of some of the funding programs and opportunities available to entrepreneurs in the European Union. Similar funding opportunities may be found in other regions and countries.

Table 9.3 EU funding for social entrepreneurship.

Funding Program	Summary Description	Timeline	Budget
European Social Innovation Competition	Boosting social innovation by awarding outstanding projects	Yearly since 2012	€200k (annual)
Social Impact Accelerator (SIA)	Public-private fund of funds addressing the growing need for availability of equity finance to support social enterprises.	Since 2013	€243m (total)
European Fund for Strategic Investments (EFSI)	Fund to finance i nfrastructures & innovative projects in Europe. Social Impact Window Innovative equity instruments developed to support social enterprises.	2015–2020	€26b (total)

(Continued)

Funding Program	Summary Description	Timeline	Budget
EU Programme for Employment and Social Innovation (EaSI)	Supporting the access to finance for social enterprises through its €193m Microfinance and Social Entrepreneurship axis	2014–2020	€919m (total)
European Social Fund (ESF)	EU's main financial instrument to support employment and social cohesion, implemented by EU member states through Operational Programs.	2014–2020	€80b (total)

Source: EVPA (2019).

Further considerations for social entrepreneurs

Subsidies & grants

As discussed previously, public grants are widely available to service the financing needs of the social entrepreneur. However, raising money from different public organizations requires time and energy and should not be underestimated. Social entrepreneurs can seek support from their local chamber of commerce, but should equally count on the word-of-mouth and online research in seeking information on the various funds available. The private sector, foundations or philanthropists are also sources of grants. Social entrepreneurs can therefore diversify their resources. The strategy here can be based on an analysis of the needs for funding and financing at various stages of business growth. Should equity capital be used for the start-up stage? Does the social enterprise require an operating grant? Is a loan required for special projects?

Crowdfunding

As mentioned above, a growing number of social entrepreneurs are turning to individuals within the online community to provide starting capital. Crowdfunding platforms have increased in number and scope, particularly as a tool to help struggling hospitality companies make ends meet throughout the COVID-19 crisis of 2020, while being closed due to large-scale lockdowns. According to Drake (2012) and cited in a common report by the OECD and the European Union, "more than 500 platforms now exist" (OECD/EU, 2013, p. 10) and the potential of financing stemming from these platforms in terms of crowdfunding market size globally is estimated to reach US$28.8 billion by 2025 (Szmigiera, 2019). All platforms function under a similar principle whereby it is a "collective effort of a large number of individuals who network and pool small amounts of capital to finance a new or existing business venture" (Szmigiera, 2019, para 1). Each crowdfunding campaign has a set goal in terms of the amount of money raised over a fixed timeframe. The money raised is tallied on a daily basis and published for investors or visitors to follow. Beyond the purely monetary factor, the use of a crowdfunding platform has the merit of (1) providing great visibility to the project and (2) validating its potential. However, here too the social entrepreneur cannot underestimate the time spent in creating the required crowdfunding marketing material adapted for the public and the time spent responding to messages posted by the hundreds of potential donors.

Bank loans

Conventional financing players have increasingly opened up to social entrepreneurs as financial intermediaries and adapted some of offers accordingly. Commercial banks may have specific products lines for social enterprises as well as a philanthropic agenda. Social-ethical banks have grown over the past decade to provide loans to companies or organizations that also fit their mission. The social entrepreneur may be able to secure loans to also finance more intangible investments such as a marketing campaign and a new training plan.

Impact Investment funds

When the social entrepreneur decides to scale the social business in order to reach a larger number of beneficiaries, this may translate to welcoming new shareholders. A new type of investment has emerged in recent years: impact investing funds. Impact investing are investments "made with the intention to generate positive, measurable social and environmental impact alongside a financial return" (GIIN, 2020, para 2). Impact investment "provides capital to address the world's most pressing challenges in sectors such as sustainable agriculture, renewable energy, conservation, microfinance, and affordable and accessible basic services including housing, healthcare, and education." (GIIN, 2020, para 3). Impact investing is interesting as it challenges the "long-held views that social and environmental issues should be addressed only by philanthropic donations, and that market investments should focus exclusively on achieving financial returns." (GIIN, 2020, para 5). Individual and institutional organizations have been attracted by impact investment, including private foundations, wealthy individuals, pension funds, non-governmental organizations or fund managers as well as traditional banks.

Industrial/corporate shareholders

Traditional corporations with a clear goal of maximizing shareholder value are increasingly attentive to the social and environmental changes taking place in their operating environment (Bulger, Singh, & Camillus, 2016; Legrand, Sloan, & Chen, 2017).

As a result, "both social enterprises and corporations are now more inclined to pursue multi-objective goals aligned with economic, social, and ecological sustainability" (Bulger et al., 2016, p. 2). Corporate or industrial partnerships consequently can help social entrepreneurs to meet the needs in terms of finding the capital to support growth. This can be done in the form of joint ventures or opting for minority stakes in the social enterprise. The most critical aspect to consider in setting some form of partnership with a corporation is to ensure that the social objective is core to the endeavor and will remain so.

Business incubators and business accelerators

Business incubators

A business incubator is a structure that welcomes and supports companies in the creation stage or 'recently created' stage (OECD/EU, 2019). The goal of a business incubator is to increase the chances of success for those enterprises (Bruneel, Ratinho, Clarysse, & Groen, 2012). The assistance provided via the business incubator structure can be diverse. Assistance in incubators falls under the following generic categories: (1) counselling, (2) space, (3) networks and (4) mentorship. For example, one or more of the following services could be part of a business incubator: exchange of experiences, analysis of the business model, search for funding, access to a workplace, training for business entrepreneurs, access to tools such as creative lab or access to networks. At times, the incubator can also provide financial support in the form market studies funding, for example. The incubator thus allows the social entrepreneur to be surrounded by people of various skills, who believe in the project and are able to ensure its development. A summary of the main features is provided in Table 9.4 – Differences and similarities between business incubators and business accelerators

Business accelerators

The accelerator is a program dedicated to entrepreneurs, with the aim to increase and *accelerate* the growth of a start-up and thus, an accelerator "condenses multiple years' worth of business building into just a few months" (Stanford, 2020, para 1). An accelerator program often involves seed-funding (the investor provides capital in a start-up company in exchange for an equity stake) and the opportunity for the social entrepreneur to be introduced to potential investors (Levinsohn, 2014). This program is often short and intensive (from a few weeks to a few months) and revolves around six key services. These include:

1. *access to financing* by introducing the social entrepreneurs to likely investors, investments funds or 'business angels' (an individual who invests personal capital in start-up companies in return for an equity stake)
2. *access to space*, which often brings together several entrepreneurs thus further promoting connections and sharing of knowledge and experience

3. *access to training* in areas directly related to entrepreneurship such as ways to raise funding or how to conduct a pitch, for example.
4. *access to mentoring* by way of support from an experienced entrepreneur, with benefits such as experience and network sharing as well provision of advice
5. *access to technical support* such as the development of a products, software or application
6. *access to legal and administrative support* such as access to specific lawyers or advice on accounting or generic administrative matters

A summary and comparison of features between incubators and accelerators is provided in Table 9.4.

Table 9.4 Differences and similarities between business incubators and business accelerators.

	Business Incubators	Business Accelerators
Objective	Support business creation and development.	Accelerate business growth.
Service portfolio	1) counselling 2) space 3) networks 4) mentorship	1) financing 2) space 3) training 4) mentorship 5) technical support 6) legal and administrative
Structure	No specific time frame; loose structure (On-demand feature).	A set time frame; rigid structure (Structured program feature).
Length of support	One or more years (and often up to three or four years, or more).	Usually three to six months (but as short as a few weeks or as long at eight months).
Selection	Admissions are typically on-going and selection is made according to the focus and criteria set by the incubator.	Admissions are typically done through a competitive selection process.
Entrepreneur features	Often enter at pre start-up stage; few, if any, employees; little experience.	Often enter after start-up stage; Often one or two employees; typically experienced.

Source: Adapted from Cohen (2013), Casasnovas and Bruno (2013), Madaleno, Nathan, Overman, and Waigths (2018), OECD/EU (2019), and Stanford (2020).

Examples of business incubators and business accelerators

Estimating the number of business incubators and accelerators is a difficult task partly due to the fact that the definition and delimitation between the two concepts is blurred. As stated in an OECD/EU policy brief (2019) on incubators and accelerators, the United States is considered to be the world leader in the number of incubator and accelerator programs, followed by the United Kingdom (Table 9.5). According to Tracxn, there are more than 1000 accelerators and incubators in the United State as of June 2019 (Tracxn, 2019). Accordingly, it is estimated that more than 900 can be found across the European Union (GUST, 2016; Al-Mubaraki & Busler, 2014).

Table 9.5 Selection of social incubator and accelerator organizations.

Incubator/ Accelerator Organization	Country	About
Accelerating Appalachia	US	"The first nature-based program accelerating the regenerative economy by connecting "basic needs businesses" in food, beverage, clothing, shelter and wellness to regenerative, inclusive business development training, peer businesses, mentors, aligned value supply chains, and investors committed to people, place and prosperity. (Accelarating Appalachia, 2020, para. 1)
Agora Partnerships	Latin America	"Entrepreneurship is fundamental to human progress. In order to meet the UN Sustainable Development Goals - to challenge global inequality, fight extreme poverty, and protect our planet - we need to unlock entrepreneurial potential. Agora provides business acceleration services access to investment to help entrepreneurs build a more inclusive and sustainable society." (Agora, 2020, para. 2–3)
Bongo Hive	Zambia	"We work with great minds building viable solutions that change the world. The programs that we have created have been crafted to guide start-ups through the entrepreneurial journey; from idea right through to getting investment." (Bongo Hive, 2020, para. 1–3)

(Continued)

(Continued)

Incubator/ Accelerator Organization	Country	About
Change Labs	Egypt, Middle East	"A 4-month immersion program aimed at accelerating conscious entrepreneurs to traction and revenue. We invest $100K in purpose driven start-ups in exchange for 8% equity and the opportunity to become a part of a new community of sustainable businesses, thinkers, mentors and investors." (Conscious Venture Lab, 2019, para. 2)
Conscious Venture Lab	US, Global	"We believe entrepreneurship can change the world – Our brick and mortar at Changelabs, offers a unique way to get students, youth, communities & businesses to launch a transformational impact-centered business in the 21st century. We do that by delivering corporate and youth training, acceleration and learning programs, youth festivals, inspiration, and funding" (Change Labs, 2020, para. 2)
Echoing Green	US, Global	"We discover emerging social entrepreneurs and invest deeply in the growth of their ideas and leadership. Over 30 years, we've built a broad, dynamic ecosystem to support these leaders as they solve the world's biggest problems." (Echoing green, para. 1)
European Investment Fund – Social Impact Accelerator	Europe	"The first pan-European public-private partnership addressing the growing need for availability of equity finance to support social enterprises." (European Investment Fund, 2020, para. 1)
FYA-Young Social Pioneers	Australia	"The program is designed to back and support young people with the initiative, drive and ideas to lead change in their communities and across the planet." (FYA, 2020), para. 2)

(Continued)

Incubator/ Accelerator Organization	Country	About
Hult Prize Foundation – Hult Prize Challenge	US, Global	"Building Startups That Have A Positive Impact On Our Planet With Every Dollar Earned" (Hult Prize, 2020, para. 1)
Impact 8	Canada	"A tailored approach to bridge the gap between social impact and economic viability for the development of entrepreneurship skills and mind-sets." Impact 8, 2018, para 1)
Impact Academy – Impact Accelerator	Australia	"Impact Accelerator - a 20-week program - focused on entrepreneurial learning and enterprise development. This program has been designed and continuously improved over four years to help start-ups, and early stage social enterprises achieve sustainable and scalable impact". (Impact Academy, 2020, para. 2)
TechnoServe Nicaragua	Nicaragua	"Since 1976, TechnoServe has been helping smallholder farmers and entrepreneurs in Nicaragua access formal markets, improve product quality, manage businesses, boost profits and become competitive. TechnoServe also works with entrepreneurs across various industries, providing business training, advice and support through several entrepreneurship development programs." (TechnoServe, 2020, para 2)
Uncharted (multiple accelerator programs)	US, Global	"We believe that our world, and how we improve it, is not fixed. There is no single way to solve the problems we face. That is why our programs bring together the people best positioned to put a dent in an issue and gives them access to what they need—mentors, funders, partners, policy makers, you name it—to attack that issue from all sides." (Uncharted, 2020, para. 1)

(Continued)

(Continued)

Incubator/ Accelerator Organization	Country	About
U.S. African Development Foundation (USADF)	Sub-Saharan Africa	"An independent U.S. government agency established by Congress to invest in African grassroots organizations, entrepreneurs and small and medium-sized enterprises. USADF's investments promote local economic development by increasing incomes, revenues and jobs, and creating pathways to prosperity for marginalized populations and underserved communities." (USADF, 2020, para 1)
Village Capital	US, Global	"Entrepreneurship is a critical tool for solving the world's biggest problems. For more than a decade our team at Village Capital has been designing, testing and sharing tools and processes to correct this imbalance and drive more investment to entrepreneurs from diverse backgrounds." (Village Capital, 2019, para. 3)

Incubators and Accelerators for Social Enterprises in Hospitality and Tourism

Institutional Accelerator

One project pertaining to sustainable tourism has been awarded European Union funding under the call of proposal for European incubation networks for creativity-driven innovation. The project is known as CAST (Creative Accelerators for Sustainable Tourism) and is funded under the EU program COSME (Competitiveness of Enterprises and Small and Medium-sized Enterprises). Within a timeframe of three years (2018–2021), the goal of CAST is to support sustainable tourism businesses via incubators and accelerators from creation to development and scaling up (European Commission, 2018). Under CAST, over one hundred small and medium-sized enterprises receive support across Europe (CAST Network, 2020). Numerous case studies and best practices were identified in a report on regional case studies published in 2019, which showcased "what the tourism industry is doing to incorporate technology in their day to day and promote sustainability as main assets for the sector's growth" (CAST Project, 2019, p. 4). Cases include the 'Ireland Leave No Trace' initiative, the 'Connemara rural tourism-based program' and the Spanish 'E-Azul Project'.

Corporate accelerator

The online booking platform and travel giant Booking.com has established its own accelerator program in sustainable tourism known as the Booster Program (Booking Booster, 2020). Accordingly, the Booking Booster program aims "to turn tourism into a force for good by supporting a select group of extraordinary start-ups as they look to scale their businesses and impact globally" (Booking Booster, 2018, p. 4). The Booking Booster program consists of a three-week accelerator program in Amsterdam, mentorship, networking, media exposure, support from Booking.com volunteers and grant funding. At the end of the accelerator program, selected entrepreneurs

> have the opportunity to pitch their scaling plan to our judges and ask for a grant of anywhere between €100,000 and €500,000 to execute their plan. In both 2017 and 2018, €2M in scaling grants were available from the Booking Booster program fund.
> (Booking Booster, 2018, p. 4)

In 2018, start-ups joining the program included the Hotel con Corazón with a social mission based in local education program support and the Community Homestay Network in Nepal, a social enterprise that supports community-based travel.

Conclusion

To start a social business or to develop a social project, funds will be required at some point. Whether crowdfunding, charity donations, entrepreneurship competition, venture capital or the help of a business angels, there are multiple of alternative methods to finance a social enterprise. Independent of the capital source, "a growing number of social entrepreneurs and investors realize that social enterprises of all sorts can generate financial returns that will make them attractive to the right investors" (Bugg-Levine et al., 2012, p. 4). The 2008–2009 global financial crisis gave social enterprises an unprecedented opportunity. Van Putten II and Green (2010) asked whether it takes "an economic recession to advance social entrepreneurship" (p. 1). The authors came to the conclusion that a series of factors linked to recession, including tax benefits, availability of skilled labor and less expensive supplies to name a few may play in favor of social entrepreneurial ventures (p. 1). A post-pandemic world may create yet another push for businesses, socially minded or not, to tackle some of the great human and planetary challenges.

CHAPTER CASE 9.1

Establishing a financially sustainable conservancy: Borana Ranch case study

(Source: The Long Run; Borana Lodge, https://www.borana.co.ke/)

Synopsis

This case study describes the model that the Borana Conservancy has developed to become financially sustainable and to secure its operation in perpetuity. The Borana Conservancy runs as a non-profit company, limited by tradable shares, where all retained earnings are reinvested for conservation purposes to enhance the Kenya Wildlife Service's endangered species strategies, specially the recovery of the black rhino. Core operating costs are covered by nine conservation shareholdings, of which Borana Ranch Ltd, retains five shares while the other four are taken up by investor partners. Each of the five shareholders engages in sustainable commercial activities, mainly through tourism maximum of ninety-six beds along with cattle ranching (Figure 9.1).

Figure 9.1 A room at Borana Lodge.
(Photo Credit: © Stevie Mann).

Donations and sponsorships are used to enhance conservation projects that are rhino-specific or outside the fence, expanding social and environmental positive impacts. The highly specific conservation mandates are guarded through underwriting commitments from each of the nine shares. Each shareholding commits to underwrite the core conservation budget – four-ninths comes from each of the four conservancy investor partners and five-ninths comes from Borana Ranch Ltd. (owned by the Dyer family). The Dyer Family Foundation was created to support shortfalls in conservation commitments and as a risk mitigation policy.

About Borana

The Borana Conservancy in Kenya is a non-profit conservation organization, run by the Dyer family for three generations. It is dedicated to the sustainable conservation of critical habitat and wildlife comprised of 30,000 acres located on the eastern edge of the Laikipia Plateau and recognized as a buffer zone of the Lewa and Ngare Ndare Forest ecosystems, which are listed as a World Heritage Site (Figure 9.2).

Figure 9.2 Borana Lodge.
(Photo Credit: ©James Lewin).

Borana's mission is to provide a sustainable ecosystem, in partnership with neighbors and local communities, for protecting critically endangered species. The Borana Conservancy has a holistic approach that commits tourism, ranching and other enterprise to build local livelihoods and enhance the integrity of the ecosystem.

Challenges

The Borana Ranch started out as a traditional ranch, raising cattle, sheep and goats. The ranch had inconsistent profitability and the integrity of the ecosystem faced huge threats.

In the late 1980s one of the shareholders, Michael Dyer, alarmed by the dramatic decline of the wildlife habitat, and in partnership with Ian Craig of Lewa, formalized the relationship with the Il'Ngwesi people and together, they developed the first community owned ecolodge Il'Ngwesi. This venture was a huge success and became globally recognized, but more importantly created momentum for the community conservancy movement and ultimately the formation of The Northern Range Lands Trust (NRT). There are now over 30 conservancies protecting thousands of square kilometers of wilderness stretching across northern Kenya, from the coastal regions to the Great Rift Valley. A founder population of 11 rhinos was introduced on Lewa in 1984 and eventually the whole of Lewa and the Ngare Ndare Forest were made available for the growing population of rhinos. In 2011 Rge Borana Conservancy was established and by 2013 a founder population of twenty-one black rhinos was introduced and the fence between Lewa and Borana was removed, creating the largest contiguous privately funded and managed rhino sanctuary in East Africa (Figure 9.3).

Figure 9.3 A Black Rhino on Borana Conservancy.
(Photo Credit: © Shaun Mousely).

However, one of the main challenges for the Dyer family was to establish a financially sustainable model to ensure that the conservancy could exist in perpetuity. The Lewa Wildlife Conservancy, bordering Borana Ranch, served as an example of a different model, where the conservancy was highly dependent on donors. With only 21% of the revenue coming from conservation fees and commercial activities, more than 60% of Lewa's income came from international aid, NGOs and sponsors, running a potential risk of not being financially sustainable in the long term. Relying on donations to pay salaries and meet operational core costs could create instability, potentially placing the whole operation of the conservancy at risk if donations were to not meet the core costs of operations, especially at moments of global crisis when grants tend to become more limited.

Solutions

In order to ensure that the Borana Conservancy would have the means to operate and protect the environment for the long run, the Dyer family designed a model where more than 90% of the core costs were covered by commercial activities, while the surplus would be used to enhance conservation of the area and expand the social and environmental positive impacts. The sustainable model compiles three main elements: an endowment fund, tradable shares and collaborative work and partnerships.

TRADABLE SHARES AND UNDERWRITING COMMITMENTS

- The Dyer family created a lease company called Borana Makazi Ltd (BML) in order to lease all the land owned by Borana Ranch Ltd. The Borana Makazi was limited by nine shares, of which Borana Ranch Ltd. held five (one from the mother and one from each of the four sons). The remaining four shares were sold to 'conservation investors', who have the right of abode, which can be run commercially with a maximum of sixteen beds per share at a pre-agreed footprint.

- Borana Conservancy Ltd. was created to manage the conservation resources.

- Protection of land was secured through a series of conservation easements and underwriting commitments.

- Each shareholder commits to contribute one-ninth of the annual conservation budget that is set, to meet the core operating costs. These include salaries of rangers and staff, trainings, administration costs, taxes, fuel, water pumping and the maintenance of infrastructure, roads and fences. Through the conservation underwriting commitments, Borana Conservancy guarantees the resources for basic operations.

- The conservation underwriting commitments are up to US$100,000 per shareholder per year. This can be met through the conservation fees that are charged to the guests who stay at the lodges (US$105/guest). Any surplus raised through guest conservation fees will also be reinvested in the conservancy and cannot go as credit to fulfil next year's underwriting commitment, nor it is refundable. If guest conservation fees are not enough, the shareholder will have to assume the remaining amount.

- Borana Ranch Ltd., which has to contribute with five-ninths of the conservation budget, covers 60–70% of their underwriting commitments through commercial activities, which include one tourist lodge, a horse riding operation, cattle and farming. Of this, tourism contributes around 75% and livestock business the remaining 25%. The balance required to meet the underwriting commitments comes from the endowment fund.

- There is a separate budget to manage the 'social and critical imperatives', which are related to social development projects for the surrounding communities, such as education and healthcare.

- Three of the conservation investors were frequent visitors of the Borana Ranch and were high-net-worth individuals interested in engaging with the conservation projects (Figure 9.4).

Figure 9.4 Horse riding on Borana Conservancy.
(Photo Credit: © Max Melesi).

ENDOWMENT FUND

- An endowment fund was created to manage financial shortfalls, as well as to serve as a risk mitigation policy for the Dyer family in case they were unable to continue managing the landscape or were forced out. The money from the sales of the four shares to conservation investors was secured in the endowment fund.

- The initial amount of the endowment fund was calculated on the basis of the money that was needed to be available to support the shortfalls on the underwriting commitments of Borana Ranch Ltd. It was estimated that the endowment fund should generate around US$250,000–300,000 to support the conservation commitments.

COLLABORATION AND PARTNERSHIPS

- Even though Borana set out a financially sustainable model for its entire core operating costs, it recognizes the need to maintain strong relationships with donors and develop partnerships. Maintaining these are very important to supporting special or additional projects not included in the general budget and to avoid compromising core conservation efforts if revenues are low. Similarly, in order to have a sustained and bigger impact, collaborative work was deemed necessary.

- Borana has developed a strong conservation partnership with the Lewa Wildlife Conservancy. They have added 50% more habitat to Lewa's existing landscape, which contributed security and enabled them to remove the fences between the two conservancies. Today, their conservation goals and security are managed collaboratively, and it is expected in the near future that the boards and budgets will amalgamate.

- Borana has also established collaborations to help conserve state-owned land. The Borana Conservancy is a trustee of the Ngare Ndare Forest Trust, which is run entirely through community-based organizations, in partnership with the Kenyan Forest Service, which owns the state-owned land that is managed under concession by the Trust. Borana also supports the trust's conservation efforts by sending guests to visit their forests.

Borana has also developed positive relationships with immediate neighbors of community-owned land holdings. These 'group ranches' comprise 20,000–30,000 acres of land, run by more than 2000 members. Borana has helped provided guidance and support to enhance their capacity to govern the land and boost access to investments from third parties or grants and has helped developed a tourism enterprise. Eventually the members created the Northern Rangeland Trust, which now looks after about five million acres of community land under structured corporate governance with thirty-three member conservancies. These partnerships

232 FINANCING HOSPITALITY SOCIAL VENTURES

have helped with forestry management, land-use planning and dialogue with the county government, as well as raising money and enabling communities to enter commercial agreements with third parties.

Positive impacts

- The conservation on Borana is a responsible and replicable model. The emphasis on sustainability through the use of commercial activities to support Kenya's wildlife and investments in community development help protect wildlife in the long term, and help others do so as well.

- US$2 million from the Endowment Fund has been reinvested in the conservancy since 2010.

- Core operating costs are financed through commercial activities, securing financial sustainability. Eighty-two percent of the Conservancy's income in 2016 came from investors and partnerships, while only 18% came from donations. *(Design: link with graphs)*

- Together with its conservation partner Lewa Wildlife Conservancy, Borana's black rhino population represents 20% of the national meta-population.

- The total area encompassed in the collaboratively managed conservation landscape exceeds 100,000 acres, including Borana, Lewa and the Ngare Ndare Forest (Figures 9.5 and 9.6).

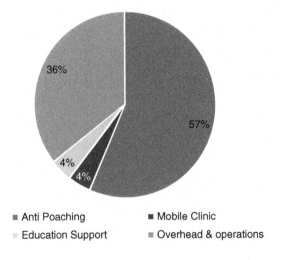

Figure 9.5 Breakdown of how conservancy fees are spent (2011–2019).

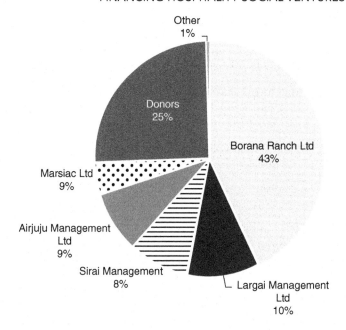

Figure 9.6 Total funding from 2011 to 2020.

Lessons learned

- It is recommended to raise more than 90% of the core operating cost from commerce activities and/or from investors. Everything raised over and above would help to have a bigger impact.
- Try to avoid falling into the donor circuit, as it places the Conservancy's sustainability at high risk.
- However, maintaining donors is also important in the viability of the conservancy as well, as it allows expanding conservation projects to increase impacts and supports the Conservancy in periods of low revenues.
- Collaborative work between private-sector land, community-owned land and state-owned land strengthens conservation efforts and governance of the area.
- Successful conservation initiatives that demonstrate positive results and expertise increase the Conservancy's credibility, attracting more donors and sponsors.
- Think and plan for the long term.

EXERCISES

Group research & discussion

Take some time to research business incubators and accelerators (refer to Table 9.5 – Selection of Social Incubator and Accelerator Organizations for a preliminary list) and discuss the following questions.

1. Find an incubator or accelerator program of your choice and discuss how the process works for interested social entrepreneurs.
2. Find an incubator or accelerator program of your choice that involves a social entrepreneur in the hospitality and tourism industry and describe the venture.
3. Contact a social entrepreneur which has experience with incubators or accelerators to find out about the dos and don'ts.

Group research & discussion

Take some time to review chapter case 9 and visit the website: (https://www.borana.co.ke/).

1. What were the challenges faced in establishing the Borana Ranch venture?
2. One if the key issues was to establish a financially sustainable model that would ensure the conservancy would exist for years to come; what were the solutions implemented to deal with this challenge?
3. Are there other sources of funds available to the Borana Ranch?
4. What were the lessons learned and would you have further suggestions in regards to the future of Borana Ranch?

Individual research

Write an essay on the topic of crowdfunding and social entrepreneurship, keeping in mind the following questions:

1. What is crowdfunding and how does it work?
2. How can a social entrepreneur use crowdfunding to support the social venture?
3. What are some interesting examples to share?
4. What are your recommendations in regards to crowdfunding for social entrepreneurship ventures?

References

Accelerating Appalachia. (2020). *Who We Are.* https://www.acceleratingappalachia.org/
Agora. (2020). *Empowering Entrepreneurs to Transform the World.* https://agora2030.org/
Al-Mubaraki, H., & Busler, M. (2014). Incubator successes: Lessons learned from successful incubators towards the twenty-first century. *World Journal of Science, Technology and Sustainable Development, 11*(1), 44–52.
Bongo Hive. (2020). *About.* https://bongohive.co.zm/about/
Booking Booster. (2017). *Booking Booster 2017 Impact report: Building a Sustainable Future for the Global Tourism industry.* https://booster.bookingcares.com/
Booking Booster. (2020). *About.* https://booster.bookingcares.com/
Brown, L. B. (2009). *Plan 4.0: Mobilizing to Save Civilization.* New York NY: Norton.
Bruneel, J., Ratinho, T., Clarysse, B., & Groen, A. (2012). The evolution of business incubators: Comparing demand and supply of business incubation services across different incubator generations. *Technovation, 32*(2), 110–121.
Bugg-Levine, A., Kogut, B., & Kulatilaka, N. (2012). A new approach to funding social enterprises. *Harvard Business Review, 90*, 1–7.
Bulger, E., Singh, S. P., & Camillus, J. C. (2016). Shareholder value and social entrepreneurship: Toward a point omega in strategic planning systems? *Midwest Academy of Management, October*, 1–38.
Casasnovas, G., & Bruno, A. (2013). Scaling social ventures. *Journal of Management for Global Sustainability, 1*(2), 173–197.
CAST Network. (2020). *Creative Accelerators for Sustainable Tourism.* https://castnetwork.eu/
CAST Project. (2019). *Regional Case Studies.* https://castnetwork.eu/resources
Change Labs. (2020). *Home.* https://www.changelabseg.org/
Cohen, S. (2013). What do accelerators do? Insights from incubators and angels. *Innovations, 8*(3–4), 19–25.
Conscious Venture Lab. (2019). *Capitalism Transformed.* http://www.consciousventurelab.com/
Echoing Green. (2020). *Mission.* https://echoinggreen.org/mission/
European Commission. (2018). *European Network of incubators Call for Proposals: Two Projects Selected.* https://ec.europa.eu/easme/en/news/european-network-incubators-call-proposals-two-projects-selected
European Investment Fund. (2020). *The Social Impact Accelerator (SIA).* https://www.eif.org/what_we_do/equity/sia/index.htm
European Union. (2020). *Social Enterprises and their Ecosystems in Europe: Comparative Synthesis Report.* Luxembourg: Publications Office of the European Union. https://ec.europa.eu/social/main.jsp?catId=952&intPageId=2914&langId=en
EVPA. (2019). *EU Funding for Social Entrepreneurship: An Overview August 2019.* European Venture Philanthropy Association. https://evpa.eu.com/download/start/EU_Funding_for_Social_Entrepreneurship_2019.pdf
FYA. (2020). *Young Social Pioneers. The Foundation for Young Australians.* https://www.fya.org.au/young-social-pioneers/
GIIN. (2020). *What You Need to Know about Impact Investing.* Global Impact Investing Network. https://thegiin.org/impact-investing/need-to-know/
Godeke, S. (2006). Hybrid Transactions in the US Social Capital Market. *Alliance Magazine, 11*(3), 49–51.
Godeke, S., & Bauer, D. (2008). *Philanthropy's New Passing Gear: Mission-Related Investing.* New York NY: Rockefeller Philanthropy Advisors.

Godeke, S., Pomares, R., Bruno, A. V., Guerra, P., Kleissner, C., & Shefrin, H. (2009). *Solutions for Impact Investors: From Strategy to Implementation*. New York NY: Rockefeller Philanthropy Advisors.

GUST. (2016). *European Accelerator Report 2016*. http://gust.com/accelerator_reports/2016/europe/

Hult Prize. (2020). *The Hult Prize 2020 Challenge*. http://www.hultprize.org/challenge/

Impact 8. (2018). *Approach*. https://www.impact8.org/en/approach/

Impact Academic. (2020). *Welcome*. https://www.impactacademy.net.au/#home

Legrand, W., Sloan, P., & Chen, J. S. (2017). *Sustainability in the Hospitality Industry: Principles of Sustainable Operations* (3rd ed.). London: Routledge.

Levinsohn, D. (2014). The role of accelerators in the development of the practicing social entrepreneur. *Jönköping International Business School, 8*(6), 1–17.

Lyons, T., & Kickul, J. (2013). The social enterprise financing landscape: The lay of the land and new research on the horizon. *Entrepreneurship Research Journal, 3*(2), 147–159.

Madaleno, M., Nathan, M., Overman, H., & Waigths, S. (2018). Incubators, accelerators and regional economic development. *IZA Institute of Labor Economics, IZA Discussion Paper No. 11856*. http://ftp.iza.org/dp11856.pdf

Mendell, M., & Nogales, R. (2009). Social enterprises in OECD member countries: What are the financial streams? In A. Noya (Ed.), *The Changing Boundaries of Social Enterprises* (pp. 89–138). Paris France: OECD.

OECD/EU. (2013). *Policy Brief on Social Entrepreneurship: Entrepreneurial Activities in Europe*. Luxembourg: Publications Office of the European Union. https://www.oecd.org/cfe/leed/Social%20entrepreneurship%20policy%20brief%20EN_FINAL.pdf

OECD/EU. (2019). *Policy Brief on Incubators and Accelerators that Support Inclusive Entrepreneurship*. Luxembourg: Publications Office of the European Union. https://ec.europa.eu/social/main.jsp?langId=en&catId=952&furtherNews=yes&newsId=9360

Reis, T. (1999). *Unleashing the New Resources and Entrepreneurship for the Common Good: a Scan, Synthesis and Scenario for Action*. Battle Creek MI: W.K. Kellogg Foundation.

SoPact. (2020). *About Us*. https://www.sopact.com/company/about-us

Stanford. (2020). *Accelerators & Incubators Guide*. Stanford Social Entrepreneurship Hub. http://sehub.stanford.edu/accelerator-incubator

Szmigiera, M. (2019). *Crowdfunding—Statistics & Facts*. Statista. https://www.statista.com/topics/1283/crowdfunding/

TechnoServe. (2020). *Where We Work*. https://www.technoserve.org/our-work/where-we-work/nicaragua/

Traxcn. (2019). *Accelerators & Incubators in United States*. Traxcn Investor Lists. https://tracxn.com/d/investor-lists/Accelerators-&-Incubators-in-United-States

Uncharted. (2020). *Our Accelerators*. https://uncharted.org/accelerators/

USADF. (2020). *About*. https://www.usadf.gov/

Van Putten II, P., & Green, R. (2010). Does it take an economic recession to advance social entrepreneurship? *Research in Business and Economics Journal, 3*, 1–10.

Village Capital. (2019). *Our Mission*. https://vilcap.com/about-us/our-mission

Chapter **10**

A world of change in hospitality: a concluding statement

Canadian astrophysicist Hubert Reeves wrote: *"We're at war with nature. If we win, we're lost."* (in Reeves, 2014, p. 139). The 2020 pandemic has had catastrophic consequences on societies as a whole, but particularly on the travel and hospitality sectors. The ways these industries are currently dealing with this offers a glimpse into crisis management endeavours and building a business case for disaster and climate resiliency. The hospitality industry has proven to be one of most innovative sectors in times of crisis, adapting to keep operating; from functioning as emergency housing, coronavirus quarantines, and daytime offices to hotel-to-hospital conversions. The industry is also assuming a leading role in keeping spirits high across the communities it operates in. Many of the characteristics found in social enterprises, discussed in this book, have been coming to the surface, enacted by large corporate players. Climate emergency is not dissimilar to the coronavirus threat, whereby "both demand early aggressive action to minimize loss" (Cobb, in Sengupta, 2020, para. 3).

With hotel companies facing existential crisis, or large-scale downsizing, what will be left of sustainability programmes and social initiatives once this pandemic is overcome? Will we be starting from scratch or is the coronavirus crisis an opportunity to implement a swift change in risk assessment and management facing the climate crisis? What are the key lessons from the coronavirus crisis on how to deal with generational challenges, including but not limited to climate emergency, social inequalities and poverty? What are the opportunities for social entrepreneurs in times of adversity?

In a book published in 2019 titled *Upheaval: How Nations Cope with Crisis and Change*, author and UCLA professor Jared Diamond writes, "Successful coping with external or internal pressures requires selective change" (p. 6), with a focus on the word 'selective'.

Diamond argues that "individuals or nations under pressure must take honest stock of their abilities and value" (p. 6). And thus, the challenge "is to figure out which parts of their identities are already functioning well and don't need changing and which parts are no longer working and do need changing" (p. 6).

So here we are; a few months away from a potential start of the recovery. And then what?

Travel restrictions are being eased; local travel is slowly picking up and long-distance trips are still lagging but hotels are running at low but steady occupancy.

This is the chance to bet on the long term; set the record straight and have "the courage to recognize what must be changed" (Diamond, 2019, p. 7).

Social entrepreneurs, across the globe, can be at the forefront of this change, as much needed transformational pioneers.

Posterity demands it.

References

Diamond, J. (2019). *Upheaval: How Nations Cope with Crisis and Change*. UK: Allen Lane.
Reeves, F. (2014). *Planet Heart: How and Unhealthy Environment Leads to Heart Disease*. Vancouver, Canada: Greystone Books.
Sengupta, S. (2020). *Climate Change Has Lessons for Fighting the Coronavirus*. New York Times, March 12. https://www.nytimes.com/2020/03/12/climate/climate-change-coronavirus-lessons.html

Index

accelerator 220–21, 224–25, 234; corporate 225; institutional 224–25
Accor 165, 169–70
accountability 53, 64, 108, 113, 135–36
agriculture 6, 21, 40, 57, 82, 114, 123, 203, 218
audit 19, 104
Authenticitys 94, 96–7, 112–13, 123

B Impact Assessment 102–03, 105, 109
benchmarking 103, 105, 108
best Practice 1, 25, 91, 224
biodiversity 6–7, 9, 59, 62, 65, 82–3, 85, 87–91, 114–15, 119–20, 153, 192–94, 203–04; collapse 2, 19, 37, 83, 189, 192; conservation 24, 68, 87; loss 5, 22, 144; protection 73, 90–1
Borana Ranch 211, 226–34
Brundtland Report 2, 4, 196
buildings 13–14, 26, 170, 202; nearly zero-energy 26

Caiman Ecological Refuge 94, 113–23
capitalism 4, 9, 19, 34, 55, 133
carbon: emissions 6–7, 11, 19, 26, 145, 171 ; footprint 13, 19, 190 ; intensity 171 ; low-carbon 196; mitigation 145; neutral 26, 86; pricing 26; sequestration 11, 83; storage 6; targets 171

certification 94–103, 105, 108–09, 111–13, 123, 171
Certified B Corp 94, 102–04, 112–13
Chumbe Island Coral Park Ltd. 46, 58–70
climate change 6–7, 11–12, 17, 22–3, 39–40, 144, 163, 189, 192–93, 195, 207
code of ethics 70, 190
conservation 15–16, 18, 24, 59–68, 86–90, 114–22, 177, 182, 192, 205, 218, 226–27, 229–33; and energy 171; and water 15; plan 149; preservation and 18; project 24, 189, 198, 227, 233
corporate social responsibility (CSR) 18, 36–7, 40–1, 50–1, 95, 133, 170, 212
crowdfunding 216–18, 225, 234

decarbonisation 26
deforestation 9, 83, 193, 206

ecosystem 3–4, 6, 8, 19, 60, 83, 88–9, 152, 193, 204, 222, 227–28
ecotourism 14, 18, 24, 59–70, 83–90, 113–23, 142, 147–56, 173–75, 189–203
environmental: burden 8; crisis 3–4; education 59–60, 63, 67, 118; entrepreneurship 52, 80, 97, 189–208;

impact 1, 13–15, 21, 51, 61, 103–04, 109, 148, 168–69, 172, 174, 191–92, 196, 204, 218, 227, 229; impact assessment 103–04; justice 5; management 13; movement 4, 14, 16, 18; protection 15–16, 19, 154, 169; regulations 15, 167
entrepreneur: attributes 73–83, 135–37; characteristics 54, 73–83; corporate social responsibility and 36–7; environmental 189–98; identity 34–35; innovation and,34; motivation 48–49, 73–83; Pull 75–7; Push 75–7
entrepretality 131
Estencia Peuma Hue 189, 197–203
externalities 39–40, 90

financing 23, 55–6, 106, 134, 173, 184, 211–34
food 10–13, 19–21, 57–8, 111, 115–19, 167–70, 172, 177–78, 183–84, 186, 191–95, 201, 221; and agriculture 40, 82, 56; and nutrition 82, 118; system 10; waste 169, 172
footprint *see* carbon
funding *see* financing

Global Social Venture Competition (GSVC) 105–07
Good Hotels 110–11
governance *see* corporate social responsibility
grants *see* subsidies

Hiç Olive Company 56–8
Hilton 165, 167, 169–72
HM Design 147–56
Human rights 3, 14, 171, 190

impacts: environmental 15, 51, 148, 174, 180, 191–92, 227, 229; measurement 97, 99, 108; social 94–100, 105–06, 108–09

incubators 211, 214, 219–25, 234
industrial revolution 4, 9
Inkaterra 24–5, 73, 83–91
innovation *see* entrepreneur
investment: community-based 215; funds 215, 219, 222–24; impact investment 218; individual 215–16; institutional 215; social return on 100–01, 124

The Long Run 58, 69, 113, 147, 154, 174, 181, 226

market failures 39–40, 43, 50–1
marketing 13, 52, 82, 97–8, 108–09, 112, 123, 139, 218
Marriott 164–65, 167, 169–70
Mashpi Lodge 198, 203–08

nature tourism 203–05
nine planetary boundaries 6–7
Nomad Lodges 163, 174–82, 186–87
non-governmental organization (NGO) 9, 24, 69, 80, 87, 95–6, 98, 102, 106, 109, 112, 121, 138, 142, 229

Paris Agreement 17, 26, 144
performance: environmental 104, 113, 197; and impact 54; metrics 54

quadruple bottom line (QBL) 99

recycling 104, 145, 171, 177, 165, 205
renewable energy 23, 82, 145, 200, 218
reporting 21–2, 96, 101, 191, 214

SLOW model 139–41
social: action 40–2; change 9, 42, 48, 106, 130–31, 163–87; impacts 94–6, 98, 100, 105–06, 109; justice 74; responsibility 18, 33, 36, 39; tourism enterprise 166–67; ventures 136, 211–34; welfare 38
social bricoleurs 56, 78

social constructionists 56, 78
social engineers 56, 78–9
Social Impact Assessment (SIA) 99–100, 105, 107, 124
Social Return on investment (SROI) 80, 94, 100, 124
Soneva 23, 25, 128, 143–46, 156
Spill-over effect 192
stakeholders 7, 9–10, 51–60, 105–06, 138–40, 147–48, 184–85; of social enterprises 97–101
subsidies 180, 212, 214, 217
sustainable development 1–27, 51, 82, 85–6, 128–129, 131, 138–139, 144, 169, 221
Sustainable Development Goals (SDGs) 1, 17, 20–7, 27, 144, 169–70, 221

sustainable tourism 17, 20, 64, 111, 143, 147, 150, 154, 156, 168, 186, 189, 191, 196, 224–25

triple bottom line (TBL) 18–19, 99, 169

United Nations Environment Programme (UNEP) 4, 191–92
United Nations World Tourism Organization (UNWTO) 18, 70, 164, 190–92

waste: management of 15, 82, 142, 177, 205; reduction 19, 172
water: crisis 15; footprint 19, 190; insecurity 11; management of 21, 195; pollution 11, 15, 205; and sanitation 82; scarcity 19, 195
World Travel and Tourism Council (WTTC) 21–2, 24

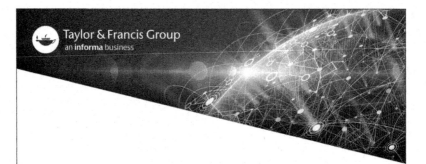